Physics in the Automotive Industry
(APS/AAPT Topical Conference)

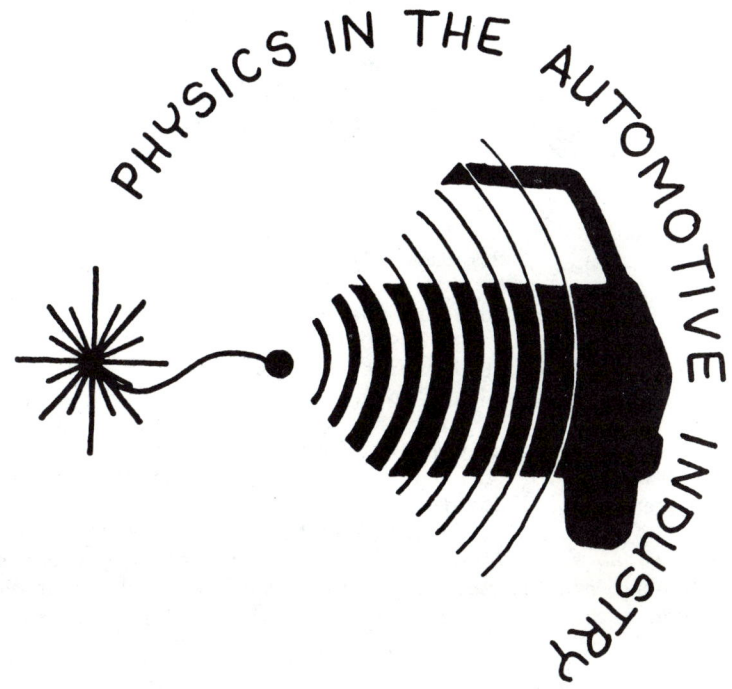

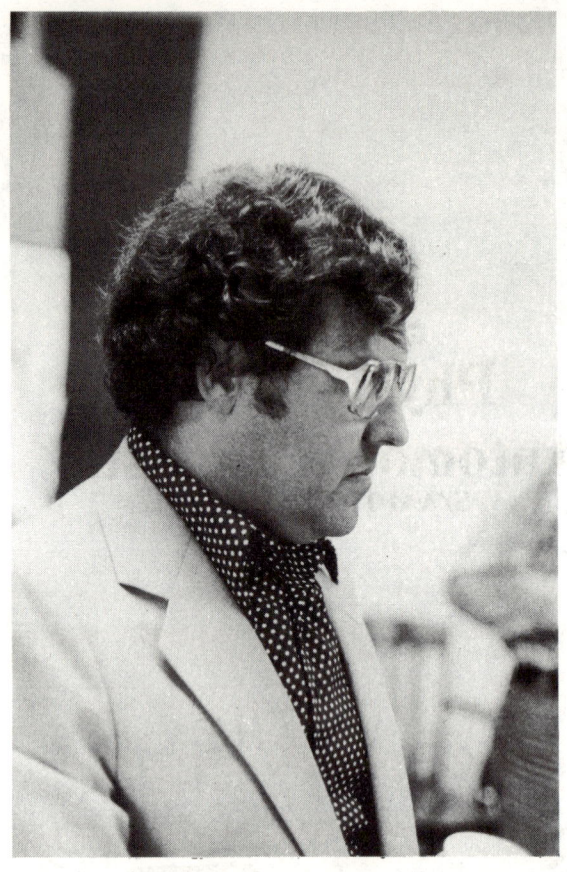

IN MEMORIAM

Dr. Daniel R. Gustafson
1937-1980
Chairman, Department of Physics
Wayne State University

Dan Gustafson served as an untiring Secretary-Treasurer of the
Organizing Committee of this Conference. Dan's sincere dedica-
tion and organizational ability significantly contributed to the
success of the Conference. Subsequent to the Conference, Dan
Gustafson died as a result of a water accident while on vacation.
Dan's colleagues and friends will remember him as a thoughtful,
dedicated man with a strong commitment to his professional field,
physics.

AIP Conference Proceedings
Series Editor: Hugh C. Wolfe
Number 66

Physics in the Automotive Industry
(APS/AAPT Topical Conference)

Editor
Frank E. Jamerson
General Motors Research Laboratories

American Institute of Physics
New York   1981

Copying fees: The code at the bottom of the first page of each article in this volume gives the fee for each copy of the article made beyond the free copying permitted under the 1978 US Copyright Law. (See also the statement following "Copyright" below). This fee can be paid to the American Institute of Physics through the Copyright Clearance Center, Inc., Box 765, Schenectady, N.Y. 12301.

Copyright © 1980 American Institute of Physics

Individual readers of this volume and non-profit libraries, acting for them, are permitted to make fair use of the material in it, such as copying an article for use in teaching or research. Permission is granted to quote from this volume in scientific work with the customary acknowledgment of the source. To reprint a figure, table or other excerpt requires the consent of one of the original authors and notification to AIP. Republication or systematic or multiple reproduction of any material in this volume is permitted only under license from AIP. Address inquiries to Series Editor, AIP Conference Proceedings, AIP.

L.C. Catalog Card No. 80-70987
ISBN 0-88318-165-7
DOE CONF- 8005123

Conference Organization

An American Physical Society Topical Conference on Physics in the Automotive Industry was held at the Engineering Society of Detroit, Detroit, Michigan on May 15-16, 1980.

The planning for this Topical Conference was initiated in the Spring of 1979 by Dean William H. Kelly, Montana State University (then Chairman of the Physics Department at Michigan State University). Dean Kelly was charged by the American Physical Society via the Committee on the Applications of Physics to organize a Topical Conference relating to the automotive industry.

The objective of the Conference was: To introduce relevant physics within this industry to university and college faculty; to enhance the interaction between industrial and university researchers; and for university personnel to capture some of the research atmosphere in this industry. The Conference should be of interest to research students contemplating future industrial employment, faculty who are frequently asked about employment in industry, and to those actively pursuing or contemplating research in allied areas.

With this objective in mind, the members of the organizing committee and program committee developed the program now recorded in these proceedings. The members of these committees were:

Organizing Committee
R. I. George, American Motors Corporation
D. R. Gustafson, Wayne State University (Secretary-Treasurer)
F. E. Jamerson, General Motors Corporation
W. H. Kelly, Montana State University (Chairman)
J. Lunan, Chrysler Corporation
J. R. Reitz, Ford Motor Company
R. H. Sands, University of Michigan
P. A. Schroeder, Michigan State University

Program Committee
D. R. Gustafson, Wayne State University (Chairman)
R. E. Hetrick, Ford Motor Company
F. E. Jamerson, General Motors Corporation

Sponsors

This Topical Conference was sponsored by the American Physical Society and the American Association of Physics Teachers. Wayne State University served as the host institution for conference planning and local arrangements. Additionally, the universities and corporations listed below were sponsors of this Topical Conference.

Income for this Conference was derived from generous contributions of a number of those automotive manufacturers and automotive supplier firms and universities shown as well as a nominal registration fee of $35.

American Physical Society
American Association of Physics Teachers
Michigan State University
Montana State University
University of Michigan
Wayne State University
American Motors Corporation
Bendix Corporation
Chrysler Corporation
Ford Motor Company
General Motors Corporation
Kelsey-Hayes
Rockwell International
TRW

PREFACE

These Proceedings document the second meeting on Physics in the Automotive Industry. The first, a Symposium, was jointly sponsored by the American Institute of Physics and the Department of Physics, University of Michigan in 1938. Papers in that Symposium addressed the applications of physics measurement methods to processes such as combustion, materials, and mechanical structures. Of particular interest was Professor Richtmyer's talk at that Symposium on Physics in the Automotive Industry where he had some prophetic words, "Among the many fields of present-day physics which promise significant contributions to the automotive industry in the near future, is the physics of the 'solid state.'" Now, forty-two years later the automobile industry is producing vehicles with the electronic technology derived from the postwar explosion of solid state physics discoveries. Professor Richtmyer also closed his remarks with an emphasis on the "importance of better teamwork among pure scientists, applied scientists and engineers". He also was prophetic enough to know that, "When better automobiles are built, physics will help build them."

That Symposium was a very successful one and it was "hoped that it will bring about more applications of physics in the automobile industry."

There have been great advances in physics and in the automotive industry since this first Symposium but the need for a second Conference has only recently been raised. Communication between industrial and academic physicists has been enhanced in recent years through activities such as the Committee on Applications of Physics of the American Physical Society and the Corporate Associates of the American Institute of Physics. In addition, the American Association of Physics Teachers has been intimately involved in the APS Visiting Physicists program where company physicists visit college and university physics departments. The Committee on Applications of Physics has used the Topical Conference format for enhancing industrial/academic interactions by organizing conferences for specific industries at locations in which these industries are prominent. The first such Topical Conference was held at Akron, Ohio, May 16, 1979 on Physics in the Tire Industry. In 1979, the Committee suggested that a Conference be held on Physics in the Automotive Industry and to be organized by Professor William H. Kelly, then Chairman of the Department of Physics, Michigan State University and also Vice-President of the AAPT. An organization committee was established that included representatives from universities and the automotive companies in the area around Detroit, Michigan where the conference was to be held.

In addition to invited talks, the conference provided for tours of the General Motors Research Laboratories and the Ford Scientific Laboratory as well as a panel discussion by representatives of the automotive industry. Moreover, the status of the automobile industry in 1980 was presented in the evening talk by Mr. Howard H. Kehrl,

Executive Vice President of General Motors Corporation. Considerable opportunities were provided for the industrial researchers and faculty to interact and become acquainted with each other. The presented papers, discussion, and tours all served extremely well to fulfill the objective of this Topical Conference.

In 1938, the industry was using the physics tools of that period, such as absorption spectra of flames. Today we see the industry contributing to research at physics frontiers, in their application of new laser methods for combustion studies and theoretical studies of surface structure. This significant increase in depth and breadth of physics research, particularly at General Motors Corporation and Ford Motor Company, suggests that opportunities are available for fundamental as well as applied physics research in this industry. Although 1980 marks a year of significant economic stress for the automotive industry, the research physicists at this conference spoke with enthusiasm about how the results of their research would make a significant contribution to their company as well as to science. The present and future challenges in energy and materials impact greatly on the automotive industry, and it is clear that physics and physicists will have a significant part to play in the development of new technology. Beyond that, we believe it will be to the betterment of physics in both industry and academe if personal interactions such as those that took place in this conference were to be continued. We are pleased to learn that similar topical conferences on Physics in the Oil Industry and Physics in the Steel Industry are being planned.

Such a conference makes use of the generous time and talents of many people in the organizations that were involved. We appreciate the great deal of assistance and advice that William W. Havens, Jr. of the Americam Physical Society gave us in drawing the Conference together and for arranging for the publication of these Proceedings. We also wish to acknowledge that the design of the Conference logo was done by Oscar Fernandez of the School of Arts at Montana State University. However, we especially appreciate the efforts of Gayle Chlebnik of Wayne State University and Jane Fiebelkorn of General Motors Research Laboratories in making the conference itself run smoothly as well as in attending to the details of this Proceedings.

William H. Kelly

Frank E. Jamerson

October 1980

Organizing Committee
Front: (L-R) John R. Reitz, William H. Kelly, Daniel R. Gustafson
Back: (L-R) Frank E. Jamerson, William W. Havens, Robert E. Hetrick, James Lunan, Peter A. Schroeder

Panel Discussion
(L-R) Patrick N. Keating, Frank E. Jamerson, George A. Ball, Roger I. George, John R. Reitz

William H. Kelly, Montana State University; Daniel R. Gustafson, Wayne State University; W. Dale Compton, Ford Motor Company; Nils L. Muench, General Motors Corporation (left to right).

Conference Attendees at Morning Session
Engineering Society of Detroit

Evening Reception at Howard Johnson's, Detroit, Michigan

Lobby Conversations, Engineering Society of Detroit
Detroit, Michigan

PROGRAM AND TABLE OF CONTENTS

WEDNESDAY, 14 MAY 1980

Evening Reception

THURSDAY, 15 MAY 1980

Morning Session
William H. Kelly, Montana State University, presiding

    Research in the General Motors Corporation
        Nils L. Muench, General Motors Research
        Laboratories... 1
    Physics and the Car Business
        W. Dale Compton, Ford Motor Company..................... 17
    Physics Research in the Automotive Supply Industry
        Patrick N. Keating, Bendix Corporation.................. 27
    The Cooperative Automotive Research Program
        Lawrence H. Linden, Office of Science and
        Technology Policy 31

Afternoon Session

    General Motors Research Laboratory Tour
        J. Charles Tracy... 37
    Tour of Research Laboratories at the Ford Motor Company
        John R. Reitz.. 43

Evening Banquet
William H. Kelly, presiding

    Challenges to the Automotive Industry
        Howard H. Kehrl, General Motors Corporation............. 51

FRIDAY, 16 MAY 1980

Morning Session
Richard H. Sands, University of Michigan, presiding

    Non-linear Spectroscopy in Combustion Research
        Kenneth A. Marko and Lajos Rimai, Ford
        Motor Company... 57
    Infrared Diode Lasers
        Wayne Lo, General Motors Research Laboratories.......... 72
    Vehicle Emissions Measurements with Infrared Diode Lasers
        John C. Hill, General Motors Research Laboratories...... 82
    Electric Vehicle Systems
        William J. Walsh, Argonne National Laboratory........... 92

FRIDAY, 16 MAY 1980 (Cont.)

    The Role of Exoelectrons and Oxide Films in Fatigue
Detection
        William J. Baxter, General Motors Research
        Laboratories.. 107
    Panel Discussion and Question Period
        Richard H. Sands, University of Michigan, Moderator
        George A. Ball, Chrysler Corporation
        Roger I. George, American Motors Corporation
        Frank E. Jamerson, General Motors Corporation
        Patrick N. Keating, Bendix Corporation
        John R. Reitz, Ford Motor Company 120

Afternoon Session
James Lunan, Chrysler Corporation, presiding

    Laser Spectroscopy in Combustion
        James H. Bechtel, General Motors Research
        Laboratories.. 127
    Exhaust Gas Oxygen Sensors
        Robert E. Hetrick, E. M. Logothetis, and
        D. K. Hohnke, Ford Motor Company........................ 140
    Transition Metal Surface Electronic Structure
        John R. Smith, General Motors Research Laboratories..... 147
    Thin-Film Light Emitting Display Devices
        S. L. McCarthy and John Lambe, Ford Motor Company....... 157

APPENDIX

    Frontpiece: A Symposium on Physics in the Automotive
    Industry, March 14-15, 1938....................................168

RESEARCH IN THE
GENERAL MOTORS CORPORATION

Nils L. Muench
Technical Director
General Motors Research Laboratories
Warren, Michigan 48090

ABSTRACT

In GM, research responds to the issues facing the auto industry: energy, air quality, safety and competition. To ensure that research is effective, GM does not isolate fundamental from applied research, and individual researchers are encouraged to understand the Corporation in their areas of expertise. Most research projects are initiated "bottom-up." Physics research is conducted primarily within the Physics Department of the General Motors Research Laboratories. However, physicists also work elsewhere on challenging research, and examples of this are given.

I. INTRODUCTION

I should begin by explaining that at GM the term research is very broad. It includes market research, economic research, and service research, but I will concentrate on the physical sciences today.

Tomorrow you will hear from five of our physicists who will talk about solid state lasers, laser spectroscopy, exo-electrons, combustion research, and surface theory. Also, today some of you will tour the GM Research Laboratories--we call ourselves GMR--for a first hand impression of physics research in the auto industry.

Thus, my job is easy: I will set the stage for these events by addressing the three universal questions: Why, how, and what? First, why do we do research in GM? Second, how do we organize and manage research? And third, what is the research done by physicists in GM?

II. WHY

Let's begin with the question "Why?". All industrial research must anticipate and respond to the technical issues which will impact the industry and the Corporation in the future. Research at GM is no exception. Although we do a great deal of long range, fundamental research, this work nevertheless responds to the issues we anticipate will be facing us in the future.

Let's examine some of these technical issues.

Only a few years ago one dominant issue faced GM: competitive economics--providing the customer the type of product that he or she wanted at a competitive price. We have never neglected this issue and as a result today the U.S. automobile is more functional and desirable than ever.

ISSN:0094-243X/81/660001-16$1.50 Copyright 1981 American Institute of Physics

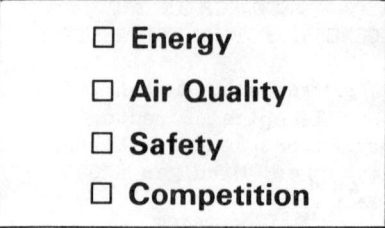

Fig. 1. Major Technical Issues Confronting Auto Industry.

But the past fifteen years have been stormy and volatile. Old issues have intensified, new issues have emerged. Today I see four major technical issues (Fig. 1) -- energy, air quality, safety and competition.

The energy issue is complex and the basis for understanding is a grasp of overall energy technology and energy resources. You will be hearing more of this from our Executive Vice-President, Howard H. Kehrl, this evening, so let me skip to the sub issues.

- Diesel
- Gasohol
- Ethanol
- Methanol
- Shale Oil
- Coal Synthetics
- Hydrogen
⋮

Fig. 2. Alternate Fuels.

First (Fig. 2) is alternate fuels. Diesel, gasohol, ethanol, methanol, shale oil, coal synthetics, and hydrogen head the list. Each alternative fuel generates an entire family of applied research questions. Consider gasohol--what does the addition of 10% ethanol to unleaded gasoline do to fuel economy? Engine knock? Emissions, whether regulated or unregulated, or perhaps even unknown? What are the health and visibility effects, if any, of these emissions?

And putting on a statesman's hat, what are the energetics of producing ethanol: Is there a net gain? What are the national economics: Is it better for the motorist to pay a U.S. farmer sixty dollars a barrel for alcohol than to pay OPEC twenty-five dollars a barrel for oil?

These are challenging applied research questions, not what you would call basic or fundamental, and certainly not all physics, but questions requiring knowledge and skill to answer confidently.

- Diesel
- Direct Injection Stratified Charge
- Gas Turbine
- Sterling
- Rotary
  ⋮

Fig. 3. Alternate Engines.

Also (Fig. 3) springing from the energy issue are questions of alternate engines: diesel, direct-injection-stratified charge, gas turbine, stirling, and rotary, among others. The diesel which provides a very substantial gain in fuel economy--25% on a miles per gallon basis--also provides a full menu of new research questions. For example, there is the matter of diesel particulates

- How Formed
- Filters and Traps
- Health Effects
- Visibility Effects

Fig. 4. Diesel Particulates.

(Fig. 4). They are formed in the combustion chamber but how and why are they formed? What can we do to decrease the quantity of particulates formed?

Then there is the matter of filters and traps in the exhaust system. Filters appear fairly straight forward and pedestrian, until you endeavor to do something new. Then fluid flow and thermodynamics provide the understanding needed to do now what we could not do previously; like design a filter that can be ignited every hundred miles to burn collected particulates without damage to the filter itself. Unfortunately the filter likes to self-destruct within 5 seconds, so we're still working on that.

Some regulation of diesel particulates probably makes sense, but at what level? This will depend primarily on health effects and possibly also on visibility effects. Federal regulatory agencies do not do the research needed as a basis for sensible regulation. Therefore, to deal with health effects, we conduct extensive biomedical research at GMR and, also, we fund selected university research.

The effect of diesel particulates on visibility involves classical physics, notably scattering theory, as well as questions of atmospheric transport requiring fairly sophisticated models. All of this is important, for extensive use of diesels can be a major factor in reducing U.S. oil imports.

> ☐ **ELECTRIC VEHICLES**
>   - **Nickel-Zinc Batteries**
>   - **High Temperature Batteries**
>
> ☐ **HYBRID VEHICLES**
>   - **Flywheel — I.C.**
>   - **Flywheel — Turbine**

Fig. 5.   Possible Future Vehicles.

The energy issue (Fig. 5) also drives us to explore other approaches to vehicle propulsion, including electric. You may be aware that we have announced that GM will have on the market, by the mid-1980's, an electric vehicle powered by nickel-zinc batteries. This announcement puts powerful salt on the tails of researchers who are still endeavouring to solve some of the knotty problems of the nickel-zinc battery.

Hybrid vehicles are very attractive, at least conceptually. Hybrids obtain high peak power from an energy storage device such as a flywheel while a low average power is supplied from a relatively small engine. Unfortunately, thus far the systems that we have explored fall short of being commercially practical for general use. In special applications involving a great deal of stop-and-go operation, there may be an advantage, however.

> - **"CCC" System**
> - **Oxygen Sensor**
> - **Microprocessor**
> - **Catalytic Converter**

Fig. 6.   Emission Control of I.C. Engine.

The (Fig. 6) air quality issue has driven us to very strict emission controls. Frankly I believe this strict control is unjustified from a health effect and cost basis--at least that's what the data tell us. However, the technology involved is a researcher's delight. Essentially all 1981 GM passenger cars will utilize a computer command control--"CCC" for short. This is a closed loop engine control system with an oxygen sensor in the exhaust. A micro computer responds to the oxygen level--and also to atmospheric pressure, temperature, and engine speed--to adjust fuel mixture and spark advance for maximum economy while providing a stoichiometric mixture to the catalytic convertor.

Just think of the beautiful technical problems involved in creating such a system! For example, as you will hear tomorrow, the semiconductor lasers built in the GMR Physics Department are emerging as the only tool with the fast response time needed to probe the CCC exhaust dynamics.

Incidentally, because of CCC, next year GM will be the largest computer manufacturer in the world--at least, of eight bit micro computers. In fact, our production rate of five million computers per year is about twenty times the 1979 rate of all other manufacturers combined.

```
- Sensor Controlled Robots
- Computer Vision Inspection
    •
    •
    •
```

Fig. 7.   Manufacturing Technology.

Let's (Fig. 7) turn to competition and the subissue of improved manufacturing technology. The list is long and I include only two items which I have personally been very close to: Sensor controlled robots and computer vision inspection. The use of robots in the U.S. suffered a setback because the first generation robots were too primitive. In particular, they were blind. They simply repeated a predescribed motion, for example, to spot weld sheet metal. If the parts were not positioned correctly, the robot went blindly ahead anyway. The second generation robots, those that are computer programmable, are a great step forward. But the real potential lies in the third generation machines that can both see and feel. I'll mention this again later.

```
- Polymers
- Steels
- Aluminum
- Composites
    •
    •
- Recycling
    •
    •
```

Fig. 8.   Materials.

Another (Fig. 8) subissue of competition--and the final one I will mention--is materials. The competitive requirement for increasing energy efficiency without taking anything away from the customer is leading us to more extensive use of polymers, high strength steels, aluminums, and composites. The discipline of the marketplace forces us to strive for new, better, and less expensive materials. Thus, materials research involves much of our more fundamental as well as applied research. For example, our research into the fundamentals of phase behavior in steel led to the first so-called dual-phase steels--economical, high strength materials of great importance.

Incidentally, I note on the figure the matter of recycling. This is important in itself but is included as indicative of the many topics which time does not permit us to cover this morning.

If you kept score, you'll note I haven't addressed safety. It is still a major issue but we have gone so far in making the vehicle mechanically safe that we have reached diminishing returns, even as we are still striving to do better. The real problem is the unsafe driver plus the 86% of car occupants who fail to wear seat belts. Although our leverage is not great, we are researching those subjects with some interesting results I'll mention later.

III. HOW

Now I would like to deal with the question of "How?". How do we organize? How do we operate? How do we manage research?

- ☐ **GM Corp. 1979 R&D Expenditures: $1.95 Billion**

- ☐ **"Research" Approximately 5 to 10% of "R&D"**

Fig. 9. GM Expenditures on R and D.

You've (Fig. 9) perhaps read of GM's R&D expenditures: $1.95 billion last year. This number includes a large amount of engineering. Only a fraction of it is for research--perhaps 5 to 10% depending upon your definitions. But still it is a large expenditure.

How do we make those research expenditures effective? That is a major part of my job, but it is also a responsibility of each researcher. One key is a strong coupling with the total GM organization. To understand you need to have at least a simplified concept (Fig. 10) of the GM organization.

There are four major groups of divisions and staffs: North American Car and Truck, Components, Overseas and Technical, and the Operating Staffs and Financial. As the figure indicates, North American Car and Truck comprises ten divisions including the names best known to the public--Buick, Cadillac, Chevrolet, Oldsmobile, and Pontiac. Components comprises 21 divisions including such

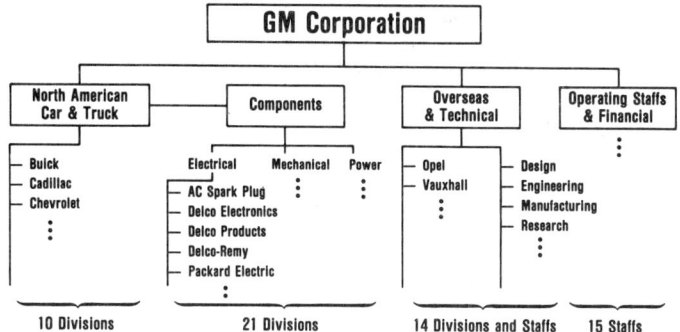

Fig. 10. Abbreviated Schematics of GM Organization.

electrically and electronically oriented divisions as AC Spark Plug, Delco Electronics, Delco Products, Delco Remy, and Packard Electric. Under Overseas and Technical we have overseas divisions such as Opel and Vauxhall. Also, we have the Technical Staffs: Design, Engineering, Manufacturing, and Research.

You will appreciate that this is a much simplified diagram, but it will suffice for me to make just two points. First, important research is conducted at GM operating divisions. Second, these divisions have become very technically sophisticated in recent years. From the standpoint of GM Research Laboratories--and that will be my focus from this point onward--the increased technical prowess of our divisions is good. It has enabled GMR to shift toward longer range research, and it has provided stronger technical contacts for better GMR coupling to the divisions.

The cornerstone of this coupling is that each researcher comes to know the divisional people that relate to his or her special expertise. For example, the surface physicists know the engineers at Packard Electric who are concerned with electrical contacts and those at AC Spark Plug who are responsible for the CCC oxygen sensor. The physicists researching rare earth magnets know the engineers at Delco Remy concerned with starter motors and those at Delco Electronics responsible for speaker magnets. But these are the same surface physicists and magnetics researchers who do the fundamental research and publish fairly extensively.

This illustrates another point: Organizationally we do not separate basic or fundamental research from applied. That is, researchers doing fundamental research work beside those doing applied research. Also, all researchers including those doing fundamental research are expected to understand the Corporation in their area of expertise. The result is that all of our research has a good chance of payoff to GM--fundamental as well as applied.

Also, (Fig. 11) the researcher's knowledge of GM ensures that a healthy fraction--in fact most--of our research moves from the bottom-up. Aided by management's efforts to identify corporate goals, problems, and deficiencies, the researchers tell management what should be done, rather than vice versa.

Fig. 11. "Bottom-Up" Philosophy.

Research management's job is, first, to attract the right staff and provide the right environment, and second to act as a high-stakes gambler, betting money and resources on the research judged most likely to be highly successful.

Another important inter-relationship is with the outside technical community. Charles Kettering said, "If we shut our doors, we shut out more than we shut in." GMR's management strongly supports that statement.

Fig. 12. GM Research Laboratories "GMR" Aerial View.

I've been discussing how we operate GM Research Laboratories (Fig. 12). Let me now give you a closer view of our facilities and people. We are spread across twelve different buildings. Most physics research is in this building by the lake. The newest building was completed just two years ago to house our biomedical research.

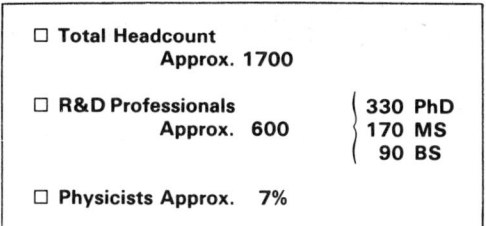

Fig. 13. GMR Staffing.

GMR (Fig. 13) has a total headcount of approximately 1700 persons. The R&D professionals number approximately 600 with over half having PhD degrees, and with physicists amounting to approximately 7% of the total professionals. Our engineering colleagues at GMR tell us that is about all the physicists any industrial research lab can bear. Of course, we don't agree with them.

U. of Michigan	24	Michigan State	7	U. of Maryland	4
U. of Calif.-Berkeley	20	Princeton	7	R.P.I.	4
U. of Illinois	18	Carnegie-Mellon	6	Rutgers State	4
Purdue	17	Iowa State	6	V.P.I.	4
Stanford	12	U. of Minnesota	6	Washington	4
Pennsylvania State	11	U. of Calif.-Los Angeles	5	Brown	3
M.I.T.	10	Cornell	5	Ill. Inst. of Tech.	3
Ohio State	9	Northwestern	5	U. of Missouri-Rolla	3
U. of Wisconsin	9	Wayne State	5	U. of Pennsylvania	3
Cal. Tech.	9	Ga. Inst. of Tech.	4	U. of Southern Calif.	3
Educated in England	9	Harvard	4	Yale	3
Case Western	8	Lehigh	4		

Three or more graduates

Fig. 14. Schools of GMR Professionals.

You may be interested in the origins of our PhD professionals (Fig. 14). The figure shows only those schools which have provided us with three or more PhD graduates. If your university is not shown, nevertheless it may have provided us with Bachelor's or Master's degrees or with less than three PhD's. In any event I want you to know that we appreciate the good job the universities are doing in providing us with talented and well educated researchers.

To summarize my answer to the question of "How do we manage research at GMR?": We hire very good people and ensure they are well-coupled to GM as well as to the outside technical community. The pay-off to GM then comes naturally.

IV. WHAT

Now I want to wind-up by giving examples of what is being done at GMR by physicists. I will include work done outside the Physics Department to make the point that there is a wide range of research that physicists are well able to do that is important and interesting.

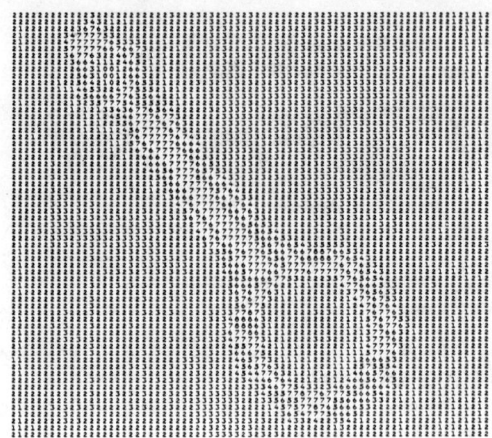

Fig. 15. Array Camera View of Connecting Rod.

I'll give you a few seconds to guess what is displayed in this figure (Fig. 15). It is a picture of a connecting rod taken by an

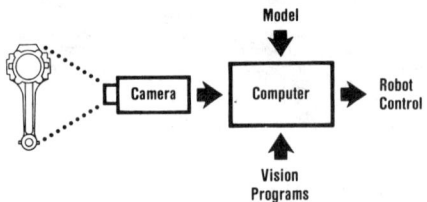

Fig. 16. Computer Vision System.

array camera. A computer vision (Fig. 16) system consists of three elements: an electronic array camera which serves as the computer's eye. The camera output is analyzed by a computer through various vision programs which take gradients, thin edges, connect edge points, label connected regions, and then calculate region properties. These results are compared with a stored model, and the output is sent to a robot. GM is a world leader in computer vision technology and we already have had some remarkable (Fig. 17) in-production successes. However, while we are able to identify one part among a few, as illustrated in this figure, we have not (Fig. 18) yet solved the more complex problem illustrated on the next figure. This remains a challenge.

I mentioned (Fig. 19) the need to understand and solve the diesel particulate problem. Measurements provide the key to understanding. Therefore we have developed a measurement of particulate mass concentration with fast time resolution so as to track different engine operating conditions. With our laser photo-acoustic device, energy from a chopped laser beam heats

Fig. 17. Confused Scene of Auto Manufacturing Parts that Present Vision Systems Can Unravel.

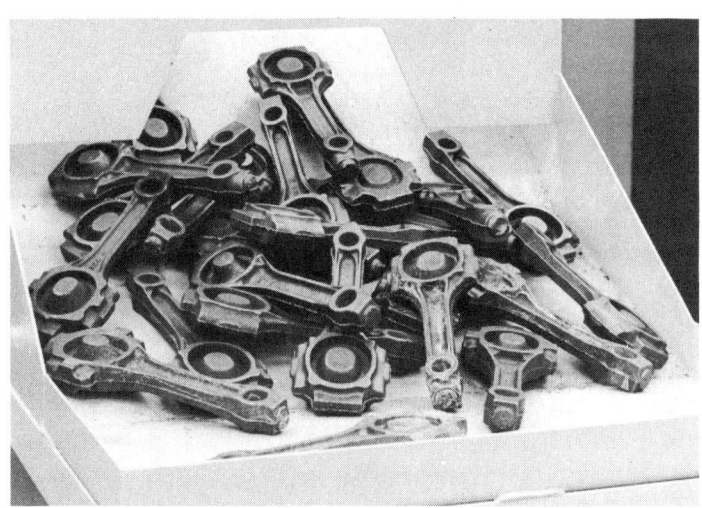

Fig. 18. The "Bin of Parts" Problem.

particulates in the exhaust sample. The heated particulates in turn heat the gas to generate an acoustic signal at the chopping frequency.

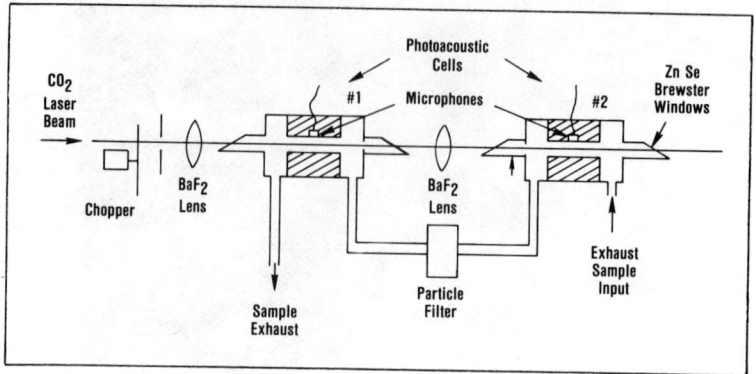

Fig. 19. Photo-Acoustic System for Particulate Measurements.

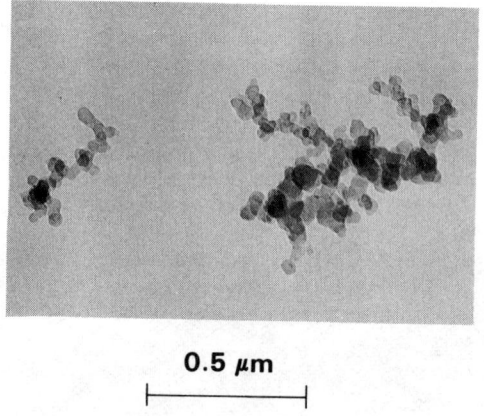

Fig. 20. Typical Diesel Particulates.

It (Fig. 20) is also important to study diesel particulates on a microscopic scale. The figure gives a transmission electron microscope image of a fairly typical particulate. As you see, a diesel particulate is a complex structure of more-or-less linear arrays of small spherical carbon particles. Formation of the linear array is a mystery yet to be unraveled. We are beginning to study the crystal structure of the individual spheres that comprise the particulate, but that's a story for another time.

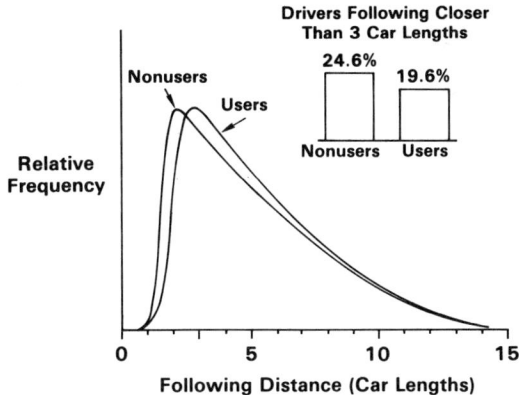

Fig. 21. Comparison of Car Following Distances for Users and Non-users of Seat Belts.

GMR (Fig. 21) physicists pioneered the study of traffic flow and we are continuing to use our techniques of observation and analysis to study current issues. For example, do drivers who buckle up their seatbelts trade-off their additional security by driving more recklessly? Here we plot relative frequency of observation as a function of following distance in car lengths. If we think driving with a short following distance is risky--and it is--then non-users of seat belts take greater risks than users of seat belts.

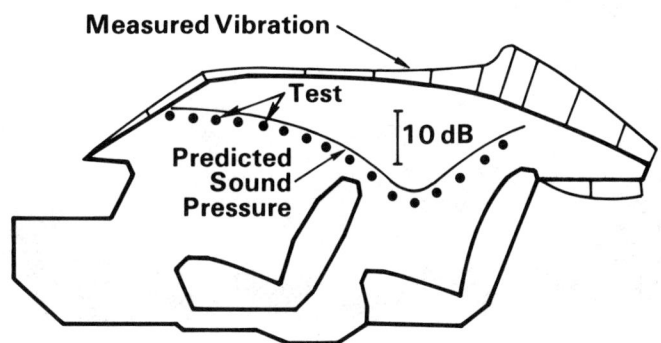

Fig. 22. Acoustic Response of Passenger Compartment.

Ever (Fig. 22) been annoyed by the noise level in your car? I hope you haven't, but as we move to lighter vehicles, perhaps with less mass devoted to acoustic insulation, acoustic design becomes more important than ever. Because of the complex geometry of the passenger compartment, acoustic analysis is, to say the least, quite difficult.

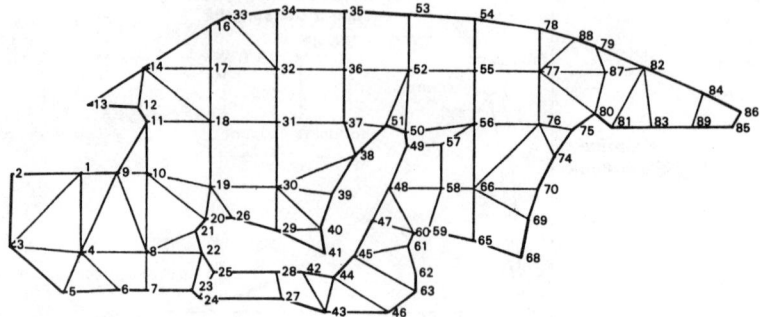

Fig. 23. Finite Element Model of Passenger Compartment.

Our approach (Fig. 23) is to make a two-dimensional, finite-element model of the passenger compartment. Then a measured vibration is used as input data to generate a predicted sound-pressure level. As illustrated, the prediction agrees well with the test data. You may ask: if we can get test data, why go to all this trouble? The answer, of course, is that we need a predictive capability to do a proper job of engineering.

Fig. 24. Plasma Carburizing of Pinion Gear.

Many (Fig. 24) parts of an automobile are carburized--for example, gear teeth in order to obtain hardness for durability. Conventional carburizing is done at high temperature for a period of hours in a hydrocarbon atmosphere. Our approach is to use a plasma which makes carbon atoms more abundantly and uniformly available at the surface of the steel part. Here you see a pinion gear being plasma-carburized in the laboratory.

The resulting hardness is greater for the plasma carburizing in 45 minutes than for the conventional in 4-1/2 hours. Also, the use of hydrocarbons is reduced by 99%--a critically important side benefit.

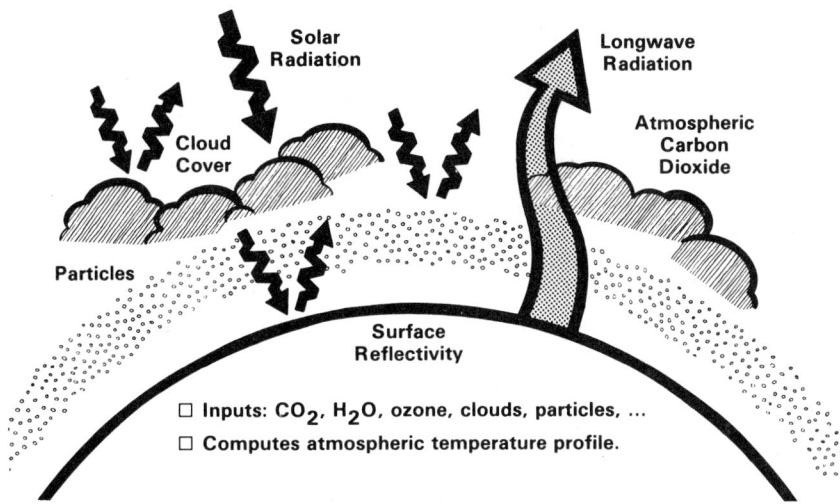

Fig. 25. GMR Atmospheric Model.

Whereas (Fig. 25) we were once concerned with only the photochemical smog formed in particular locations such as the L.A. Basin, we are now concerned with the global atmosphere, including the effects of particulates, cloud-cover, carbon dioxide and freon, among others. With these inputs plus surface albedo, researchers in the Physics Department have developed an atmospheric model which computes temperature profiles and predicts the long-term change in global temperature.

100%	Increase in Carbon Dioxide	→	+2°C
10%	Increase in Cloud Cover	→	-2°C
13%	Increase in Surface Reflectivity	→	-2°C
200%	Increase in Airborne Particles	→	-2°C

Fig. 26. Atmospheric Sensitivity Analysis.

One (Fig. 26) value of such a model is that it permits an atmospheric sensitivity analysis--just to keep the prophets of doom honest! It is well publicized that a 100% increase in carbon dioxide will increase global temperatures by approximately 2°C. Less well publicized is the result that a 10% increase in cloud cover will decrease temperatures by 2°C, as will a 13% increase in surface reflectivity or a 200% increase in airborne particles.

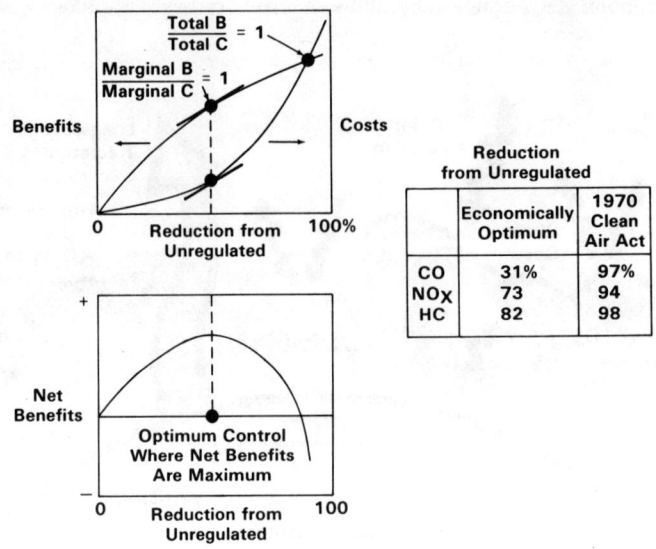

Fig. 27. Cost Benefit Analysis.

I have (Fig. 27) time to mention only one final example of work in which physicists have played a role: cost-benefit analysis. Reduction of exhaust emissions has costs indicated by the lower curve, and benefits indicated by the upper curve. Where these curves cross, the benefits equal the cost. Emissions should be reduced until benefits equal costs. Right? Wrong. At this point the net benefit is zero. Society certainly does not want zero benefit, but rather maximum net benefit. The net benefit--the difference between these curves--is maximum at a much lower level of emission reduction, substantially below the standards of the Clean Air Act.

This analysis involves partly economic theory, but also a great deal of hard work in projecting the physical effects of changes in exhaust emissions. Thus you see one of our jobs is to generate logical approaches and factual data to help ensure that resources devoted to societal objectives are wisely expended.

Those of us who are a part of physics research at General Motors count ourselves fortunate. The decade ahead will be an exciting one, and the auto industry a challenging place to be. As you tour GMR today and listen to the papers tomorrow, I know you will feel the enthusiasm of our physicists. They are playing a vital role in research at General Motors while making important contributions to science in their chosen fields.

PHYSICS AND THE CAR BUSINESS

W. Dale Compton and John R. Reitz
Engineering and Research Staff, Research
Ford Motor Company, Dearborn, Michigan 48121

ABSTRACT

Physicists have made important contributions to many areas of Ford Motor Company activity, particularly in areas of basic and applied research and product development. A number have assumed positions with management responsibility. Many of the technical problems facing the automotive industry today require a fundamental understanding, and the ability of physicists to contribute to the solution of these problems is greater now than it has been in the past. The present paper discusses some of these problems, and also traces a few case histories of physicists at Ford Motor Company; these illustrate the wide diversity of career paths for persons entering industry with a physics background.

The general environment in which the automotive industry operates presents many pressures. There is the pressure to develop new competitive products. There is the pressure to quickly improve fuel economy. There is the need to meet the many government regulations. It is hoped that this meeting will offer some insight into what physics or physicists are able to contribute in this context. In order to do this, it is necessary to talk briefly about the people, the opportunities, and the challenges.
Ford Motor Company is readily characterized as an engineering and manufacturing company. It is not a physics company although it does employ physicists. By this we mean there is really no direct line between the product, cars and trucks, and basic physics research.
But the individual physicist contributes to the overall success of the Company in many important ways. There is the familiar research function in which new knowledge is generated in areas of potential interest to the Company. It is important to note that this research can be either applied or basic. The results of these studies are published in the scientific journals and reported at technical meetings such as this one which is sponsored by the American Physical Society. There is the consulting role where the research physicist works on an occasional basis with the applied scientist or engineer in the search for a solution to a particular problem or in the application of a new technology. And there is the management role where the individual with a physics background proceeds to lead particular groups or elements of the technical community in product development or in manufacturing development. The vast majority of the physicists employed by Ford are in applied areas, and their role here is directly related to the product or to new processes. In applied research the physicist may find himself

ISSN:0094-243X/81/660017-10$1.50 Copyright 1981 American Institute of Physics

as part of an interdisciplinary team, or he may function as a surrogate engineer, but because of his physics background he is able to bring a broader perspective to bear on his program, and in some cases he may bring a special combination of talents, such as, e.g., special knowledge of both materials and electronic instrumentation.

The physicist is employed in various capacities. There are 356 people at Ford with at least one degree in physics. Eighty-two of these people are employed in the Research Staff, but only 28 of them are in the Physics Department. The others in Research are in interdisciplinary departments which are concerned with systems problems relating to the automobile, on the development of nondestructive or other diagnostic testing techniques, on the exploration of alternate energy developments or on the study of engines and their characteristics.

A characterization of the Research Staff personnel by their highest educational degree is given in Tables I and II. Of all science majors in Research, physicists are the second most populous class. Furthermore, even though engineers are the biggest single group of people within Research, the engineers outnumber the scientists by less than 20 percent. Outside of Research Staff,

Table I. Highest Education Level and Major in the Professional/Technical Workforce, Research Staff

Science Major	PhD	MS	BS	Total
Chemistry	73	22	31	126
Physics	50	11	13	74
Metallurgy	15	4	1	20
Math	2	2	7	11
Materials	2	1	-	3
Ceramics	1	-	-	1
Other	10	8	2	20
Sub-Total	153	48	54	255

the 274 people with at least one degree in physics are employed by various activities, e.g., in the other staffs and in many of the operating divisions. They are involved directly in the technical problems of the Company and in the management of its various units. Among this group is a Chief Engineer, a Plant Manager and a Forward Engineering Planning Manager. A number of the people have combined a degree in physics with a degree in business or engineering, thereby expanding their opportunities. A few brief case histories may be helpful in illustrating the large number of possibilities that exist for a person with a physics background.

Table II. Highest Education Level and Major in the Professional/Technical Workforce, Research Staff

Engineering Major	PhD	MS	BS	Total
Mechanical	27	62	54	143
Electrical	6	10	30	46
Metallurgical	10	7	6	23
Chemical	4	6	14	24
Engrg. Mech.	6	2	2	10
Aeronautical	2	1	3	6
Automotive	-	4	3	7
Ceramics	1	2	1	4
Nuclear	-	1	-	1
Other	14	6	9	29
Sub-Total	70	101	122	293

Case 1 has a Ph.D. in Physics from Birmingham University (England). He has worked at a number of different industrial and government laboratories. He joined Ford as a Research Scientist and is presently Senior Staff Scientist - Theoretical Physics, in Engineering and Research Staff.

Case 2 has a B.A. in Physics from Brown University and an MBA from University of Pennsylvania. He joined Ford as a Planning Analyst in Truck Operations and is currently Forward Engineering and Research Program Planning Manager.

Case 3 has a B.S. in Physics and Chemistry from Punjab University (India) and an M.S. in Engineering from Wayne State. He joined Ford as a Project Construction Engineer in the Glass Division and is currently Plant Manager, Milan Plant.

Case 4 has a B.A. in Mathematics and Physics from St. Joseph College and an M.S. in Engineering from Michigan. He joined Ford Division in the Product Design Department, and is currently Executive Engineer, Fuel Economy and Compliance Engineering, Truck Operations.

Case 5 has a Ph.D. in Physics from Ohio State University. He joined Ford as a Research Scientist. Switching to Product Development, he progressed from Supervisor to Manager to Executive Engineer in the Product Development Group and the Chassis Division; he has been Chief Engineer, Components Engineering Office, and Chief Engineer in the Climate Control Division. He is presently Chief Engineer, Light Truck Product Development.

Case 6 has a B.A. in Physics from Carleton College and an M.B.A. from Michigan State. He joined Engineering and Research Staff as a Research Technician and is currently Manager, Computer Operations, Car Engineering.

Case 7 has a Ph.D. in Physics from the University of Maryland. He joined Ford as a Research Engineer and is presently Senior Staff Scientist, Research Staff.

Case 8 has a Ph.D. in Physics from University of Illinois. He joined Ford as a Research Scientist; he has been Manager, Engine Logic, General Parts Division, and Manager, Control Systems Department, Research Staff and is currently Manager, Analytical Sciences, Research Staff.

Case 9 has a Ph.D. in Physics from University of Michigan. He joined Research Staff as a Research Scientist but four years later switched to Product Engineering as a Principal Design Engineer. He has been Manager, Steering Gear and Pumps, Chassis Engineering, and is now Executive Engineer, Climate Control Division.

Case 10 has a Ph.D. in Physics from Cornell University. She joined Ford as a Research Scientist and is currently Principal Research Scientist, Engineering and Research Staff.

Case 11 has a B.S. in Physics from Maryland and a Ph.D. in Psychology from University of Pennsylvania. He joined Ford as Supervisor, Human Factors Engineering, and is now Executive Engineer, Safety Research in Environmental and Safety Engineering Staff.

Case 12 has a B.S. in Physics and an M.B.A., both from Stanford. He joined Ford as a Financial Analyst and is now Executive Director, Special Vehicle Operations, Ford of Japan.

Let us turn now to a brief discussion of the research that can challenge the physicists. The industry has undergone a remarkable change in the past decade; it has changed from a mature industry, in which the product tended to evolve from one period to the next, to a high-technology industry that is prepared to utilize the latest developments in areas such as new materials, electronics, energy conversion and robotics. Many of the problems facing the automotive industry are technical problems of a fundamental nature, and who are better equipped to handle such problems than physicists? Problems of energy-conversion efficiency, the relationship between work and inertial mass, and the use of a material property to measure the state of a system are just a few examples of what might be considered to be the physicist's bread and butter.

Perhaps the most pressing problem currently confronting the industry is the development of more fuel-efficient vehicles. The dependence of fuel economy upon vehicle weight is depicted in Figure 1. This is a plot of the EPA published data, averaged for each vehicle inertia weight and plotted as a function of inertia weight. Data for gasoline-powered vehicles are used in this Figure. Since a decrease in vehicle weight (or vehicle inertia) leads to improved fuel economy, it is easy to understand the interest in new lightweight structural materials such as high-strength low-alloy steels, aluminum alloys, titanium, and graphite/plastic composites. A reduction in vehicle weight through new design and the use of lightweight materials is essential to improved fuel economy in a car that is to retain its utility in terms of passenger comfort and cargo capacity.

Fig. 1. Fuel economy as a function of vehicle inertia weight for gasoline-power vehicles (EPA data).

But the curve of Figure 1 represents only one of a family of curves; the fuel economy of diesel-powered vehicles falls on another curve, somewhat above the original curve of the figure. Therefore, another way to improve fuel economy is by means of more efficient power plants, such as the diesel engine, the stratified charge engine or the lean-burn engine. There are also opportunities to improve transmission efficiencies, reduce aerodynamic drag and minimize frictional losses. Clearly all of these avenues of improvement, lighter-weight, more-compact vehicles, improved power-trains, and improved design must be pursued if we are to reduce appreciably the energy requirements of the transportation sector in this country.

It may be of interest to spend a few minutes in discussing the overall efficiency of the car power plant. Discussions with non-technical people often leave the impression that there is a very large opportunity for improving the efficiency of the vehicle powertrain. And indeed it may be startling to note that in the typical 1979 gasoline powertrain only about 12% of the energy in the fuel is converted to net work at the wheels. But, as physicists, we understand that some of the energy in the fuel is unavailable for motive power because a thermodynamic cycle is involved, and the laws of physics require a certain fraction of the heat to be rejected to the atmosphere at ambient or somewhat elevated temperatures in order for the engine to operate as a thermo-mechanical converter. In addition, even some nonthermodynamic losses are unavoidable because we must deal with combustion products which are not pefect gases, engine friction, engine thermal losses and parasitic losses in pumps. On the other hand, there are many places where the efficiency of a typical powertrain can be improved, and a sequence of small improvements can add up to substantial energy savings.

The energy distribution in a typical gasoline powertrain is shown in Figure 2 along with that for an improved stratified charge gasoline powertrain, known as PROCO, for "programmed combustion". Through improvements in engine efficiency and reduction in idle/deceleration/warmup losses, the PROCO powertrain achieves about a 40% improvement in the net work delivered to the wheels. It is interesting to note how much energy is consumed in warming up the engine, deceleration and idle; the development of new systems based on regenerative braking, engine shut-down at idle, etc., may further reduce these nonthermodynamic losses. Such possibilities pose interesting challenges to the scientist and engineer.

A complicating feature in the pursuit of better fuel economy is the simultaneous need to control the emissions of certain pollutants. At the present time, one of the best engine control systems for achieving federally-mandated emissions and fuel economy requirements utilizes a catalyst that simultaneously oxidizes the hydrocarbons and carbon monoxide while reducing the oxides of nitrogen. A catalyst operating in this mode is described by the term "three-way catalyst" or TWC. The need for accurate control of the air-fuel mixture that enters the engine is indicated in Figure 3, where the efficiency of a TWC for the oxidation of CO and hydrocarbon and for the reduction of nitrogen oxides (NO_x) is plotted as a function of the air to fuel (A/F) ratio. It is apparent that high overall efficiency for the simultaneous removal of all three gases with a TWC is achieved only within a very narrow A/F ratio range near the stoichiometric value, that is, the A/F ratio at which complete combustion occurs. This then establishes the need for a control system that maintains the A/F constant over a wide range of engine parameters. This, in turn, requires an A/F sensor that can accurately sense a quantity that is related to the air/fuel ratio.

At the present time, the only automotive A/F sensors contemplated for use are oxygen sensors that sense the oxygen pressure in the exhaust gas. Figure 4 shows the dependence of the oxygen pressure in the exhaust of an internal combustion engine on the A/F ratio. Since the oxygen pressure changes by many orders of magnitude at the stoichiometric point, the point at which complete combustion occurs, it is a relatively straightforward strategy to detect (and hence control) the air/fuel ratio with a sensor made from a material with a physical property which depends on oxygen pressure. Nevertheless, the harsh conditions prevailing in the automotive environment impose severe requirements on the electrical, chemical and mechanical properties of sensor materials. Additional complications arise from the fact that the exhaust consists of many gaseous components which are not in thermodynamic equilibrium.

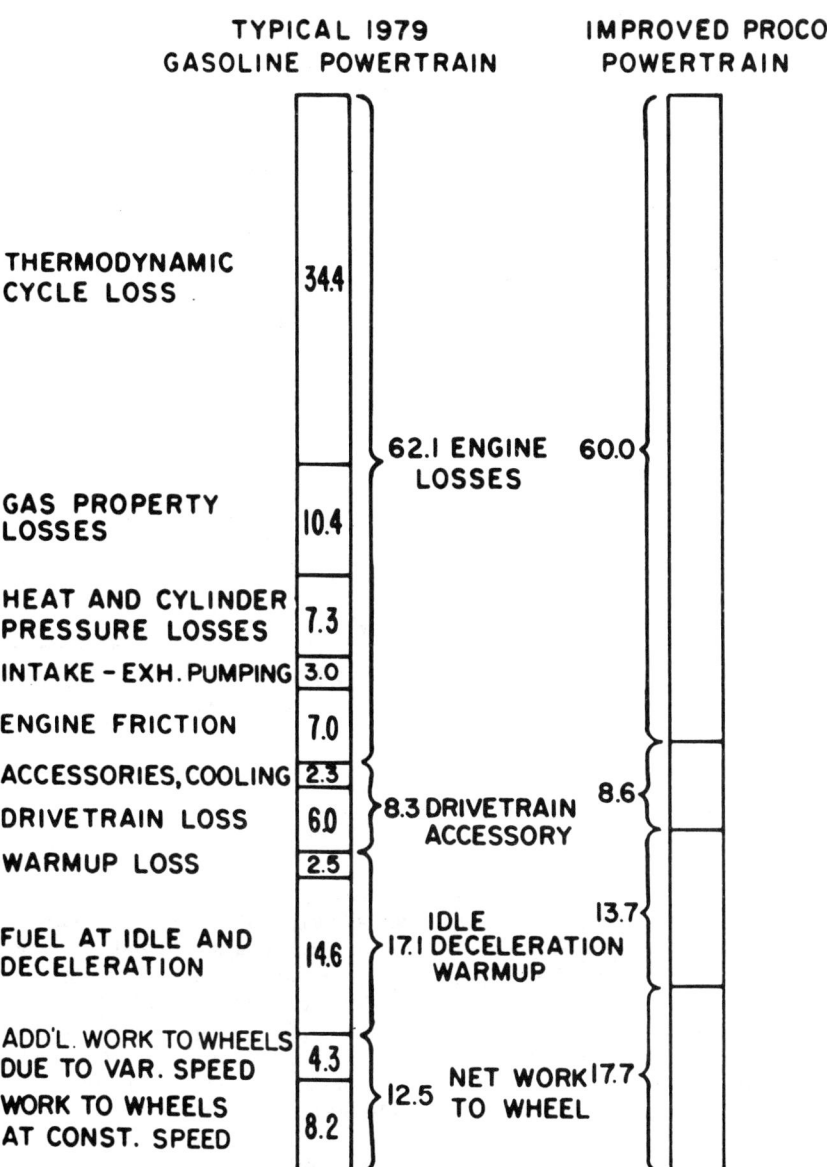

Fig. 2. Energy distribution chart for typical gasoline powertrain.

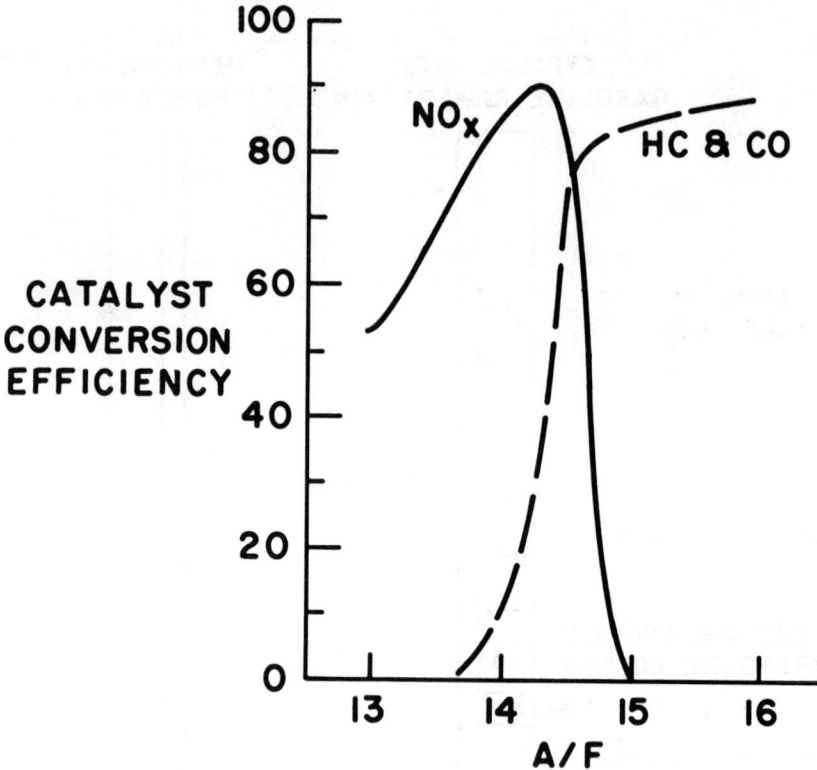

Fig. 3. Catalyst conversion efficiency as a function of air/fuel ratio.

The materials which are being used as sensors are ZrO_2 and TiO_2. The zirconia device which was developed by Westinghouse, Robert Bosch, and others produces a voltage which depends on the difference in oxygen pressure in the exhaust and the outside atmosphere. The titania device was developed at Ford Research Laboratories; it measures oxygen pressure in the exhaust through changes in its electrical resistance. The possibility of detecting other exhaust gas constituents by measuring a change in some material parameter is a direct challenge to the physicist and material scientist.

Ford Motor Company is primarily a manufacturing company. Our principal products are cars, trucks and tractors, but our survival throughout our 77-year history has depended upon our being able to mass-produce a quality product at a reasonable cost. Our future survival depends upon the continual introduction of new manufacturing techniques and processes which increase productivity while at the same time insuring high quality and reliability. In the

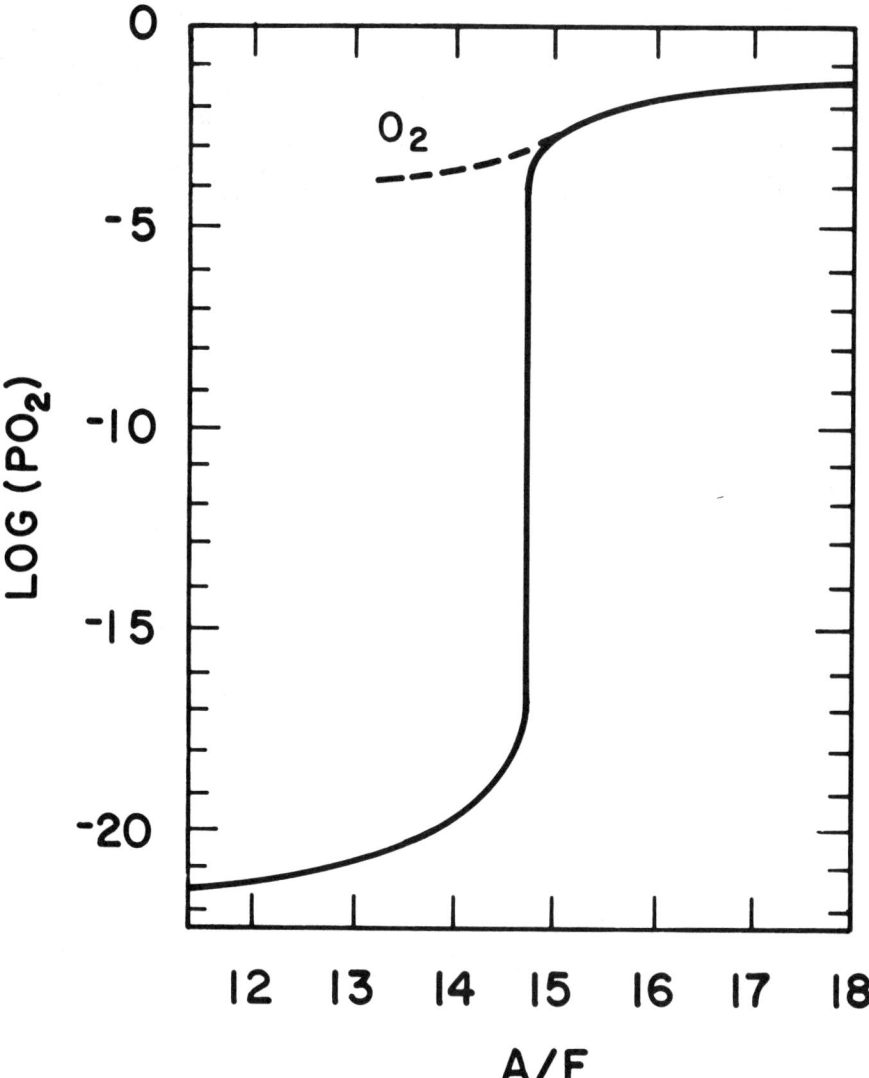

Fig. 4. Exhaust oxygen pressure as a function of the air/fuel ratio.

past, many developments which increased productivity were energy intensive, but what is needed now are productivity-increase developments which produce net energy savings. This poses a tremendous challenge to our technical people, but at the same time it offers opportunities for those innovative persons with both imagination and technical knowledge.

We have talked to you today mainly about people, and a little about the challenges facing an important American industry. The sessions which follow this will focus in more detail on some of the technical areas which we have discussed, as well as on others that are of great interest. You are visiting Detroit at one of the worst economic times in the history of the automotive industry. But we will be healthy by the time that Detroit hosts the next major physics meeting -- American Physical Society Meeting, March 1984. We hope to see you and many of your colleagues again in 1984.

PHYSICS IN THE AUTOMOTIVE SUPPLY INDUSTRY

Patrick N. Keating
Bendix Advanced Technology Center
Southfield, Michigan 48037

ABSTRACT

A brief account of the characteristics of the automotive supply industry and its use of physics is presented.

INTRODUCTION

The U.S. automotive industry consists of two main segments. The first, and best-known, consists of the original equipment manufacturers (OEM's) who are, of course, General Motors, Ford, Chrysler, and American Motors. The second section of the automotive industry consists of the automotive suppliers, those companies who supply parts to the OEM's, and is not as well-known.

In the two previous talks, Nils Muench and Dale Compton have given excellent descriptions of the role of physics at GM and Ford. The purpose of this paper is to give a brief account of the role of physics in the supply side of the automotive business. The paper is basically in two parts - (a) a general discussion of the characteristics of the supply industry and of the physics-related work which is carried out there, and (b) a review of some of the specific physics-related activities which take place in these companies. The general discussion reflects the biases of the author to some degree.

GENERAL CHARACTERISTICS

The automotive supply industry consists of a large number of companies, each of whose automotive sales volume is significantly smaller than that of the OEM's, although some of the companies are quite large because of other, non-automotive product areas. Because of the relative sizes, and because the original manufacturers have historically retained systems responsibility in their own hands, the suppliers generally provide components, and not systems.

The two most-important characteristics required of these components are cost and reliability. When several million automotive units are being produced each year, a 10¢ increment in the cost of any component of a unit means a substantial fraction of a million dollars during the year. Thus, it is not surprising that the OEM's exert substantial pressure, both internally and on their suppliers, regarding the cost of components. Those of us who have had a car give up on us during a trip can readily understand the need for reliability.

As a result of these three factors (the emphasis on cost and reliability and the fact that components, not systems, are supplied), the automotive supply industry is generally quite low-technology in its outlook. Advanced technologies tend to emphasize improved performance rather than low cost, and have not yet achieved the cost reductions which tend to follow the learning curve. Furthermore, they also bring unknown reliability characteristics, because of their lack of history. Many design innovations have significant system implications and are difficult to implement if the supplier has no control over the system. Because of these factors, most of the technical effort is devoted to materials and manufacturing engineering, for this is the best way to achieve low cost and high reliability.

Where does this leave physics? First of all, there is some, but not very much, physics research in the automotive supply industry, although there is significant opportunity to use physics in various problem-solving activities. On the other hand, the lack of physics research activity in the automotive supply industry makes the work done at the universities particularly valuable. University research is the base upon which the technologies used in this industry are built and, like all foundations, is very important.

SOME EXAMPLES OF PHYSICS IN THE SUPPLY INDUSTRY

An exhaustive survey of the physics-related work being carried out by companies which supply the automotive parts to the original-equipment manufacturers is not intended here. Instead, our aim is to give the flavor ot this work by briefly discussing some examples.

Rockwell International is an example of a large corporation with only a portion of its products in the automotive industry, primarily in trucks. Rockwell is very interested in the fluid dynamics of oil films which are 10-100 Å, i.e., just a few molecules, thick and which are subject to high shear stresses. This appears to represent a physics problem of significant fundamental interest, and university research would be of considerable value. Another area of interest to Rockwell Automotive is a study of the mechanics of the steering effort from the steering wheel down to the road, with especial emphasis on the slip which arises when the front wheels of a moving vehicle are turned.

Dana Corporation is heavily involved in the automotive supply business, with emphasis on transmissions. While most of their technical effort is in mechanical engineering, a continuing effort is devoted to the physics of noise and noise analysis.

Another large corporation with only part of its product line in the automotive supply industry is United Technologies Corporation, whose Essex division is most closely identified with this industry. UTC is probably doing as much automotive-oriented research as anyone, including combustion research (using Raman scattering) and fuel emulsification studies.

The development of sensors and transducers is an important activity at UTC, as it is at a number of automotive suppliers. Pollution and fuel-economy requirements are causing a substantial shift to the electronic control of automotive engines. Such control systems require sensors to provide the appropriate input information, including the sensing or measurement of temperature, airflow (preferably in terms of mass flow of oxygen), pressure, crankshaft position, throttle position, and so forth. Many suppliers are developing low-cost transducers for these functions, including UTC, Bendix, Borg-Warner, Motorola, and National Semiconductor. In addition to their development of sensors and transducers, Borg-Warner also has a strong interest in surface physics, particularly the physics of seals, bearings, and condensation and nucleation.

The Bendix Corporation is another large corporation with substantial sales in markets other than the automotive industry, such as aerospace and electronics, forest-products, and industrial equipment. However, Bendix produces a wide range of automotive products, including brakes, spark-plugs, steering systems, and engine control systems and components. Most of the physics research is oriented towards aerospace and electronics needs, but some research is devoted to physics problems associated with the automotive supply industry. Bendix has, among other things, researched the physical phenomena which occur during spark discharges and has developed a number of sensors, including absolute-pressure and air mass-flow transduction. As an example, research on spark discharges shows that, during the sustaining phase which follows breakdown, the spark migrates over the electrodes and, in the presence of turbulence, is extinguished and restruck several times during one spark event.

The tire companies are important members of the supply industry and are involved in a number of physical studies, including the generation and transfer of heat within tires. One interesting example of this at Firestone is an experimental approach which is very similar in concept to computerized axial tomography (CAT), now heavily used for medical diagnostics.

The steel companies form another important segment of the automotive supply industry. Physics does not appear to play a very strong role here, but metallurgical research has led to new lightweight steels which are highly desirable for weight-saving and fuel economy.

SUMMARY

There is not a great deal of physics research in the automotive supply industry, primarily because of the lack of systems responsibility and the need for low-cost and conservative design. Much of the physics effort which does exist is devoted to sensor and transducer development.

THE COOPERATIVE AUTOMOTIVE RESEARCH PROGRAM

Lawrence H. Linden
Office of Science and Technology Policy
Executive Office of the President
Washington, D. C. 20500

INTRODUCTION

This paper briefly presents the Cooperative Automotive Research Program (CARP), an initiative by the U.S. Government and the automotive industry in basic research related to automotive technology. In the following three sections, the framework for federal automotive research and development policy, current government research and development programs, and CARP are described.

AUTOMOTIVE RESEARCH AND DEVELOPMENT POLICY FRAMEWORK

The U.S. Government's policy for ensuring a technologically vital and sound automotive sector is based on the following five precepts:

First, the automotive manufacturers are best able to exploit science and technology for the development and mass production of passenger cars. The modern passenger car is, for the most part, a product which is remarkably efficient and reliable, and modern automotive production facilities remain among the best examples of mass production technology.

Second, the principal forces needed to spur technological change in the industry are market forces, especially realistic energy prices. Profit motivation in the face of domestic and foreign competition forces individual firms to maintain technological progress, balancing short-run expenses against long-term consumer desires. The Federal Government has hindered the industry's response to the energy situation over the past six years by holding down energy prices; the decision to decontrol crude oil prices and such measures as the proposed gasoline conservation fee have rectified this circumstance.

Third, regulatory programs are required where market forces are inadequate. Emissions, safety, and fuel economy regulations have helped to stimulate technological change in socially productive directions over the past fifteen years and will, in varying degrees, continue to be a necessary part of the industry's incentive structure.

Fourth, these market and regulatory forces should be supplemented by Federal support for development programs on technologically high risk systems with potentially high contribution to our national objectives for the transportation sector, where appropriate. Such support should depend on a reasonably convincing case that the particular system or technology would not otherwise be supported at an appropriate level by the private sector.

Fifth, the government should ensure the existence of an adequate program of basic research related to automotive technology to provide ideas and fundamental knowledge to the technology and systems development efforts supported by the public and private sectors.

An automotive technology policy based on this framework will seek the balanced and integrated use of a set of policy tools, with each playing its appropriate role in the overall structure.

CURRENT FEDERALLY-SUPPORTED AUTOMOTIVE RESEARCH AND DEVELOPMENT PROGRAMS

The most important current program of Federal support for automotive technology development is that of the Department of Energy, whose Fiscal Year 1981 budget for automotive research, development, and demonstration is $101 million. In the heat engine area, there are two contractor teams at work on advanced gas turbine systems for automotive propulsion and one working on the Stirling system. The gas turbine contracts are cost-shared with the contractor teams, each of which includes a major domestic automotive manufacturer. There are a range of efforts on the research, development and demonstration of electric and hybrid vehicles as well, including research on advanced battery concepts, development of efficient power conversion technology, systems integration, and demonstration of current technology.

The Department of Transportation also has a research and development program in the automotive area. It is managed by the National Highway Traffic Safety Administration, primarily to support its rulemaking functions in the safety and fuel economy area. The Administration is committed to maintaining a sound scientific and technological basis for the government's regulatory programs, and therefore considers this an important effort. It is focused on near- and mid-term technologies, knowledge of which would allow more effective and efficient safety and fuel economy regulation.

Basic research in the physical sciences related to automotive technology is supported by six Federal agencies -- the Departments of Defense, Energy, Transportation (through the Research and Special Programs Administration), Commerce (through the National Bureau of Standards), the National Aeronautics and Space Administration, and the National Science Foundation. The total level of effort for Fiscal Year 1981 will be approximately $42 million. This figure is based on data that was assembled by a team of agency staff, assisted by consultants, which made judgments concerning the relationship of particular projects to automotive technology and to distinguish between basic and applied work; the reported levels are functions of these judgments.

THE COOPERATIVE AUTOMOTIVE RESEARCH PROGRAM – BACKGROUND, OPERATING PRINCIPLES, AND OBJECTIVES

The concept of the Cooperative Automotive Research Program grew out of discussions within the Federal Government and between the Government and the automotive industry during the period from December 1978 through May 1979. These discussions culminated in a meeting at the White House between the President and the leaders of the American automobile industry on May 18, 1979. At that meeting, the President and the automotive industry leadership announced the principles for a new initiative.

Since the May 1979 meeting, the Director of the Office of Science and Technology Policy and the Secretary of Transportation have carried forward discussions with the industry to design an Administrative Framework which will guide the administrative aspects of the program in accordance with these principles. Simultaneously, a team of scientists and engineers from around the nation have been developing a Technical Framework which will serve to guide the research under the program.

The objectives of the Cooperative Automotive Research Program are the following:

o <u>To improve the scientific and technological base underlying automotive technology.</u> The Program is based on the premise that the automotive industry will utilize ideas which come from fundamental scientific research, and that current levels of effort in this area are inadequate. The Program will not provide solutions to short- or even mid-term problems. The Program will stimulate new segments of the scientific community to work on automotive technology-related problems. It will provide directly no new automotive systems. It will, however, greatly increase the flow of ideas, techniques, and knowledge into the industry.

o <u>To increase the level of production of new engineers and scientists oriented toward the automotive sector.</u> By comparison to other scientific and engineering areas, for example electronics or aerospace engineering, the automotive sector has not been seen by students as a dynamic one where there are attractive careers. Over the decade of the 1980's and beyond, there will be heavy demands for scientists and engineers from the major defense and synthetic fuels programs the nation has launched. It is an objective of CARP to ensure that a reasonable number of students from our major research universities recognize the exciting prospects for technological change in the automotive sector. The university-industry linkages established through CARP will aid in this.

o <u>To provide a new cooperative element to the generally adversarial relationship between the automotive industry and the Federal Government.</u> While this relationship is, of necessity, adversarial in large part due to the Federal Government's regulatory responsibilities, a cooperative element can be usefully added to this relationship; over time this modest level of cooperation may appropriately grow.

THE FINANCIAL AND OPERATING STRUCTURE OF CARP

The structure of the Program is based for the most part on generally accepted concepts of research policy. Support of basic research is a natural and widely accepted role for the government. The projects funded under the Program will be selected in part for their relevance to future automotive technology; the Program will provide results of use to the automotive industry. It is therefore reasonable for the industry to finance a major share of the effort. The government's support also recognizes the significance of long-run technological change in this particular industrial sector which is central to the nation's energy, environment, health and safety, and economic concerns. The government and the industry have agreed to a one-to-one matching program. The automobile manufacturers have agreed among themselves to split their share of the effort according to their share of production of automobiles in the United States.

The Program will operate as a voluntary confederation of relatively autonomous participants, i.e. automotive firms or Federal agencies, each of whom will select and fund the research projects supported with its share of the total effort, consistent with the mutually agreed-upon administrative and technical guidelines. The relative autonomy of project selection by each participant assures that a range of different ideas will be funded. There will be wide and open dissemination of research results, subject to appropriate patent provisions; publication of research results in technical journals; personnel exchange programs; and extramural funding of work; all of which will stimulate diffusion of the new knowledge to those who can utilize it. The Federal Government's support will be primarily extramural. The work supported by the industry under the Program will be significantly extramural.

An independent CARP Oversight Committee will be established to monitor each participant's expenditures to assure that the various aspects of the cooperative agreement are fulfilled. Projects which the Committee judges inapplicable to the Program -- for example, if they are not sufficiently basic in character -- will not be counted as a part of a participant's matching effort under the Program.

Any cooperative research program of this sort naturally raises antitrust issues. The Justice Department was therefore involved from the very beginning in the discussions leading to the design of the Program and has provided a statement of support for the effort. Likewise, the Federal Trade Commission is also supportive of the Program. The Program is consistent with the current automotive antitrust consent decree because it is confined to basic research which is explicitly exempted from the prohibitions under that decree.

Twelve research areas have been identified for inclusion in the Cooperative Automotive Research Program. These are the following:
- Combustion, Thermal and Fluid Sciences
- Structural Mechanics
- Electrochemistry
- Aerodynamics
- Materials Science and Processing
- Control Systems
- Tribology
- Acoustics and Vibration
- Surface Science and Catalysis
- Environmental Science
- Biomedical Science
- Behavioral Science

A team of approximately 100 scientists from university, industry, and government laboratories has been preparing advisory reports which will lead to a Technical Framework for the Program. This framework will describe a range of research topics for each of these areas and will serve as a guide for the Program's participants.

A variety of different types of research projects will be initiated under the Program. There will be personnel exchanges whereby, for example, a scientist from an automotive laboratory might spend a year working at a university, and a graduate student from a university might perform a set of experiments for his or her thesis on experimental equipment only available at one of the companies. Standard basic research grants will be awarded by participating Federal agencies to individual faculty members to support research at universities, and similar arrangements will be made by the automobile manufacturers. There may also be some projects jointly funded by industry and government.

Considerable thought has been given to the organization of the Federal side to this Program. It was decided at the outset, and approved by the President, that several government agencies would participate, to maintain a pluralistic approach for the goverment's participation. It was also decided that no regulatory agency or subcabinet level regulatory administration would participate; this excluded the Environmental Protection Agency and the National Highway Traffic Safety Administration. The Department of Transportation will be the lead agency for the Program. In Fiscal Year 1981, the other Federal agency participating as a member of the CARP confederation structure will be the National Science Foundation.

The proposed budget for the Program for Fiscal Year 1981 is $12 million of obligational authority and $6 million of outlays; about sixty percent of these will be allocated to the Department of Transportation and about forty percent to the National Science Foundation. The planning target remains at a combined government-industry level of $100 million in three-to-five years; how and whether we approach this or exceed it will depend on our experience with the effort as it grows.

CONCLUSION

As a result of a major reassessment of federally-supported automotive research and development, the Federal Government has joined with the automotive industry to launch the Cooperative Automotive Research Program. CARP is part of a balanced overall automotive research and development strategy which relies principally on market forces to insure a technologically sound domestic automotive sector. Over the next several years, this initiative will serve to significantly increase the efforts supporting the science and technology base supporting the automobile.

GENERAL MOTORS RESEARCH LABORATORIES TOUR

J. Charles Tracy
Physics Department
General Motors Research Laboratories, Warren, Michigan 48090

INTRODUCTION

The General Motors Research Laboratories is located at the General Motors Technical Center. Its staff is the largest of the five central staffs at the Technical Center which include: Engineering, Design, Manufacturing, and Environmental Activities. The Research Laboratories complex encompasses over one million square feet and eleven separate buildings. Of the nearly 1700 people employed, 660 are professional researchers, and 375 of these hold doctoral degrees.

Within the Laboratories are twenty technical departments ranging from mathematics, chemistry and physics to computer science, engine research and fluid dynamics.

GM Research is a future-oriented organization, with long range research goals from five to fifteen years to ensure that General Motors is abreast of scientific and technological developments. Although short term projects are sometimes handled which deal with immediate technical problems, emphasis is on long range applied research that will provide a scientific base for GM products and processes in the future.

More specifically, the main objectives of the GM Research Laboratories are to generate new technical knowledge of commercial interest to GM; to evaluate outside technical advances for possible application to GM products and processes; to anticipate future technological needs and develop the expertise required to meet those needs; to provide information for corporate priorities, policies, and operating programs; and to contribute to the solution of product and processing problems that require our specialized facilities and personnel.

LABORATORY TOUR

The tour for the attendees to "Physics in the Automotive Industry" consisted of seven presentations at locations throughout GM Research. These talks, summarized below, were intended to familiarize the visitors with some of the physics research and also other areas of interest to the physics community.

POLYMER-METAL INTERFACES
James M. Burkstrand, Physics Department

Polymers are now being extensively used as substitutes for heavier metals in many automotive applications. Often these parts are metal-coated to provide improved durability and appearance. Our polymer-metal interface studies seek to determine the microscopic interactions such as chemical bonding which may take place at a poly-

ISSN:0094-243X/81/660037-06$1.50 Copyright 1981 American Institute of Physics

mer surface when a metal film is deposited. We correlate these interactions with the adhesion properties of the film to determine the role of chemical bonding in enhancing adhesion. The formation of chemical bonds between the metal and polymer is determined using x-ray photoemission spectroscopy which measures shifts in the binding energies of core electrons in the surface atoms after the metal is deposited. Atomic species which chemically interact at the interface show these electron energy shifts. Correlation of this information with film adhesion strength measurements indicates what types of chemical interactions at the interface produce good metal film adhesion. Our results show that metal films have enhanced adhesion to oxygen-containing polymers through the formation of chelate-like complexes of the deposited metal atoms with the oxygen atoms in the polymer.

J. M. Burkstrand, "Surface Effects on the Electronic Structure of Metal Overlayers — An XPS Study of Polymer-Metal Interfaces," Phys. Rev. B, 20, 12 (1979).

ATMOSPHERIC PHYSICS
Ruth A. Reck and John R. Hummel
Physics Department

The possible influence of General Motors products and manufacturing processes on global climate is an issue of continuing importance. Research in the Physics Department to analyze both natural and man-made pollution consists of solving mathematical models of the atmosphere. The models attempt to accurately simulate the radiative convective energy balance of the atmosphere. The research includes studying the effect on the model output, e.g., computed vertical temperature profiles, of changes in CO_2, O_3, relative humidity, O_2, particulates, clouds, and trace gases. The sensitivity of the model results to changes in these quantities provides information on the sensitivity of the thermal structure of the atmosphere to changes in its composition. For example, the influence of particulates on the atmospheric temperature profile has been found to be sensitive to the reflective properties of the earth's surface and the radiative influence of chlorofluoromethane has been examined.

Ruth A. Reck and David L. Fry, "The Direct Effects of Chlorofluoromethanes on the Atmospheric Surface Temperature," Atmospheric Environment, 12, 239-253 (1979).

John R. Hummel and Ruth A. Reck, "A Global Surface Albedo Model," J. Appl. Meteo. 18, 239-253 (1979).

ELECTRIC VEHICLE BATTERY RESEARCH
John S. Dunning, Electrochemistry Department

General Motors' plans to begin offering electric cars in the mid-1980s are dependent on the development of long life, high performance zinc/nickel oxide batteries. In support of this need, GM Research is concentrating on improving the utilization of the cells' active materials, increasing cell specific energy, and advancing the technology of components with potentially low processing costs (e.g., nonsintered nickel oxide electrodes). GMR has developed special computer-controlled facilities which are used to test cells and batteries under realistic vehicle driving profiles.

We are continuing research on a high temperature lithium iron sulfide cell which could be the 'next generation' electric vehicle battery. The research challenge here is the identification of reasonable cost cell materials compatible with the very agressive environment provided by the molten lithium salt electrolyte.

Displayed was one of the 35 electric vans being built by the GMC Truck & Coach Division of GM for American Telephone and Telegraph Co. as part of a U.S. Department of Energy demonstration project.

E. H. Heitbrink and E. J. Cairns, Electrochemical Power for Transportation: Comprehensive Treatise of Electrochemistry (Plenum Press, Vol. 7, 1980).

COMPUTER VISION AND ROBOTICS
Lothar Rossol and Clifford C. Geschke
Computer Science Department

GMR computer scientists have pioneered in the development of computer vision systems, e.g., computer systems combined with electronic cameras which sense, interpret, and analyze visual scenes. Such computers, when teamed with robots, make attractive systems for performing automated part handling, inspection, and assembly operations under changing conditions without exact part positioning. A recently completed system, called CONSIGHT, looks for a part randomly placed on a moving conveyor belt and directs a robot arm to track the part, pick it up, and transfer it to a predetermined location. In addition to vision systems, we are developing robot systems with touch sensors to monitor forces in the robot's hand while acquiring and assembling parts.

Computer Vision and Sensor-based Robots, ed., G. G. Dodd and L. Rossol (Plenum Press, New York, 1979).

PHOTOACOUSTIC MEASUREMENT OF DIESEL EMISSIONS
Fred R. Faxvog and David M. Roessler
Physics Department

To aid General Motors in meeting federal standards for diesel powered vehicle emissions, we have developed a sensitive and rapid method for measurement of diesel particulate carbon mass emissions based on the photoacoustic effect.

In the photoacoustic process optical energy is converted into acoustic energy. Particulates in a cell are heated by an infrared laser and, in turn, heat the surrounding air, thus increasing its pressure. Chopping the laser beam gives rise to periodic pressure fluctuations in the cell which are detected by a microphone.

The method capitalizes on the fact that the laser radiation is uniform throughout each individual particle. The absorption is independent of particle size since the diesel particles are all smaller than the laser wavelength, 10.6 μm. Thus the photoacoustic signal is proportional to the total particulate volume, or mass.

Unlike current filter methods, which can require a full day to weight samples and process the data, the photoacoustic method measures particulate mass with a half-second response time. Such real-time measurements can identify differences in diesel exhaust emissions under various driving conditions which will aid engineers in the design of lower emission diesel engines.

F. R. Faxvog and D. M. Roessler, "Optoacoustic Measurement of Diesel Particulate Emissions," J. Appl. Phys. 50, 7880 (1979).

METAL PHYSICS
Donald P. Koistinen and Robert A. Ayres
Physics Department

Improved control of sheet metal flow during stamping operations could reduce die development efforts. The way the sheet metal flows during stamping depends on such local conditions as: extent of work hardening, strain-rate, biaxial stress state, and punch-sheet friction. In this laboratory, these properties are measured with highly specialized mechanical testing equipment and then incorporated into a mathematical model of plastically deformed sheet metal being developed in our Mathematics Department. Such models predict the performance of sheet metal flow in laboratory experiments and in some stamping operations, e.g., flanging.

R. A. Ayres and M. L. Wenner, "Strain and Strain-Rate Hardening Effects in Punch Stretching of 5182-0 Aluminum at Elevated Temperatures," Met. Trans. A, 10A, 41-46 (1979).

In addition, we are concerned with improving the properties of sheet metals. We have invented a means of increasing the strength of low carbon sheet steels by means of a simple heat treatment. By subjecting a low carbon nitrogenized steel to this treatment and taking advantage of the additional strengthening from the stamping process, parts are produced which are twice as strong as the incoming material. Yet, despite this increase in strength, the formability of the material is greater than that of more conventional alloyed high strength steels. This improved formability permits the application of our thermo-mechanically-treated (TMT) high strength steel to parts which previously were considered too complex for such a materials substitution.

D. J. Bailey and R. Stevenson, "High Strength Low Carbon Sheet Steel by Thermomechanical Treatment: I. Strengthening Mechanisms," Metal Trans. A, 10A, 47-55 (1979).

GMR's ALTERNATIVE FUELS RESEARCH
Russell F. Stebar and Alex R. Sapre
Fuels and Lubricants Department

Although commercially viable alternative fuels in significant quantities are at least ten years away, GMR is preparing for use of these fuels in two ways. First, we are studying the overall energy situation and the technology for generating fuels from our nation's vast resources of oil shale, coal, and solar energy (biomass). Second, we are studying the characteristics of the fuels that could be provided, and when available, testing these fuels in the laboratory and in vehicles.

Currently, gasoline and diesel fuel obtained from oil shale and coal are the most promising alternatives. These fuels can initially be used to supplement petroleum-derived fuels, and eventually to replace them. Alcohols from coal or biomass also show promise, but they would have to be used in vehicles designed for them. Hydrogen from coal, or from water via electrolysis using nuclear or solar power, is a long-term possibility. It is a good fuel, but its promise is limited because of problems with its distribution and on-board storage.

N. E. Gallopoulos, "Alternative Fuels for Reciprocating Engines," Progress in Astronautics and Aeronautics, Vol. 62 (1978).

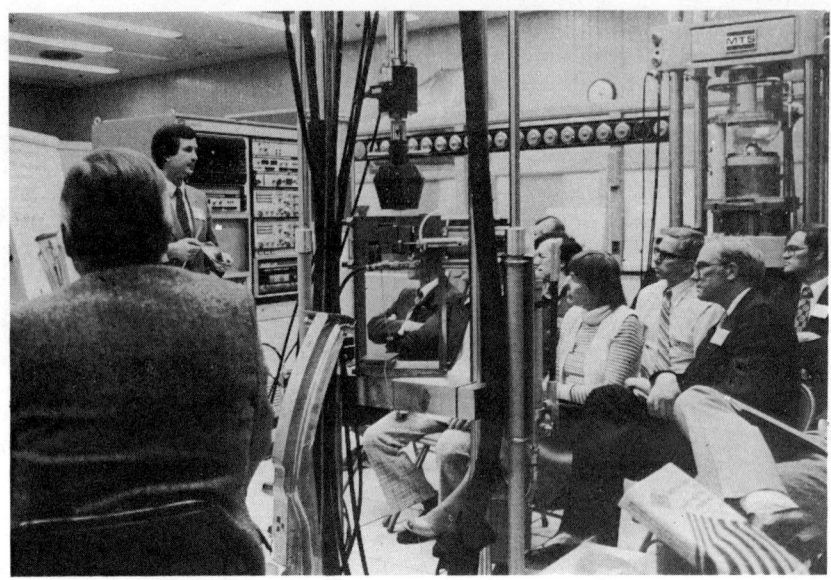

Dr. Robert Ayres explaining research during tour of General Motors Research Laboratories on plastic deformation of metals research which is aimed at understanding physical processes in the stamping of sheet metal components.

A tour group in the Metal Physics laboratory at the General Motors Research Laboratories.

TOUR OF RESEARCH LABORATORIES AT THE FORD MOTOR COMPANY

J. R. Reitz
Engineering and Research Staff, Research, Ford Motor Company
Dearborn, Michigan 48121

ABSTRACT

A brief description of the physics programs encountered on the tour of the Ford Motor Company Research Laboratories is provided.

A visit to the Research Laboratories of the Ford Motor Company is part of the Conference on Physics in the Automotive Industry. The visit will show a cross-section of the programs in Research Staff which are clearly identified as physics research as well as other areas where physicists have established themselves as dominant or team members in what might traditionally be regarded as the province of engineering R & D.

After a brief orientation, the Conference visitors will be divided into tour groups and will visit laboratories involved in combustion research, arc-discharge physics, various spectroscopic applications, metal gauging, energy management, optical display systems and solar energy research. Synopses of the specific tour visits follow.

FOUR-WAVE MIXING LASER SPECTROSCOPY IN COMBUSTION RESEARCH
K. A. Marko, D. I. Klick and L. Rimai

Laser beams are finding increased use as diagnostic probes for studying the combustion process since they provide excellent spatial and temporal resolution for the measurement of chemical species and temperature distributions in combusting systems. The basic measurement technique is Raman scattering, but various multibeam variants of this offer improved sensitivity and easier optical access to the combustion zone.

Techniques for the acquisition of gas phase Raman spectra using four-wave mixing spectroscopy with high-power pulsed lasers will be demonstrated. The experiments are carried out on a specially-designed, stable burner with laminar, premixed air-fuel flow. The experiments involve the acquisition of broadband spectral information from a small volume in the combustion zone during a single laser pulse. The data acquisition and analysis techniques for obtaining temperatures and concentrations will also be discussed.

ARC DISCHARGE PHYSICS
M. R. Gaerttner and W. J. Johnson

There is considerable automotive interest in understanding the electrical characteristics of arc discharges. A better understanding of such discharges should lead to the development of more dependable and more energy-efficient means of igniting fuel.

Furthermore, electrical breakdown in spark gaps is an undesirable source of electromagnetic radiation (EMR) which can interfere with radios and with computers now employed in automobiles.

In most automotive ignition systems, a coil generates a negative voltage ramp ($\sim$ -1 kV/µsec) across a distributor spark gap (width $\sim$ 2mm) until the gap breaks down (typically at $\sim$ 10 kV). During breakdown there can be a current transient of over 25 amperes lasting for several nanoseconds. The charge stored at high voltage on the stray capacitance of the coil-distributor lead is the main source of energy creating the current transient, and this excites EMR with a frequency spectrum between 1 and 1000 MHz.

One method for reducing EMR is to reduce the voltage at which electrical breakdown occurs, so that currents through leads to the spark gap are low and have only low-frequency components. In order for breakdown to occur, however, there must be a "trigger" event which releases at least one electron to start the avalanche. The usual sources of free electrons, cosmic rays or thermionic emission, are sufficiently improbable in the time interval near dc threshold for breakdown, hence the much larger voltages usually encountered (1.5 to 3 times dc threshold). Other techniques for inducing the "trigger" event are being studied; one method of achieving this uses electrodes coated with insulating material such as silicone grease. It is known[1,2] that certain insulators trap and store ions during electrical discharge and thereby create persisting high local electric fields near the insulator surface. This is believed to be the reason that electrodes coated with silicone grease break down at lower voltages than do clean electrodes. When voltage is applied to the coated electrode, the electric fields in the grease presumably assist in the emission of electrons from the cathode, and electrical breakdown occurs near dc threshold.

Experiments involving clean brass electrodes, coated electrodes, and electrodes irradiated with ultraviolet light will be discussed during the tour.

THIN-FILM DISPLAY DEVICES
S. L. McCarthy and John Lambe

Research on light-emitting thin-film devices began as a result of the discovery of a new quantum light source[3] having an emission spectrum controlled by an externally applied voltage. The emission is continuously variable from infrared to ultraviolet. The light emission is produced by inelastic electron tunneling excitation of electromagnetic modes of the junction. The quantum efficiency, however, is too low for automotive instrument dashboard applications.

Current research involves studies of a new, bright thin-film electroluminescent device. This light source is a metal-insulator-metal sandwich where the insulator is doped with phosphor ions such as manganese or terbium. Electronic current passing through the insulator excites the phosphor ion. The light emission spectra arises from the relaxation of the ion. Terbium ions produce green

light and manganese ions give orange color. Presently, work is in
progress to improve electroluminescent durability of the device.
During the tour test devices of terbium-doped light emitting sources
will be demonstrated.

OH SPECTROSCOPY AND RELATED APPLICATIONS
C. C. Wang

OH is an important molecule which has been studied extensively
since the advent of quantum mechanics. However, many important
physical and spectroscopic properties of OH remain to be understood.
Recently, the interest in OH has been revived because of the pivotal
role which OH plays in the atmosphere. For example, a determination
of the OH concentration with an accuracy of 5 - 10% is needed in
order to test the validity of various models for clean and polluted
atmospheres. Using either the fluorescence technique[4] or the absorption technique[5] to make this determination, one requires the
band oscillator strength and the absorption lineshape of OH transitions to an accuracy of better than 5%. We have undertaken experimental and theoretical studies[6] which have now led to an accurate
value for the band oscillator strength and its rotational dependence.
Experimental results have been obtained which verify the spin-independent nature of these quantities, and have completely established the functional dependence of the absorption lineshape.

Additionally, our program at Ford has developed the technique
of laser-induced fluorescence for OH measurements with a demonstrated detection limit of 2×10^6 OH/cm^3. Successful field
measurements of OH were conducted last year both on board a NASA
research aircraft and at ground level near Boulder, Colorado.

LUMINESCENT SOLAR CONCENTRATORS
T. Cole

The luminescent solar concentrator (LSC) combines the phenomenon of luminescence and total internal reflection to achieve collection and concentration of solar photons without the use of conventional optics or tracking systems.[7] A thin flat plate of transparent
material is doped with high-efficiency luminescent molecules. Solar
photons are absorbed by the molecules and subsequently reradiated at
longer wavelength. The fraction of luminescent photons emitted at
angles greater than the critical angle for total internal reflection
is trapped within the LSC and travels by multiple reflections to the
edge of the plate where the photons exit into photovoltaic cells.
The fraction of luminescence so collected is $F = (1 - 1/n^2)^{1/2}$
where n is the refractive index of the matrix. The photon concentration ratio in an ideal LSC is $F A_f/A_e$ where A_f and A_e are the
face and edge areas of the plate, respectively. Since A_f/A_e can be
made large, substantial photon flux gains are possible.

We describe here experiments with LSCs based on the laser dyes
Rhodamine 6G, Coumarin 6 and Coumarin 30 in a matrix of

polymethylmethacrylate. A demonstration of amplification of photon flux density and an estimate of overall efficiency will be given.

GAS ANALYSIS BY FOURIER TRANSFORM INFRARED SPECTROSCOPY
P. D. Maker

Conventional infrared spectrometers employ prisms or gratings to spatially isolate for measurement narrow wavelength intervals of infrared energy. While servicing one such element, the remainder of the spectrum is shielded from the detector and thus ignored. This waste can be avoided, and an enormous shortening of the measurement time realized, by instead using a scanning Michelson interferometer to effect the wavelength discrimination. The principle involved is elementary: for each wavelength, as the interferometer scans through an additional half-wavelength, the transmitted energy at that wavelength undergoes an additional modulation cycle. Thus each wavelenth is modulated at a unique frequency, and an appropriate frequency analysis (Fourier transform) of the digitally recorded interferogram will reveal the detailed wavelength distribution of the incident infrared (IR) radiation. If the number of wavelength intervals to be resolved in the desired spectrum is N, the use of a Michelson interferometer can result in a time savings of $\sqrt{N}$. At high resolution, as required for characterization of gaseous samples, N is $> 10^4$.

Additional enhancements also accrue. At the same resolution, an interferometer transmits significantly more energy per resolution element than does a grating instrument of conventional design; the data set is perforce digitized, and at high accuracy, ready for computer-aided analysis and processing. With such instruments, quantitative analysis of complex gas mixtures by high resolution IR absorption spectroscopy becomes practical.

In our Laboratory automotive exhaust analysis by FTIR spectroscopy has been reduced to routine. Samples of dilute exhaust taken during CVS testing are placed at atmospheric pressure in a 20 m absorption path cell of 6 ℓ volume, data are collected for 1.5 minutes, and after 45 sec of computer processing an analysis is available, listing concentrations of some 20 species with detection sensitivity of ~ 0.1 ppm and simultaneously as high as several percent. The facility has also proved to be a potent tool for the study of the radical chemistry involved in atmospheric pollution.

PHOTOACOUSTIC SPECTROSCOPY
R. Terhune and T. Kushida

We have been studying the absorption of visible radiation by aerosols in the atmosphere by measuring the sound generated when the air is illuminated by a modulated laser beam. The sound is generated by the expansion of the gas around the submicron-size particulates as the heat diffuses out in times of the order of a microsecond. Using a one watt argon laser beam and an acoustically resonant cavity absorption as low as $10^{-6} m^{-1}$ has been measured.[8] These measurements can be made in the presence of a much larger extinction due to light scattering. Good correlation between the acousto-optic signal and the amount of carbonaceous or soot-like components of the aerosols has been observed.[9,10] This technique shows great promise for modal analysis of the particulate generation in engines during emission testing cycles.

Acousto-optic spectroscopy is also being used to study the concentration as a function of depth of ultraviolet absorbing materials in paint films. The films are illuminated with a one microsecond duration pulsed UV laser beam. Following the laser pulse, the time dependence of the flow of heat from the film is measured with a time resolution near twenty microseconds. From this, one obtains a measure of the absorption as a function of depth. Near the surface, a resolution of about one micron can be obtained. Ultraviolet absorbing materials are commonly added to paints to stabilize them against degradation due to UV illumination. Diffusion studies of these materials in paint films are being carried out; also, the utility of the technique for measurements on the actual paint films with pigment particles present is being investigated.

IMPROVEMENTS IN AUTOMOTIVE FUEL ECONOMY DUE TO CHANGES IN WEIGHT, AERODYNAMIC DRAG AND ROLLING RESISTANCE
R. H. Borcherts

The work done by an internal combustion engine in a present day automobile in moving from A to B is used to overcome vehicle inertia, aerodynamic drag and rolling resistance. From data given by an engine map (emissions and fuel consumption as a function of engine speed, load, exhaust-gas recirculation, spark advance, and air/fuel ratio) improvements in automotive fuel economy due to changes in vehicle weight, aerodynamic drag and rolling resistance are obtained for a given set of emission constraints and performance criteria. These values are 0.7, 0.28 and 0.17 percent improvements in fuel economy over the federal test cycle for one percent reductions in weight, aerodynamic drag and rolling resistance, respectively. Maximum increases in fuel economy for these changes will also be discussed.

DATA COMMUNICATION IN MANUFACTURING CONTROL
R. H. Sherman

The manufacturing system contains programmable controllers, microprocessor-based test stands, and terminals for operator interaction. A network has been designed to provide management information, and data collection for inspectors and foreman. The network employs a broadband coaxial cable as a multiaccess, shared medium. Data is communicated at 1 Mbit/sec. Contention for the cable is handled locally at each network interface. A prototype network is being used for laboratory automation.

INDUSTRIAL APPLICATIONS OF SHADOW MOIRÉ TOPOGRAPHY
G. M. Brown, J. A. Levitt, and V. J. Lumelsky

Shadow Moiré Topography is a technique for measuring deviations from flatness or deviation from a specified shape. Illuminating and viewing of a manufactured component (or part) through a grating produces a contour map to reveal the detailed shape of the part. Parts can be rapidly contoured to reveal gross defects or, by computer processing of fringe patterns, quantitative measurement information can be obtained to an accuracy of about 10 μm.

Moiré contour fringes will be demonstrated using a manufactured part, specifically a clutch plate. The fringe pattern is prepared for image processing by means of a TV imaging system, and the dynamics of the fringe system can be studied as a function of position of the light source. A technique for computer processing of the moiré fringe pattern for on-line inspection/measurement of components will be explained.

REFERENCES

1. L. Malter, Phys. Rev. 49, 879 (1936).
2. H. Jacobs, Phys. Rev. 34 (5), 877 (1951).
3. J. Lambe and S. L. McCarthy, Phys. Rev. Lett. 37, 923 (1976); S. L. McCarthy and J. Lambe, Appl. Phys. Lett. 30, 427 (1977).
4. C. C. Wang and L. I. Davis, Phys. Rev. Lett. 32, 349 (1974); D. K. Killinger, C. C. Wang and M. Hanabusa, Phys. Rev. A13, 2145 (1976).
5. D. K. Killinger and C. C. Wang, Chem. Phys. Lett. 52, 374 (1977).
6. C. C. Wang and D. K. Killinger, Phys. Rev. A 20, 1495 (1979).
7. W. H. Weber and John Lambe, Appl. Opt. 15, 2299 (1976).
8. R. W. Terhune and J. E. Anderson, "Spectrophone Measurements of the Absorption of Visible Light by Aerosols in the Atmosphere" Opt. Lett. 1, 70 (1977).
9. T. J. Truex and J. E. Anderson, "Mass Monitoring of Carbonaceous Aerosols with a Spectrophone", Atmos. Environ. 13, 507 (1979).
10. D. K. Killinger, J. Moore, and S. M. Japar, "The Use of Photoacoustic Spectroscopy to Characterize and Monitor Soot in Combustion Processes", Chem. Phys. Lett. 66, 207 (1979).

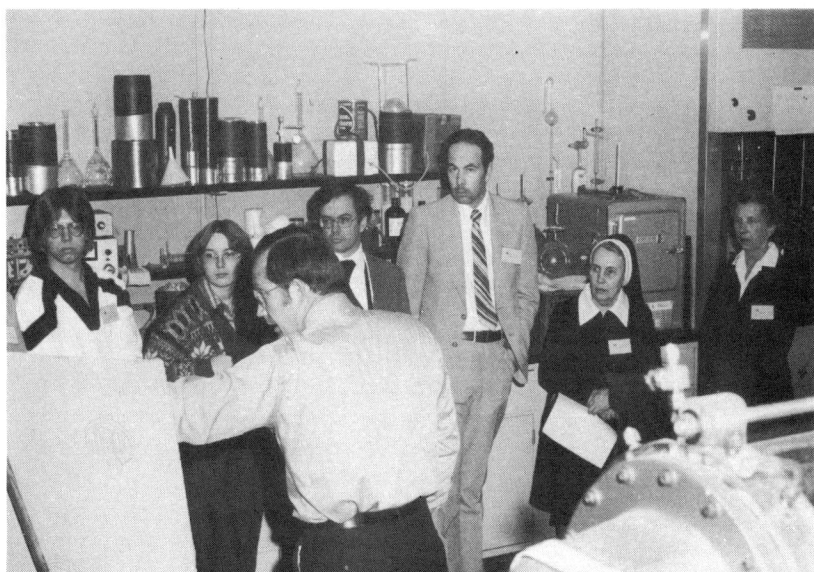

Dr. Paul Maker demonstrates the principles of Fourier transform infrared spectroscopy for measuring air pollutants and other gaseous materials during the tour of the Ford Motor Company Research Laboratories.

50

CHALLENGES TO THE AUTOMOTIVE INDUSTRY

Howard H. Kehrl
Executive Vice President
General Motors Corporation, Detroit, Mi. 48202

My early days in GM Research brings back a flood of memories. I <u>did</u> have a chance to work under Boss Ket...not as his protege, but as a young engineer in awe of a living lengend. Kettering truly was legendary...ingenious, creative, dedicated. The type of person the automotive industry needed then, and needs now. He was a man intrigued by change...not as a spectator, but as a moving spirit. He used to say the only thing constant in this world is change. How right he was.

So much has happened since Boss Ket's day. Can you imagine what he would think of the General Motors Technical Center if he could see how it has grown? Quite a few of you saw it today on your tour. He would be very impressed...in fact, downright dazzled. What is going on there -- and at the Ford Research Laboratories which others of you saw -- would amaze him even more.

Back in Boss Ket's day, fuel economy, low emissions and functional design weren't so highly prized. Just getting the car to start and keep on running was the main job then. That's not to say Boss Ket wasn't concerned about good, economical transportation. He certainly was, and he made a tremendous contribution. He and his creative crew took much of the work out of driving by developing the electric self-starter. He took out engine knock by putting lead in gasoline, but that was long before exhaust emissions were a concern. I wonder what he'd think if he knew we're removing it now so catalytic converters can do their work. He researched diesel engines, and helped poineer the two-cycle, high-speed diesel that is used worldwide in trucks, buses, locomotives, and boats. He was not only a man of his times...but a man far ahead of his time.

When he addressed this American Physical Society group back in 1938, he urged those listening to him to work at the leading edge of technology...push our technical and scientific frontiers ever forward. What could be said today that would be more appropriate? Boss Ket made a tremendous contribution. He didn't stand alone. Many people contributed then, just as today many are contributing **importantly**. I am thinking of the people here...and the people in offices, labs, shops, and testing grounds across the land and around the world.

Since the 1930's, the scientific and technological community has developed transportation systems and communication networks that have unified our world. It has probed the universe and sent men rocketing to the moon. It has lengthened the lives of human beings and has made life richer and fuller for all of us. Much has been achieved; much more will be done.

ISSN:0094-243X/81/660051-06$1.50 Copyright 1981 American Institute of Physics

I would like to look at some achievements and challenges tonight from the perspective of an automotive man...concentrate on what's been done in our industry and what seems to lie ahead.

In our industry, as in nature itself, things don't fall neatly into separate categories. They may appear to because we put names to main activities -- research, engineering, design, manufacturing, financial, overseas operations. But that's to help us fit them together and manage them better. In everything we do, there are no straight borderlines. Just about everything overlaps and intertwines...as well it should.

This is particularly true at the GM Tech Center. Project centers there interconnect to thousands of our staff and divisional people. They work as teams, each team responsible for a new car or truck line, new or advanced components, or vital safety devices. Researchers work with engineers; and both work with designers and manufacturing people. Everyone works closely with his counterparts.

A good example of this interaction is our "World Car" program. The mainstream energies of every part of General Motors are channeled toward products that have great world appeal. We plan to introduce in the not too distant future a single basic car line in many different countries. This truly will be a world car...sharing the same design but being built and marketed in various parts of the world. This approach will permit us to use more common components, expand worldwide parts sourcing, and benefit from economies of scale. More importantly, it will give consumers higher quality products and more value for their money.

Our world cars -- all our future products, for that matter -- will combine our scientific and technological achievements of the past. They also will incorporate the more sophisticated technology that's coming on stream. General Motors is committing billions of dollars to push ahead our technological frontiers and develop exciting new cars and trucks.

We are just completing construction of a new wind tunnel, capable of handling full-size cars and light trucks. I'm sorry you couldn't see it today, but we're working hard to have it operational in June. It's truly a magnificent structure -- a giant facility with a 43-foot diameter fan that can generate winds of hurricane speed. The facility will enable us to design out many problems associated with road spray, dirt deposits and noise...and let us design in aerodynamic shapes that reduce drag and improve fuel economy.

I can't think of anything we're more concerned with these days than fuel-efficiency. Saving energy through vehicle design and performance is a priority consideration everywhere. Even though passenger cars aren't the energy consumer many people think they are, they do account for about 8 percent of our nation's total energy usage and about 27 percent of the petroleum used. We have an ongoing program to bring this down further. Since 1974, we have increased our corporate average fuel economy from 12 miles per gallon to about 21.7 -- a gain of 81 percent. And we fully intend to meet, if not exceed, the government-required 27.5 mpg fleet average by 1985. Much of our progress came from downsizing our cars, starting with the Cadillac Seville and Chevrolet Chevette in 1975 and going through redesigned full-size, mid-size and front-drive personal luxury cars in succeeding years. Our latest offerings are the new "X" cars -- the cars typified by the Chevrolet Citation. This is the look of the future. We plan to steadily increase productive capacity for vehicles of this type which have front drive and transverse-mounted engines. Our fuel economy improvements in the future will be harder to make. But we are pressing ahead to gain better economy incrementally through new technology and new usage of materials.

Electronics will play a vital roll...and I recognize the fact that discoveries and contributions of the physics community helped make possible the solid state electronic revolution. Nils Muench mentioned our "computer command control" approach. A microcomputer is the heart of the system. It regulates precisely the air-fuel mixture from the carburetor. The result is optimum fuel economy, improved driveability and much better control of exhaust emissions. You can judge, for yourself, the success of this system when it comes out nationwide this autumn.

We are making greater use of finite element analysis. This lets us study on interactive video screens the dynamic behavior of all mechanical parts. With the interactive screen, we can redesign to achieve needed performance with minimum weight. Lighter weight materials will also make a major contribution. You'll find more plastics and aluminum in our future automobiles. The average GM car now has a shipping weight of about 3,200 pounds. By 1985, it could be down to 2,750 pounds.

Product mix will also be balanced for overall fleet fuel economy. Diesels will become increasingly important. We now offer them in several models. There will be more in the future. Passenger car diesels get about 25 percent better fuel economy than comparable gasoline engines. To achieve that, without diesels, we would have to reduce the weight of a typical GM car by some 900 pounds, either by downsizing or by using more expensive materials. That's why diesels are so important. I'm sure you're all aware of the diesel particulate question. We see cause for concern, but not alarm. Evidence to date indicates that diesel particulates pose no increased risk of lung cancer. Our Biomedical Science Department says extensive and ongoing studies of animals in laboratories support this result. There is no indication of significant deterioration of healthy lung or bronchial tissue and no functional impairment as a result of animals inhaling very large quantities of diesel particulates for prolonged periods. Research is ongoing to insure there are no other causes for concern. So diesel passenger cars figure prominently in our product plans.

So, too, do electric cars. We consider battery-powered cars

promising and have established a project center for their development. Our goal is to introduce small electric personal cars for urban and commuter use in the middle of this decade. The battery mainstream program involves zinc-nickel oxide batteries capable of storing more than twice as much energy per pound as current lead-acid batteries. Our engineers and scientists were able to lengthen battery life through improved components that give the plates more durability and less lost power in recharges. We think electric passenger cars can fill an important niche in our nation's transportation system. Trucks also show much promise. We've already built 35 battery-powered vans, 20 of which are being used successfully in telephone installation service out west, and soon we will have 15 in service in Detroit.

You can see that we have the plans and the products lined up for the 80's. This decade will be the most exciting -- and perhaps the most challenging -- in the history of the automotive industry.

This morning Nils mentioned technical issues facing the auto industry. Now I would like to give you my perspective on the challenges, both technical and non-technical, which face our nation and the automotive industry. They are the challenges of inflation, of government regulation, of competition, and of energy availability. Unlike some of the economists and pollsters who see nothing but gloom and doom ahead, I am optimistic about the future. I'm sure we can work our way out of our problems and make the 1980's the best decade yet. Let's examine the challenges one by one -- not to emphasize the negative, but to see what we have to cope with.

First, let's look at inflation. Inflation will remain a troublesome economic problem in the 1980's, not only for the United States, but for other major industrialized countries. Upward pressures are stemming to a great extent from OPEC price increases. Fuel prices are steadily climbing here, and may one day rival those in European countries. That will put greater pressure on the automotive industry to offer even more fuel-efficient cars and trucks. However, in the United States, the rate of the consumer price advance should moderate somewhat in the third and fourth quarters, depending on the government's committment to sound monetary and fiscal policies.

Second, government regulations. These certainly complicate our business and contribute to inflationary pressures. Reasonable standards are necessary in some areas -- emission control, for example -- but we are greatly concerned about the expense of meeting standards that have no significant value to consumers and do little but increase costs. Government regulation of business is expected to cost the nation $100 billion this year. And, at GM, the cost of federal, state, and local regulations since 1975 has averaged $1.3 billion per year in addition to the cost of hardware added to our vehicles. From a business management perspective, it also has required the full-time efforts of an equivalent of 26,600 hard-working employes. Regulatory cost has also had a significant effect on our customers. By the mid-1980's, the buyer of a typical GM car will be paying an additional $800 for fuel economy, safety, and emission regulations in terms of today's dollars.

Now, let's turn to the third major challenge, foreign competition. Such competition has never been more intense, especially as consumers shift buying preferences to cars that get better gas mileage. This isn't just domestic, but worldwide. In some sectors, the increased portion of the U.S. market captured by the imports is being viewed with so much alarm that attempts are being made to seek protectionist legislation. GM is against such protectionism. At the same time, countries that enjoy complete access to our automotive market should recognize trade is a two-way street. We feel we should have as much right to sell our products in other countries as they do in ours. Whatever happens on that issue, it won't change the fact that we will still have to compete with foreign manufacturers on a value basis, as perceived by the consumer. Our future depends on our success in serving a variety of individual, family, and commercial needs with higher quality vehicles than those imported from Japan and Germany.

Finally, there's energy. Further destabilization in the Middle East is a constant threat. It will always be that way until we diminish our dependence on foreign oil and launch an effective energy plan for our nation -- a plan which would explore all avenues of alternative energy sources and foster a positive environment for increasing production of our existing resources. Because of its direct impact on so many Americans, the energy problem frequently is thought of in terms of price and availability of gasoline. So it's in the national interest -- as well as in our own corporate interest -- that General Motors has been devoting extensive efforts and resources to conserving energy -- in both our plants and in our products. We are studying many possibilities. Nils told you about some of them, and I would like to amplify some of the things he mentioned.

Cars of the future will have to run on different kinds of fuel. We realize that oil from the ground must be used until viable alternative energy sources can be developed, but we have high hopes for gasoline and diesel fuel from oil shale and coal. Greater use of alcohols from coal and biomass are also possibilities. But we feel the gaseous fuels are collectively not well suited for automobile use. Hydrogen has some promise, but it's dangerous to handle and difficult to store on the car. Developing alternative fuels finally seems to be getting under way...and not a day too soon. A while back, a team of GM engineers and researchers went to Colorado to study two oil shale recovery operations. The people our men talked to out there were optimistic. They believe oil can be extracted from shale in commercial quantities using existing technology, and saw no insurmountable obstacles ahead. So we consider this source extremely promising.

As you know, efforts are also being made to stretch existing gasoline supplies through additives. Gasohol is getting the most attention these days. Maybe some of you have used it because stations are selling it now in many parts of Michigan and in other areas of the nation. In addition to gasoline, gasohol contains 10 percent ethyl alcohol or ethanol and this is virtually the same thing moonshiners made, or should I say make, in mountain stills. Engineers and scientists are working hard to make alcohols more cheaply using less energy. But right now it takes approximately the same amount of energy to produce the ethanol as the ethanol contains, and most of the energy used to make it comes from petroleum and natural gas. New processing units will use solid fuels such as coal or biomass in place of these more valuable fuels. Most people agree that gasohol does have potential in the United States, but it is somewhat limited.

In my opinion, some forms of biomass have much potential. Our people once did some rough calculations for me. They indicated the number of cars now being driven in the United States could travel 10,000 miles a year at an average fuel economy of 25 miles per gallon on methanol produced annually by 120 million acres of woodland. We probably could never rely this heavily on biomass, but the U.S. does have some 400 million acres of idle land that could possibly be used to produce methanol fuel on a renewable basis.

I opened with a thought from Boss Ket, and I'd like to close with one. Probably his most famous saying was that all of us should be concerned about the future, because that's where we'll spend the rest of our lives. Well, I think it's clearly up to us -- all of us -- whether that future is good or bad, exciting or dull, constructive or destructive. The physics community has always had a key role in shaping the future, and I am confident this will be even more true in the important years ahead. We in the technical area can help set the tone for future generations. If we have enough optimism, enough enthusiasm, and, most of all, enough solid determination, this decade and the decades beyond will be all that we want them to be.

NONLINEAR SPECTROSCOPY FOR COMBUSTION RESEARCH

Kenneth Marko and Lajos Rimai
Engineering and Research Staff, Research, Ford Motor Company
Dearborn, Michigan 48121

ABSTRACT

A brief review of the theory of the generation of coherent scattered light via the 3rd order nonlinear susceptibility of gases is presented. The application of nonlinear spectroscopy to the measurement of temperatures and species concentrations in hot reacting gas flows is discussed along with the methods of signal analysis needed to obtain this information. Recent results obtained for the temperature distribution and concentration of CO in our stable flame burner are presented and the techniques used to perform these measurements are outlined. The report concludes with a discussion of the capabilities of nonlinear spectroscopy and its potential applications for combustion studies in laboratory single-cylinder engines.

INTRODUCTION

In the past several years the field of nonlinear spectroscopy has seen applications to the gas phase and to combustion studies.[1-5] Nonlinear spectroscopy, while more difficult to apply as a result of the additional light sources and optics required, has many advantages over ordinary 'linear' spectroscopy (signal strength, coherence, noise immunity, for example) which makes it especially suitable for combustion diagnostics. After a discussion of those features of nonlinear optical spectroscopy that are relevant to combustion diagnostics, we shall describe a number of experiments currently underway in our laboratory and discuss their applications to combustion research.

I. THEORETICAL BACKGROUND

A. Third Order Susceptibility in Gases

The response of a medium to applied electric fields can be expressed in a power series as

$$\underline{P} = \chi^{(1)}\underline{E} + \chi^{(2)}\underline{E}\cdot\underline{E} + \chi^{(3)}\underline{E}\cdot\underline{E}\cdot\underline{E} + \ldots \qquad (1)$$

where P is the induced polarization, E is the total applied electric field usually a sum of Fourier components at optical frequencies and $\chi^{(j)}$ are the susceptibility tensors of order $j + 1$. The linear susceptibility $\chi^{(1)}$ is responsible for linear optical phenomena such as absorption and refraction. The second order susceptibility $\chi^{(2)}$ governs lowest order frequency mixing phenomena for two applied fields, in particular second harmonic generation. However, for centrosymmetric media such as fluids and gases, $\chi^{(2)}$ is zero. The third order susceptibility $\chi^{(3)}$ is generally nonzero and for gas phase diagnostics is the lowest order nonlinear interaction available for study.

In terms of Fourier components, $\chi^{(3)}$ relates the induced polarization at frequency ω_p to the product of three applied fields at frequencies ω_a, ω_b, ω_c

$$P_\mu(\omega_p) = \chi^{\mu\alpha\beta\gamma}(\omega_a, \omega_b, -\omega_c) E_\alpha(\omega_a) E_\beta(\omega_b) E_\gamma^*(\omega_c) \tag{2}$$

where $\omega_p = \omega_a + \omega_b - \omega_c$ and $\mu\alpha\beta\gamma$ refer to Cartesian components. General expressions for $\chi^{(3)}$ have been given in the literature[6,7] and since our interest for the present is limited to Raman-type spectroscopy (study of molecular resonances when the difference between two of the applied frequencies lies near a vibration-rotational molecular transition frequency) we can write $\chi^{(3)}$ as

$$\chi^{\mu\alpha\beta\gamma} = \sigma^{\mu\alpha\beta\gamma} + \sum_{\text{all species}} \left[\chi^{\mu\alpha\beta\gamma}(\omega_p, \omega_a, \omega_b, \omega_c) + \chi^{\mu\beta\alpha\gamma}(\omega_p, \omega_b, \omega_a, \omega_c) \right] \tag{3}$$

where for a given molecular species of number density N in the gas

$$\chi_o^{\mu 12\gamma}(\omega_p, \omega_1, \omega_2, \omega_c) = \frac{\hbar N}{6} \sum_{g,t} \rho_{gg}^{(o)}$$

$$\cdot \left[\frac{f_{\mu 2}^{tg}(\omega_p, -\omega_2) f_{1\gamma}^{tg}(\omega_1, -\omega_c)}{\omega_{tg} - (\omega_1 - \omega_c) - i\Gamma_{tg}} + \frac{f_{1\gamma}^{tg}(-\omega_1, \omega_c) f_{\mu 2}^{tg}(-\omega_p, \omega_2)}{\omega_{tg} + (\omega_1 - \omega_c) + i\Gamma_{tg}} \right] \tag{4}$$

and where

$$f_{\mu\gamma}^{tg}(\omega_i, \omega_g) = \sum_s \frac{\langle t|P_\mu|s\rangle \langle s|P_\nu|g\rangle}{\omega_{sg} - \omega_i} + \frac{\langle t|P_\nu|s\rangle \langle s|P_\mu|g\rangle}{\omega_{sg} - \omega_j} \tag{5}$$

is a second order tensor, p_i is the ith Cartesian component of the electric dipole operator; t, g, s refer to molecular quantum states;

ω_{sg}, ω_{st} are the corresponding transition frequencies, Γ_{tg} the damping constant; and ρ_{gg} is the population of state g. Equations (4) and (5) are valid as long as no frequency is near a one or two photon transition[7] which has been the case in our work to the present. The term σ, the so-called nonresonant background susceptibility, incorporates the tails of all additive two photon resonant terms as well as of those subtractive (Raman) resonant terms for which any applied frequency difference is far from resonance. Thus, σ is real and for a relatively narrow frequency range, such as that considered in our experiments, can be considered constant. Any Raman resonant terms close to the range of applied frequencies is explicitly accounted for χ_0. For $\omega_i = -\omega_j$ Eq. (5) is identical to the Kramers dispersion formula[8] and thus $f_{\mu\nu}$ represents a direct generalization of the Raman tensor that describes the spontaneous Raman effect. Thus, it has the same transformation properties and is subject to the same selection rules in terms of the terminal states t,g. If μ,ν,α,β refer to a coordinate system, fixed in the molecules, aligned along molecular symmetry axes, $f_{\mu\nu}$ is diagonal for totally symmetric vibrations. More generally for Σ-Σ transitions of linear molecules (in particular for diatomics such as CO, N_2, O_2) in the molecular reference frame f^{tg} has only two independent components f_{zz}^{tg} and $f_{xx}^{tg} = f_{yy}^{tg}$ (z being the molecular axis).[9,10,11] In the laboratory frame $|t\rangle$ and $|g\rangle$ involve both vibrational and rotational levels; thus they correspond to a pair of quantum numbers, v for the vibration, J for the total angular momentum: $t \to J'v'$, $g \to J''v''$. For such transitions now in the laboratory coordinates there will again be only two independent components of the f tensor.

$$f_0(J',v',J'',v'') = f_{\mu\mu}^{t,g}$$
$$f_1(J',v',J'',v'') = f_{\mu\nu}^{t,g} \quad \mu \neq \nu \quad (6)$$

and f_0, f_1 can be expressed in terms of f_{zz}, f_{xx} and products of known harmonic oscillator and angular momentum matrix elements.[11] Neglecting anharmonicity in the vibrational potential, the terms in (6) are nonzero only for $v' = v'' + 1$ or $v' = v''$, and it can be shown that for Σ-Σ transitions $f_0 \neq 0$ if $J' = J''$ or $J' = J'' \pm 2$, $v' = v'' \pm 1$ contributes to the Q band ($J' = J''$) and the O and S band ($J' = J'' \pm 2$) spectra whereas $f_1 \neq 0$ only if $J' - J'' \pm 2$. Thus for $v' = v''$, f_1 is responsible for the pure rotational spectrum whereas for $v' = v'' \pm 1$ it contributes only to the O and S bands.[11]

In addition to the denominators, $f_{\mu\nu}$ also depend on ω_1 and ω_2 through the frequency dependence of the dipole matrix elements. Because we assume to be far from one photon resonances and examine spectra in relatively narrow ranges, we may neglect the frequency dependence of $f_{\mu\nu}(f_0, f_1)$ and thus $\chi_0^{\mu\alpha\beta\gamma}$ of Eq. (4) can be taken as a function of only a single frequency difference $\omega_1 - \omega_c$. To correlate Eq. (2) with our experiments, we call ω_a, ω_b the pump frequencies, ω_c the probe frequency. Coherent Anti-Stokes Raman

Scattering (CARS) resonances are obtained when $\omega_a < \omega_c$, $\omega_a - \omega_c \sim -\omega_{tg}$. The resonances responsible for Raman gain are realized when ω_p equals one of the applied frequencies, say $\omega_p = \omega_c$ and thus $\omega_a = -\omega_b$, $|\omega_a - \omega_c| \sim |\omega_{tg}|$.

For isotropic media (freely rotating molecules) the $\chi^{(3)}$ tensor has only two independent components $\chi^{\alpha\alpha\alpha\alpha} = \chi^{\beta\beta\beta\beta}$ and $\chi^{\alpha\beta\beta\alpha}$. Since the experimental situation generally involves quasiplane waves (weakly focused beams) we assume all applied fields and the induced polarization to be coplanar. The pump frequencies are generated by the same linearly polarized laser and $\vec{E}_a$, $\vec{E}_b$ are taken to be parallel to the x axis and the probe beam is linearly polarized at an angle Θ to the x-axis. Then the CARS (or CSRS) polarization components are given by

$$P_X = E_a E_b E_c^* (\chi^{\alpha\alpha\alpha\alpha} \cos\Theta)$$
$$P_Y = E_a E_b E_c^* (\chi^{\alpha\beta\beta\alpha} \sin\Theta) .$$
(7)

From Eqs. (4) and (6) it follows that $\chi^{\alpha\alpha\alpha\alpha}$ contains only f_0 terms whereas $\chi^{\alpha\beta\beta\alpha}$ contains only f_1 terms. Thus, for $\Theta = 0$ one observes both $\Delta J = 0$ and $\Delta J = \pm 2$ bands while only O and S ($\Delta J = 2$) bands are observed for $\Theta = \Pi/2$.

B. Considerations of Spatial and Time Resolution

To simplify the discussion, let us restrict ourselves to the $\Theta = 0$ case thus having to consider only one component of the $\chi^{(3)}$, $\chi \sim \chi^{\alpha\alpha\alpha\alpha}$. Then

$$\chi = \sigma + \chi_0(\omega_a - \omega_c) + \chi_0(\omega_b - \omega_c) \quad (8)$$

if X and the field amplitudes are independent of $\underline{r}$ in the interaction volume V the radiated field generated by the induced third order polarization at a given frequency ω_p is

$$E(\omega_p) = (k^2/r)\exp(ikr - i\omega t)G(V)\sum_{\omega_a}\sum_{\omega_b}$$
$$\chi[\omega_a,\omega_b,\omega_p - (\omega_a + \omega_b)]E_a(\omega_a)E_b(\omega_b)E_c^*(\omega_c)$$
(9)

where the sums are over all the harmonic components of the pump laser bandwidth. G(V) is a diffraction integral over the interaction volume and depends on the angular distribution of the field intensity within the applied beams. For plane waves, G(V) yields the conventional phase matching condition

$$\underline{k}_1 + \underline{k}_2 + \underline{k}_3 + \underline{k}_4 = 0 \tag{10}$$

which defines the relative directions of the four beams for effective coherent interaction. For focused beams it yields the same relation in terms of ray directions and can be used to predict the gross features of the CARS or CSRS radiation pattern. The dependence of G(V) on the dimensions of V yields information spatial resolution.[12]

For dispersionless media, such as gases near atmospheric pressures, the phase matching condition can be satisfied with collinear beams; however, in this case the technique offers very poor spatial resolution in the direction of propagation which precludes its practical use as a probe of inhomogeneous gas distributions such as those occurring near flame fronts. However, simple ways to achieve high spatial resolution have been found which utilize nonparallel input beams to generate a phase matched CARS signal. A three-beam technique was first developed by Eckbreth[13] and we subsequently modified it so as to require only two focused beams (pump and probe) with suitable angular intensity distributions easily attainable in practice.[3] Both of these techniques have spatial resolution adequate to avoid CARS signals generated in denser cold gas regions surrounding the flame front in small burners, while probing the hot gas regions in or above the flames. This noncollinear phase matching technique was dubbed BOXCARS, but to avoid introducing additional confusing acronyms, we shall refer to all measurements as CARS and simply specify the spatial resolution. The spatial resolution for any focused beam intensity distribution can be calculated by determining the dependence of the diffraction integral G(V) on the dimensions of the interaction volume V.[12] Measurements of spectra within small dimension cold gas zones inside the flame cones of small torches, and of the small hot gas zones above the flame indicate agreement with such calculations.[5] For typical beam configurations in our experiments, longitudinal resolution in the order of 1 mm is obtained.

In order to acquire CARS or CSRS spectra containing a substantial number of rotation-vibration lines in a single laser pulse, it is necessary to use a broadband laser as the source for one of the beams. We apply the expression for the induced polarizability

$$P(\omega_p) = \sum_{\omega_a} \sum_{\omega_b} [\sigma + \chi_0(\omega_p - \omega_b) + \chi_0(\omega_p - \omega_a)] E_a(\omega_a) E_b(\omega_b) E_c^*(\omega_a + \omega_b - \omega_p) \tag{11}$$

with the assumption of incoherence between individual harmonic components (modes) of the sources, for two cases of interest.

1. Let us assume $\omega_a \sim \omega_b$, that is, the pump that generates ω_a and ω_b cover sufficiently narrow range of frequencies about ω_0 so that $E_c^*(\omega_a + \omega_b - \omega_p)$ can be considered constant and equal to $E_c^*(2\omega_0 - \omega_p)$. The average radiated power is proportional to $<|P(\omega_p)|^2>_{av}$.

$$<|P(\omega_p)|^2>_{av} = |E_c^*(2\omega_0 - \omega_p)|^2 \sum_{\omega_a} |E_a(\omega_a)|^2 \times$$

$$\times \sum_{\omega_b} |E_b(\omega_b)|^2 \times |\sigma + 2\chi_0(\omega_p - \omega_b)|^2 .$$

(12)

Thus the emitted power spectrum over ω_p, when properly normalized by the probe laser emission spectrum reproduces the spectrum of the absolute value squared of the susceptibility, and the full CARS spectrum from a single pulse can be obtained and analyzed.

2. Let us take ω_c to be very narrow in frequency spread, ω_a and ω_b to cover a broad spectral region. Furthermore assume that χ consists of a single sharp resonance (neglect σ)

$$\chi_0(\omega_p - \omega_b) \simeq \delta(\omega_p - \omega_b - \Omega) \qquad (13)$$

then we find

$$<|P(\omega_p)|^2>_{av} = [4\sum_{\omega_b} \delta(\Omega + \omega_p - \omega_b)|E_b(\omega_b)|^2] \times$$

$$\times |E_c(\omega_c)|^2 \times \sum_{\omega_a} |E_a(\omega_a)|^2 .$$

(14)

Thus, the single pulse spectrum of the generated radiation will reproduce that of the broadband source of ω_a and ω_b.

II. EXPERIMENTS

A. Techniques and Equipment

The capability of generating a complete molecular vibrational rotational CARS spectrum, with the conditions stated in Case 1, is attained with a broadband laser pumped dye laser. The broadband CARS signal, after dispersion by a grating monochromator, can be recorded for each laser pulse on a multichannel vidicon or reticon detector. If sufficiently small pump bandwidth (~ 0.05 cm^{-1}) is used, spectral resolution is determined essentially by the monochromator. At the cost of time resolution, high spectral resolution can be attained by using a scanned narrow band source for ω_c. Several groups have reported results with this technique and we have made measurements which easily resolve the rotational structure in the Q-band of hot N_2.[2,4] However, the broadband technique, despite the reduction in spectral resolution, offers many advantages in terms of noise reduction, reduced data accumulation times, and time resolution and, therefore, we will concern ourselves solely with its applications.

The primary light source in all our experiments is a Quanta-Ray DCR 1-A Nd:YAG laser oscillator-amplifier operating at 10 pps with a frequency doubled output at 532 nm of up to 200 mJ/pulse. The transverse intensity distribution is annular as a result of the diffraction coupled output of the oscillator. This has important significance for the two beam high spatial resolution CARS technique.[3] Using an intracavity etalon, the single pulse linewidth of the laser is reduced to below .1 cm^{-1}. The output of this laser is divided to provide the pump beam for the CARS spectroscopy and to pump a modified convertible narrow band-broadband dye laser to provide the Stokes beam for CARS studies. The dye laser oscillator and pre-amplifier consists of transversely pumped dye cells, with dye solutions circulated through the cells from a large reservoir. A dielectric mirror for the broadband studies and a diffraction grating for narrow band scanned spectroscopy can be used as the back reflector in the cavity. Broadband operation for Rhodamine dyes is typically 10-20 mJ/pulse over a roughly Gaussian spectral profile ~ 10 nm wide. A final longitudinally pumped amplifier after beam expansion is necessary for the higher powers and also provides improved beam quality and stability.

The remainder of the Nd:YAG beam and the dye beam are combined on a dichroic, as shown in the schematic diagram in Fig. 1 made parallel in the desired configuration of the beams and focused down into the combustion zone. The signal and laser beams are picked up by a matching lens and transmitted to dichroic D_5, where the signal is separated from the ω_o and ω_s beams. The latter are refocused into a cell filled with argon gas at high pressure. The signal from the cell and the signal from the combustion zone are brought together at different horizontal planes and focused by a cylindrical lens on an input slit to a 3/4 m Spex spectrometer. The output of

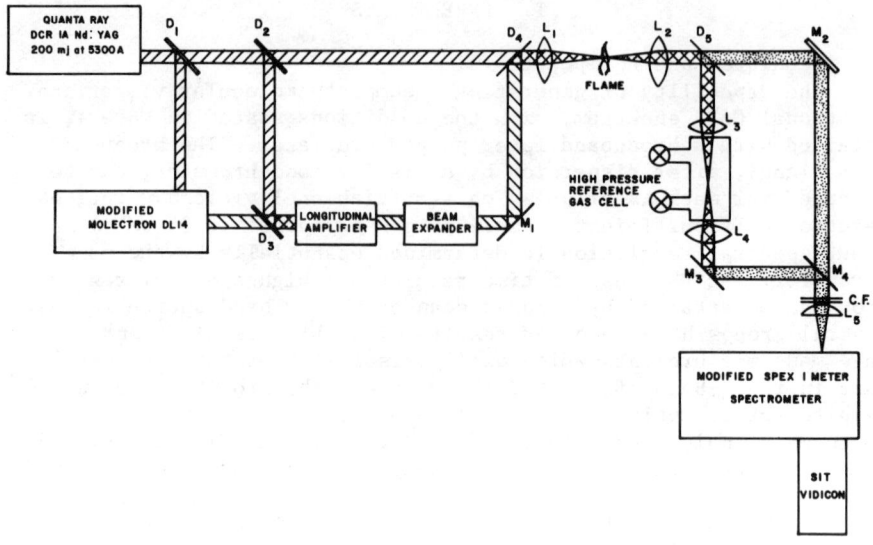

Fig. 1. Schematic diagram of system used in these experiments. D_i are dichroic mirrors; L_1, L_2 and L_3, L_4 are matched pairs of lenses; C.F. is Corning color filter or dichroic edge filter as needed for a particular frequency combination.

the spectrometer is coupled to a SIT vidicon, gated on synchronously with the laser at 10 pps. A cylindrical focusing lens ahead of the spectrometer allows us to use the full vertical height of the SIT for light collection which improves the dynamic range. The output of the SIT is recorded on the LSI-11 based OMA 2 system, corrected for background noise and stored on magnetic disks. From there it is transferred to an HP9825 system for smoothing and normalization. This system interfaces with a DEC-10 computer which is used to generate the theoretical spectra.

B. Results and Analysis
  1. CSRS Experiments

A broadband CSRS experiment along the lines of Case 2, section A.2, was performed in N_2 gas at room temperature, with ω_c narrow band at 532 nm, ω_b broadband centered at about 604 nm. The nitrogen vibrational fundamental at 2329 cm^{-1} is used to generate the broadband CSRS output near 700 nm. To demonstrate that the CSRS output accurately reproduces the dye spectral profile, the broadband nonresonant CARS signal (around 470 nm) was recorded from the reference channel simultaneously with the CSRS signal. The monochromator was adjusted so that the output in the two different spectral regions from different grating orders could be detected simultaneously, though with vertical separation on the vidicon. As shown in Fig. 2, with both the CARS and CSRS signals plotted

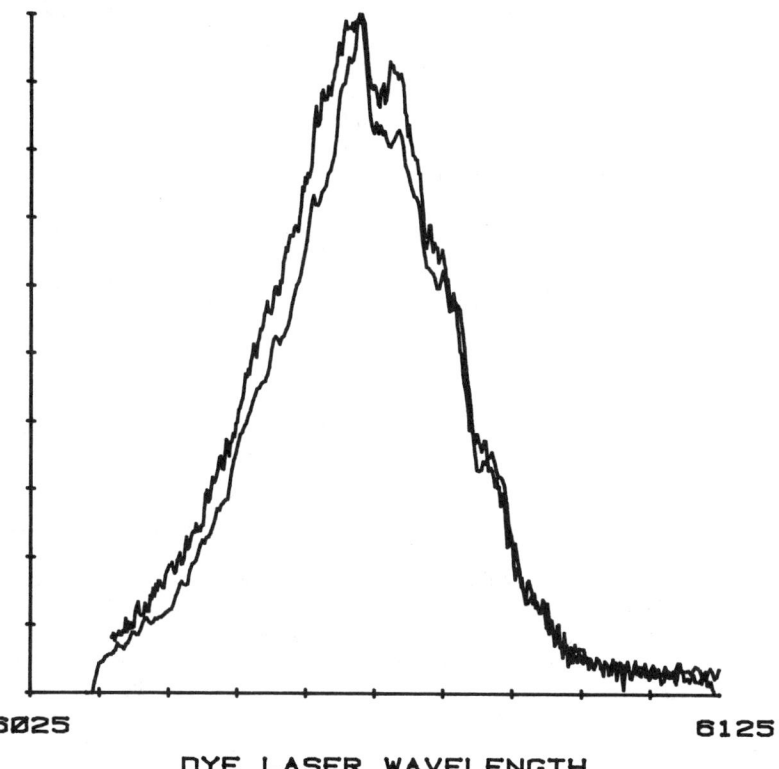

Fig. 2. Plot of observed argon CARS signal and broadband CSRS signal generated in N_2 versus wavelength of broadband dye laser. Signals were acquired simultaneously on different sections of the same vidicon tube.

parametrically as a function of dye laser wavelength, the spectral profiles agree very well. Small differences are expected due to different sensitivities and transmission efficiencies in the different spectral ranges. We have also observed CSRS spectra with a combination of broadband and narrow band excitation from the dye laser which was obtained by inserting in the oscillator cavity a partially reflecting mirror ahead of the tuning grating. A straightforward extension of the analysis in Section A.2 can be used to show that for the case in which the power per unit frequency in the narrow band component is much larger than that of the broadband component, the resonance structure of the susceptibility can be observed in the CSRS spectrum as a 'beat' in the polarization between the narrow and broad pump components coupled by the resonant susceptibility. Furthermore, the CSRS output can be obtained in convenient regions of the optical spectrum by appropriate choice of the narrow band frequency.[14] Further investigations of such combination spectra, CARS and CSRS are now being carried out. The experiments were performed with a CSRS frequency configuration to make use of the available laser setup which is normally used for CARS spectroscopy. Essentially similar results could be obtained for a CARS configuration ($\omega_a \sim \omega_c + 2329$ cm^{-1}).

2. Studies in Laminar Flames

We have performed all our combustion experiments with a premixed laminar flow burner which has a bluff body stabilized flame. This type burner, similar to a design developed by F. Clauser[15], provides excellent optical access to the free flame and the flame-wall interaction zones. Some details of the burner and its operation have been given elsewhere.[5]

Our initial work was primarily devoted to temperature measurements using the N_2 Q-band spectra which can easily be observed everywhere in the burner.[3,5] For temperatures above $\sim 1000°$K, the Q-band CARS spectral profile is recorded and compared with calculated spectra. The calculated spectra with adjustable parameters $\Gamma_{ij}, f_0, f_1, T, \sigma$ are compared with the experimental spectra to obtain values of T. The agreement between the calculated and experimental spectra indicates that the temperature can be determined to an accuracy of approximately ± 25°K from several laser pulses and to slightly poorer accuracy from a single pulse measurement.[5] Temperature measurements on multiple pulse averaged CARS spectra are only significant if the pulse to pulse fluctuations in the temperature during the averaging period are relatively small. Temperature profiles across the flame front, at two different points, for a lean propane air flame in the burner, determined from the nitrogen spectra are shown in Fig. 5.

Below the flame where temperatures less than 1000°K occur, it is necessary to consider $\Delta J = \pm 2$ (O and S band) spectra for temperature measurements due to the dynamic range limitations of vidicons. With $\Theta = \Pi/2$ (the broadband Stokes radiation polarized perpendicular to the narrow band pump beam) the Q-band is suppressed, except for leakage due to imperfect polarization and, as noted above, only the rotational structure of the O and S bands is observed. Single pulse spectra are easily obtained and for sufficiently broadband dye emission temperatures can be determined.

CARS spectra of other major species of interest, including hydrocarbons, O_2, CO_2 and CO have been obtained. For all these species, single pulse spectra for concentrations $\gtrsim 0.5\%$ can easily be observed. Spectra ($\Theta = 0$) of CO_2 above a lean flame at two positions with widely different temperatures are shown in Fig. 3. These spectra cover the range near the Fermi resonance between the symmetric stretch fundamental and the $\Delta v = 2$ transition of the bending mode. As a triatomic, CO_2 has a more complicated spectrum than the diatomics, due to a number of vibrational overtones and hot bands contributing to the Q-band structure. We have not yet

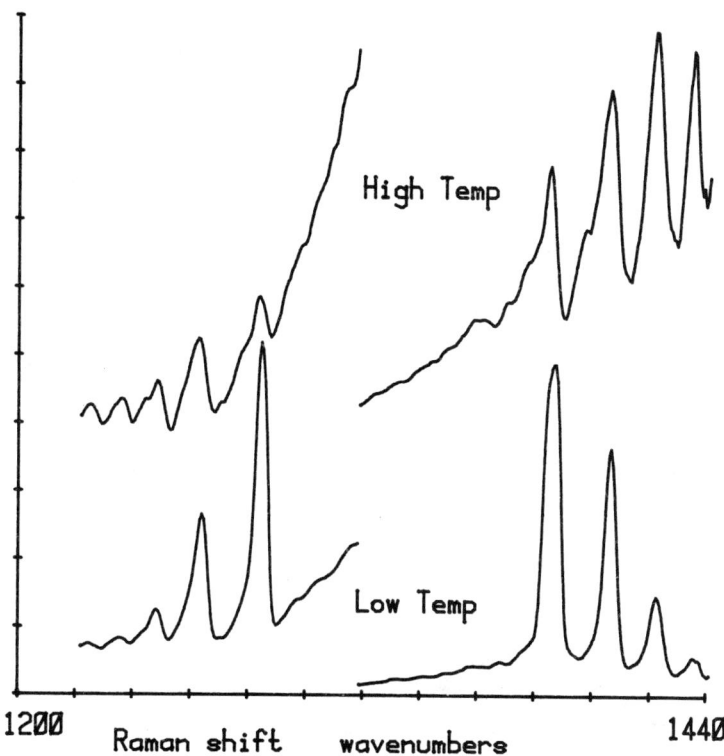

Fig. 3. Broadband CARS spectrum of carbon dioxide in the Fermi resonance region. The lower frequency position of the spectra are plotted at a ∼ x10 gain for display purposes. The lines at 1288 and 1386 cm^{-1} involve the ground state transitions while the other lines involve 'hot bands'. The temperature difference results from measurements near and far from the burner wall.

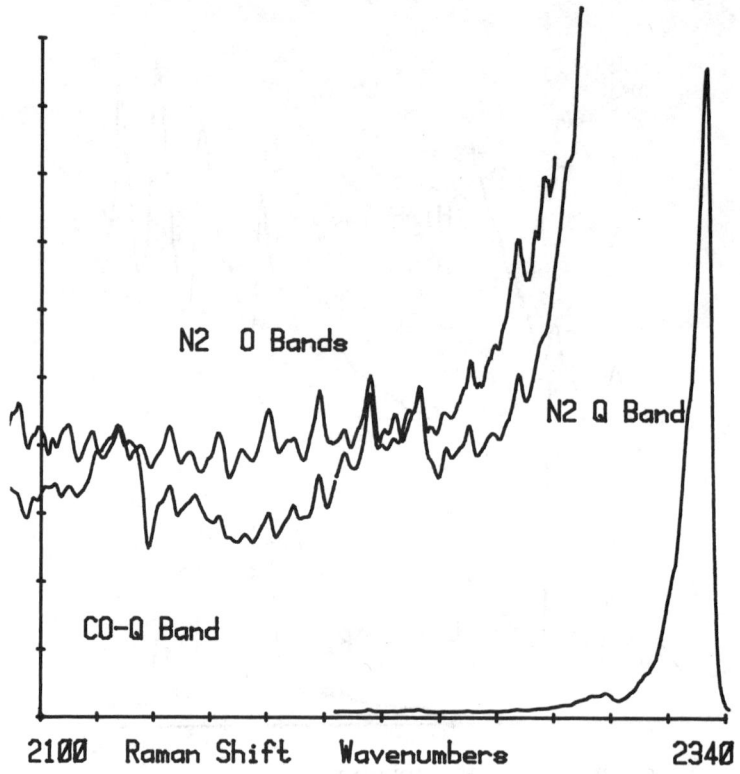

Fig. 4. Broadband CARS spectra of the CO-N_2 spectral range. The upper trace shows the N_2 O bands with $\theta = \Pi/2$ as described in the text. The lowest trace is a low gain display of the N_2 Q-bands ($\theta = 0$) and the middle trace is a magnified display of this trace showing both the N_2 O bands and the CO Q-band.

completed a detailed calculation of the CARS profile to determine the CO_2 concentration and temperature.

A more detailed investigation of the distribution of CO has been undertaken for lean propane-air flames. Carbon monoxide is an important species for combustion diagnostics since it is an intermediate which is not present in the completed reactions. The analysis of CO spectra is complicated by the fact that, as shown in Fig. 4, the CO Q-band, the N_2 O band and the N_2 Q-band tail overlap and for hot gas mixtures with low CO concentration the spectral features from N_2 may dominate the spectra. Therefore, it has been necessary to compute simultaneously the contributions of N_2 and CO to the spectra in order to obtain good agreement between calculated and experimental profiles. This complication, however, provides

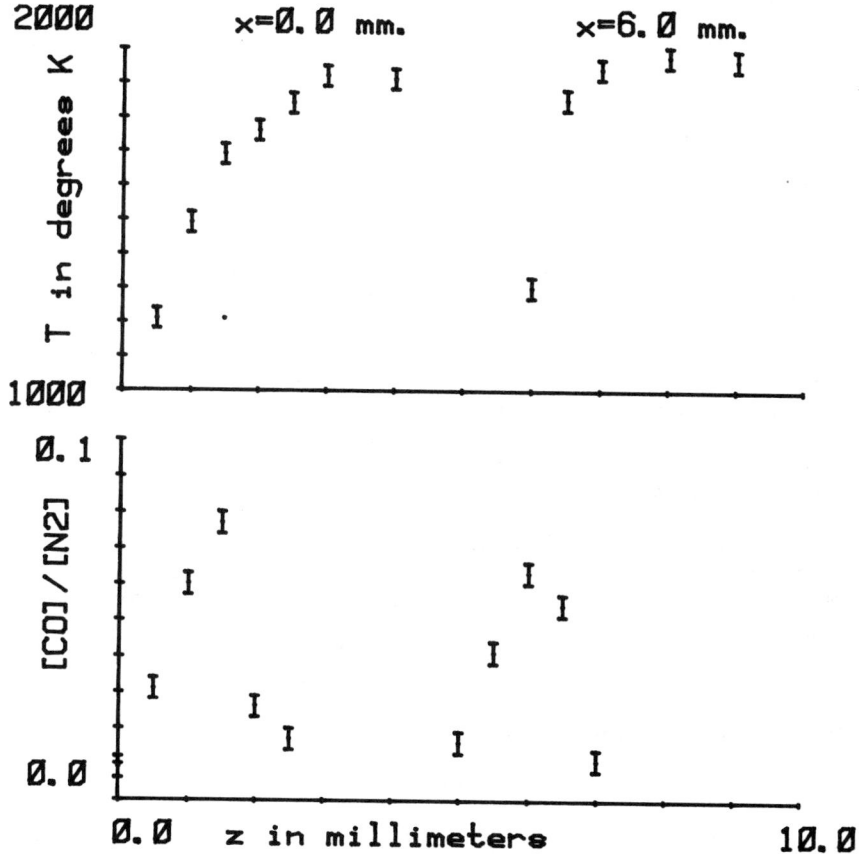

Fig. 5. Temperature distribution and CO distribution from data as shown in Fig. 4 for two different horizontal positions (across the reaction zone) in the burner. The CO plot is the CO concentration relative to N_2 in these lean propane-air flame measurements.

an opportunity to relate the CO concentration to the identifiable structure from the N_2 O bands and thus to the N_2 concentration independently from nonresonant susceptibility σ, as long as the latter is relatively large. In practice, the ratio of the peak to valley height at the CO Q-band to the N_2 O band intensity in the experimental spectrum is compared to the corresponding ratio in the calculated profile for the same temperature with the temperature usually obtained from the N_2 Q-band spectrum. In this manner, the CO concentration profiles of Fig. 5 were obtained. At the higher CO concentrations, the CO Q-band profile itself can be analyzed to obtain an independent measure of temperature. This has been done for the points of maximum CO concentration and the corresponding value of T agrees within the error limits of ± 25°K with that obtained from the Q-bands of N_2.

CONCLUSIONS

We have shown how nonlinear spectroscopy has developed into a tool for space and time resolved combustion diagnostics. The applications of the techniques to measurements of physical parameters of interest in stable flame systems have been demonstrated and these demonstrations indicate that CARS spectroscopy should be an effective probe of transient combustion systems. In fact, preliminary measurements in the exhaust of a small single cylinder engine have already been made[5] which can resolve the effects of individual cycle episodes on the exhaust gas. Use of this small laboratory engine for in-cylinder measurements during the firing cycle will begin shortly. Although the extension of the CARS measurements to engine applications is straightforward, as indicated by preliminary results obtained in scanned narrow band CARS spectroscopy[16] reliable single pulse broadband in-cylinder measurements have not yet been demonstrated. Problems relating to window damage, transient beam steering by refractive index gradients and optical access difficulties in certain specific regions within the cylinder have to be addressed. Nevertheless, it appears that noninteracting time resolved thermometry, species identification and concentration measurements are not only feasible with nonlinear optical techniques but that for rather general conditions these techniques offer the only possible method for such measurements. Practical application of CARS in engine cylinder combustion diagnostics seems imminent.

REFERENCES

1. F. Moya, S. A. J. Druet and J. P. E. Taran, Opt. Commun. 13, 169 (1975).
2. A. C. Eckbreth, United Technologies Research Center, Report #78-41 (1978).
3. K. A. Marko and L. Rimai, Optics Letters 4, 211 (1979).
4. L. A. Rahn, L. J. Zych and P. L. Mattern, Optics. Commun. 30, 249 (1979).
5. K. A. Marko and L. Rimai, Paper #800138, Society of Automotive Engineers (1980).
6. N. Bloembergen, Nonlinear Optics, W. A. Benjamin Inc., New York, 1965.
7. R. T. Lynch - Thesis, Harvard University, Cambridge, Mass., March 1977.
8. W. Heitler, The Quantum Theory of Radiation, 3rd Edition, Clarendon Press, Oxford 1954.
9. E. B. Wilson, J. C. Decius and P. C. Cross, Molecular Vibrations, McGraw Hill, New York, 1955.

10. G. Hertzberg, Molecular Spectra and Molecular Structure $\underline{1}$, Spectra of Diatomic Molecules, 2nd Ed., VanNostrand, Princeton, N. J., 1950.
11. B. P. Stoicheff, in Advances in Spectroscopy $\underline{1}$, 91, H. W. Thompson, Editor, Interscience, N.Y., 1959.
12. L. C. Davis, K. Marko, L. Rimai -- in preparation.
13. A. C. Eckbreth, Appl. Phys. Letters $\underline{32}$, 421 (1978).
14. K. Marko and L. Rimai -- MS in preparation.
15. F. Clauser, California Institute of Technology, Pasadena, California, private communications and to be published.
16. I. A. Stanhouse, D. R. Williams, J. B. Cole and M. D. Swords, Publication Preprint from Atomic Energy Research Establishment, Harwell, Didcot, Oxfordshire, England, 1979.

INFRARED DIODE LASERS

Wayne Lo
Physics Department
General Motors Research Laboratories, Warren, Michigan 48090

ABSTRACT

This paper reviews the development of infrared diode lasers for automobile exhaust gas analysis and high resolution spectroscopy at the General Motors Research Laboratories. Advances in lead-salt crystal growth technology and laser fabrication techniques to achieve high temperature operation and wide frequency tuning range will be discussed. Recent developments in improving the long-term reliability of the lasers will also be reviewed.

INTRODUCTION

In recent years, the technology of fabricating lead-salt diode lasers has advanced rapidly.[1] This is due to the demand for more reliable and well-behaved devices for certain applications. In the case of automotive research, high sensitivity real-time exhaust gas analysis[2] and catalyst dynamic reaction measurements[3] have been demonstrated recently by using a diode laser spectrometer system. For environmental studies, the use of these lasers for the measurements of the chemical reactions in the upper atmosphere has also been proposed.[4]

Figure 1 shows lead-salt material systems, the wavelength ranges covered by diode lasers, and the absorption lines of important automobile exhaust components. For the wavelength range between 3 and 10 μm, the use of $Pb_{1-x}Sn_xTe$, $PbS_{1-x}Se_x$ and $Pb_{1-x}Cd_xS$ will be adequate for complete coverage. Also shown in Figure 1 is the comparison of spectral power density for a laser and a conventional infrared (IR) spectrometer. Due to the narrow linewidth of these lasers, a factor of 10^4 more resolving power can be obtained than with a conventional spectrometer.

In this paper, advances in the art of crystal growth that led to improvement in laser performance will be reviewed first. This is followed by the results of reliability studies that led to an increase of laser lifetime from a few weeks to over a year. Finally, the use of a carrier concentration gradient to achieve high-temperature operation and the observation of room-temperature electroluminescence from these diodes will also be described.

CRYSTAL GROWTH

Although there are many different ways of growing lead-salt crystals, the ingot-nucleation technique offers a more convenient way of growing them with a low dislocation density.[5] The advantages of this technique is that the as-grown facets are not in contact with the quartz growth ampoule and hence are not subjected to the strain caused by a mismatch in thermal expansion coefficients.

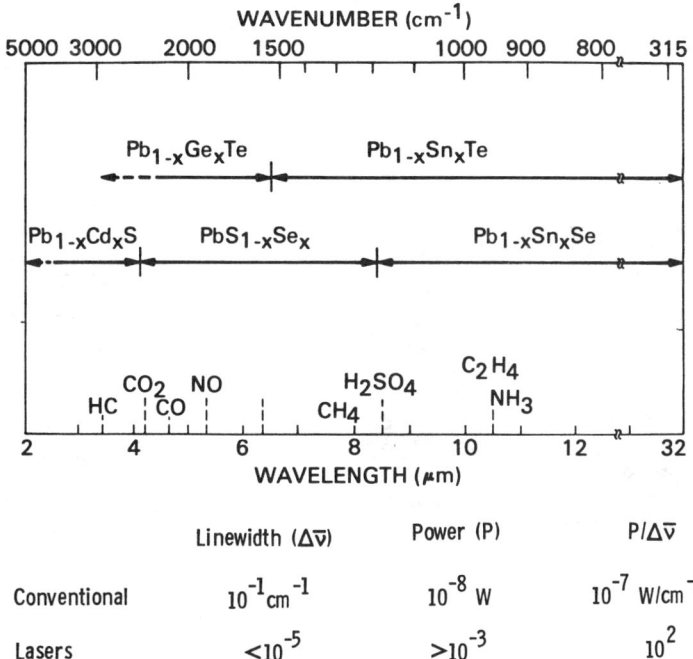

Fig. 1 Infrared wavelength range for the lead-salt system and comprison of parameters for conventional IR systems and diode lasers.

Figure 2 shows the furnace temperature profile used to grow ingot-nucleated single crystals. The temperature drop near the end of the ingot is the driving force for localized condensation of vapor, and the temperature rise at the end of the ampoule is needed to prevent vapor transport too far away from the ingot. By using this technique, single crystals of $Pb_{1-x}Sn_xTe$ and $PbS_{1-x}Se_x$ with a dislocation density of $10^3/cm^2$ or less have been grown.

The output power of diode lasers is directly related to the dislocation density of the starting crystals. We found that the density must be $10^3/cm^2$ or less in order to fabricate a diode with 1 mw or more output power. The dislocation density also depends on the furnace cooling rate (from growth temperature to room temperature) as shown in Table I. Of course, care must be taken in the fabrication process to minimize the generation of additional dislocations and other defects.

The diffusion process used to form p-n junctions is also important in fabricating high performance diode lasers. Impurity diffusion, in particular Cd-diffusion, is much superior to the self-diffusion process for fabricating high quality PbSnTe diode lasers.[6] However, for PbSSe materials, the self-diffusion process also produces high performance diode lasers.[7]

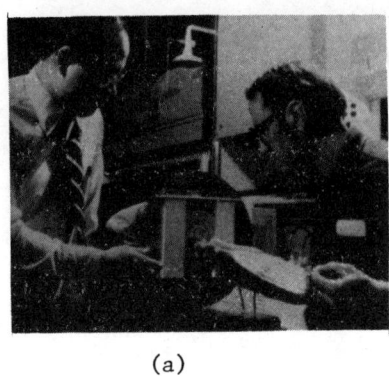 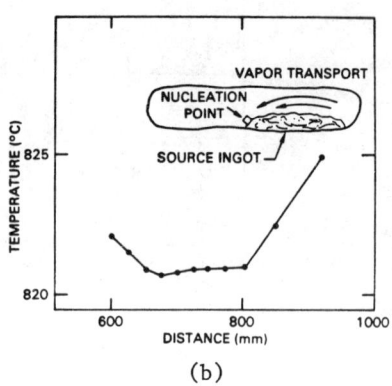

(a)   (b)

Fig. 2   (a) The author and Mr. Don Swets load a crystal growth furnace.
(b) Temperature profile used to grow ingot-nucleated single crystals.

Table I   Effect of Cooling and Growth Conditions on Dislocation Density

	Dislocation Density of Crystal Grown on Quartz Ampoule Wall	Dislocation Density of Crystal Grown on Source Ingot
Fast Cool (200°C/hr)	10^6–10^7 cm^{-2}	10^5 cm^{-2}
Slow Cool (10°C/hr)	10^5 cm^{-2}	10^3–10^4 cm^{-2}

CONTACT RELIABILITY

For cw operation at temperatures approaching 40 K, we found that a contact resistance of 10^{-4} ohm-cm^2 or less is necessary. This is attributed to the low thermal conductivity of lead salt materials (typically 0.07 W/cm-K versus 3.0 W/cm-K for GaAs at 77 K).[8] Since lead-salt crystals have very high electron affinities, low resistance and ohmic contact to the n-type side of diodes can be obtained easily by using either Au, In or In-Au combinations. It is the p-tye contact that normally causes problems.

For the p-type side In-Au,[9] In-Pt[10] and In-Pt-Au[11] structures have been reported as producing low resistance ohmic contacts. More recently only In-Au combinations have been used.[12,13] We are not aware of any systematic studies on the long-term reliability of In-Au contacts. However, we found that they are not stable in our devices. During storage at room temperature over periods that range from days to months, the resistance of In-Au contacts can increase. Such increases are typically accompanied by increases in cw threshold current densities and laser emission frequencies, while at the same time laser output powers tend to decrease.

We found that the increase in contact resistance is caused by the diffusion of In into the surface layer of the p-type side. Figure 3 shows an electron microprobe analysis of the In concentration profile near the metal-semiconductor interface after degradation. Note that for a degraded sample, traces of In were found in the first few μm of the crystal below the contact. Since In is a donor in lead-salt materials, a reduction in hole carrier concentration near the surface is expected. We think that this is the reason for the increase in contact resistance.[14]

Further study revealed that Au or Pt alone cannot form a barrier against In penetration, but a combination of Pt-Au does. It was also noticed that the reliability of the lasers depends on the thickness of the Pt and Au layers. We found that both layers have to be at least 0.2 μm thick in order to form a barrier against In diffusion. After depositing the Au and Pt layers on the p-type side of the diode a 10 μm layer of In is added. The n-type contact consists of a 0.2 μm layer of Au plus 5 μm of In. The p-type side of the crystal surface was purposely oxidized by exposure to air before evaporating the first layer of Au. This increases the hole carrier concentration near the surface and tends to stabilize the contact resistance.

Over a period of ten months, groups of $PbS_{1-x}Se_x$ and $Pb_{1-x}Sn_xTe$ lasers (made with three-layer contacts on the p-type side) have been tested for thermal cycling, room temperature storage and cw operation. For up to sixty thermal cycles and five hundred hours of cw operation, no significant changes in contact resistance, threshold current density or optical properties were observed. The test results are summarized in Table II. This is a significant improvement over lasers that have been fabricated in

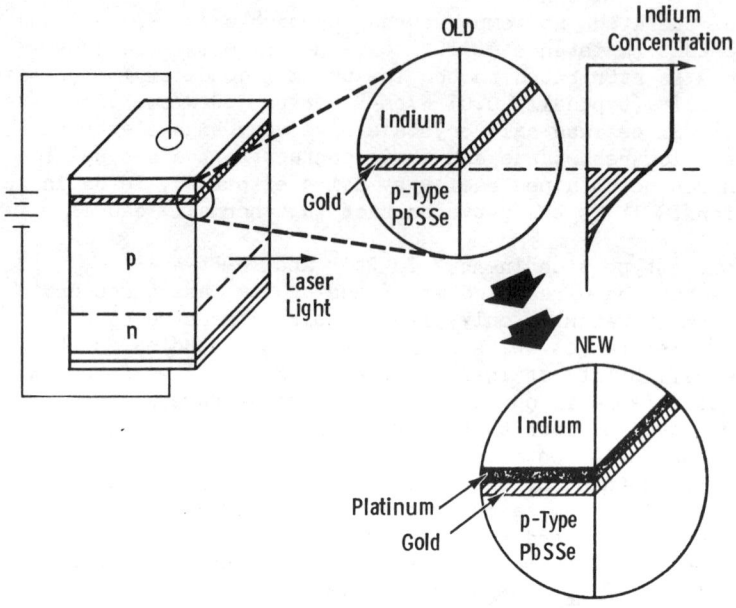

Fig. 3   Electron microprobe analysis of contact diffusion and lifetime improvement for PbSSe diode lasers.

the past, whose performance could degrade in a matter of a few days at room temperature.

OPERATING TEMPERATURE

Diode lasers of $Pb_{1-x}Sn_xTe$ and $PbS_{1-x}Se_x$ have been fabricated with maximum lasing temperatures of 130 K[15] and 140 K,[7] respectively. These lasers were fabricated with a two step diffusion-annealing process which produces a graded carrier concentration profile as shown in Figure 4. This graded region (approximately 100 to 150 μm deep) can serve as a waveguide for photons if the laser active region is placed within the carrier gradient. This is achieved by using another diffusion process to form a p-n junction approximately 5 to 8 μm deep. As shown in Fig. 4, this carrier concentration gradient produces an index of refraction gradient which guides the photons in the active region and improves the laser efficiency. We wish to emphasize that the strong dependence of index of refraction on carrier concentration is a unique property of lead-salt crystals and may not be applicable in other semiconductor materials.

Table II Laser Test Results (Ten-Month Test Period)

		R_c (Ohm-cm^2)x10^5 Contact Resistance		J_{th} (A/cm^2) Threshold Current Density		P(mW) Total Output Power at I=1 Amp, T=20K		Remarks
		Initial	Final	Initial	Final	Initial	Final	
PbS$_{0.82}$Se$_{0.18}$	#1	1.10	1.18	260	280	0.85	0.80	500 hours c.w. operation Thermal cycling 26 times
	#2	0.87	0.91	365	380	3.2	2.6	Thermal Cycling 45 times
Pb$_{0.86}$Sn$_{0.14}$Te	#1	0.74	0.80	95	105	0.65	0.58	300 hours c.w. operation Thermal Cycling 25 times
	#2	0.65	0.73	125	135	0.90	0.86	420 hours c.w. operation Thermal Cycling 33 times

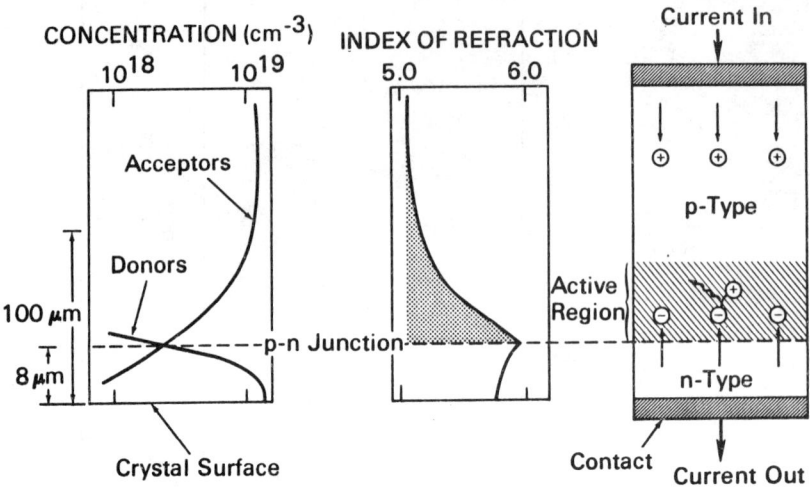

Fig. 4 Carrier concentration and index refraction profile for a widely tunable $Pb_{0.86}Sn_{0.14}Te$ diode laser.

In an effort to predict the highest temperature of operation for lasers at long wavelengths, we have made an empirical plot shown in Figure 5. From this plot, it is seen that the longest wavelength for a room temperature semiconductor laser is 2.5 μm. Although laser sources are desirable for many applications, room temperature, long wavelength incoherent light sources are of interest for low resolution applications, as well as for low loss optical fiber communication systems.[16,17] The narrow band gap, lead-salt materials are suitable for fabricating emitters in the 3-16 μm spectral range. Photoluminescence[18] and cathodoluminescence[19] have been observed at room temperature, but not electroluminescence. We report here the first recorded electroluminescence from PbSSe at room temperature.[20]

High temperature spontaneous emission spectra were recorded as shown in Figure 6. Notice that the 330 ppm atmospheric CO_2 absorption band near 4.2 μm appears in the 260 K and 300 K spectra (Fig. 2, e-f).

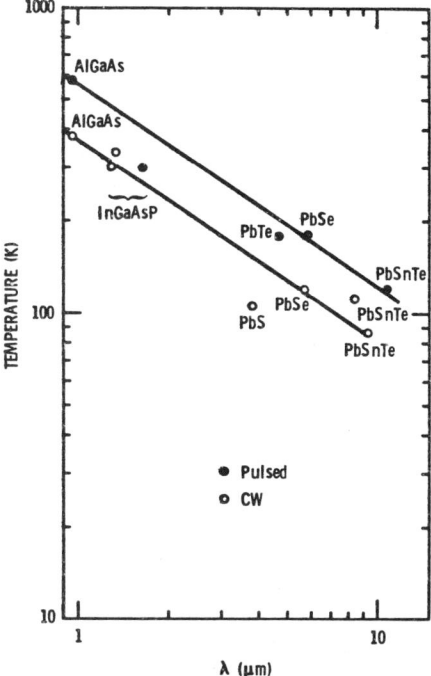

Fig. 5. Empirical plot of the highest observed operating temperatures for semiconductor diode lasers at different wavelengths.

The power output for this (laser) diode geometry is low, on the order of a few hundred nW. This is attributed to the high index of refraction (4.6) for lead-sulfide-selenide, which produces substantial internal reflection at the semiconductor-air interface. The critical angle for total internal reflection (i.e., the largest angle which incident radiation can subtend with the normal and still exit the crystal), is 12°. A large fraction of the randomly oriented junction radiation is totally reflected back into the semiconductor and absorbed. By using a hemispherical structure and extracting light from the top surface rather than the side, a factor of 1000 improvement in power is possible. This will allow these diodes to emit 200 µw at room temperature.

CONCLUDING REMARKS

In conclusion, we found that the slow degradation of contact resistance for lead-salt diode lasers fabricated with In-Au contacts is due to the migration of In into the surface layer of the p-type side of the lasers. By using combinations of Au-Pt or

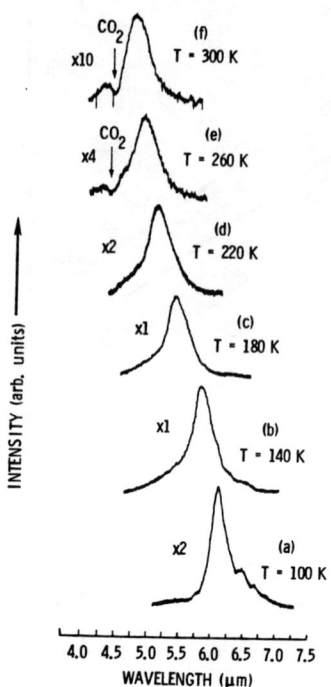

Fig. 6   Spontaneous emission spectra at different temperatures. Also shown is the 330 PPM atmospheric CO_2 absorption band near 4.2 μm in the 260 K and 350 K spectra.

Pt-Au as barriers to prevent In migration, we have substantially increased the lifetime of these lasers. For high temperature operation, we have shown that although lasing action at room temperature is possible only up to 2.5 μm, spontaneous emission at room temperature has been observed near 4.6 μm.

REFERENCES

1. W. Lo, Proceedings of the Conference on Heterodyne Systems and Technology, National Aeronautics and Space Administration, Langley Research Center, Hampton, VA (1980).
2. J. C. Hill and R. F. Majkowski, Society of Automotive Engineers Conference Paper #800510 (1980).
3. J. A. Sell, R. K. Herz and D. R. Monroe, Society of Automotive Engineer Conference Paper #800463 (1980).
4. F. Allario and S. J. Katzberg, Proceedings of the Conference on Heterodyne Systems and Technology, National Aeronautic and Space Administration, Langley Research Center, Hampton, VA (1980).

5. W. Lo, G. P. Montgomery, Jr. and D. E. Swets, J. Appl. Phys. 47, 267 (1976).
6. W. Lo, Appl. Phys. Lett. 28, 154 (1976).
7. W. Lo and D. E. Swets, Appl. Phys. Lett., 33, 938 (1978).
8. American Institute of Physics Handbook, McGraw Hill, 1975, pp. 4-156.
9. R. W. Ralston, I. Melngailis, A. R. Calawa, and W. T. Lindi, IEEE, J. Quant. Electron., QE-9, 350 (1973).
10. G. A. Antcliffe, and S. G. Parker, J. Appl. Phys., 44, 4145 (1973).
11. R. W. Ralston, J. N. Walpole, A. R. Clawa, T. C. Harman, and J. P. McVittie, J. Appl. Phys., 45, 1323 (1974).
12. J. N. Walpole, A. R. Calawa, T. C. Harman and S. H. Grove, Appl. Phys. Lett., 28, 552 (1976).
13. K. J. Lindon, K. W. Nill and J. F. Butler, IEEE, J. Quant. Electron., QE-13, 720 (1977).
14. W. Lo, J. Electron Mater., 6, 39 (1977).
15. W. Lo, IEEE, J. Quant. Electron., QE-13, 591 (1977).
16. D. A. Pinnow, A. L. Gentile, A. G. Standler, A. J. Timper, and L. M. Hobrock, Appl. Phys. Lett., 33, 28 (1978).
17. L. G. Van Uitert and S. H. Wemple, Appl. Phys. Lett., 33, 57 (1978).
18. F. Galeski, L. Drozd, L. T. Lebedeva, V. P. Ten, and A. E. Yunovich, Sov. Phys. Semicond., 11, 327 (1977).
19. L. N. Kurbatou, A. D. Britou, and S. M. Karavaev, Sov. Phys. Semicond., 9, 1045 (1976).
20. W. Lo and D. E. Swets, Appl. Phys. Lett. 36, 450 (1980).

VEHICLE EMISSIONS MEASUREMENTS WITH INFRARED DIODE LASERS

John C. Hill
Physics Department
General Motors Research Laboratories, Warren, Michigan 48090

ABSTRACT

Absorption of tunable diode laser radiation can detect small concentrations of gases with fast response. The selectivity of the method is demonstrated by the detection of sulfuric acid in the presence of water vapor. The speed of the method is demonstrated by the first measurements of carbon monoxide (CO) concentrations in automotive exhaust with a time response (<25 ms) fast enough to be useful in the analysis of engine and emission control system dynamics. The CO was measured before and after a catalytic converter under operation at: 1) constant air/fuel (A/F) ratio, 2) step changes in A/F, and 3) oscillations of A/F at frequencies on the order of 1 Hz.

INTRODUCTION

As vehicle emission control technology becomes more sophisticated, the ability to measure emissions on a time scale short enough to understand the dynamic response of engines and control systems becomes more important. However, any new method must also be able to detect small concentrations of species, down to the ppm level, and simultaneously avoid interference by molecules that are not of interest.

One method with potential for analyzing a wide variety of exhaust components in real time is absorption of diode laser radiation. The basic principle is to use tunable semiconductor lasers which emit light at infrared wavelengths. The tunability of these devices allows their output to be matched exactly with a given molecule's infrared absorption. Furthermore the spectral width of their output is narrow, on the order of $10^{-5} cm^{-1}$ compared to about $1\ cm^{-1}$ for a conventional spectrometer. This very narrow linewidth makes it possible to pick out an absorption line from one molecule, while avoiding overlap with and interference from lines of other molecules. Diode lasers also have an advantage in their high output power, typically on the order of $10^{-3}W$ compared to $10^{-8}W$ from a spectrometer. At laser power levels detector noise is negligible, allowing the use of short time constants and fast detection of gaseous species. The combination of spectral selectivity and high speed detection makes these lasers suitable for real-time measurement of vehicle emissions.

As examples of the recent advances that have been made with these lasers, we shall describe measurements of sulfuric acid (sulfate) and carbon monoxide.

H_2SO_4 Measurements

The small amount of sulfur (~0.03%) in motor vehicle fuel is almost totally oxidized to SO_2 during combustion. While passing over a catalyst there is the further possibility of oxidation to SO_3, followed by hydration to H_2SO_4. The problem with prior methods for measuring sulfate was a requirement for passing exhaust through a filter or condensation tube for 10 min or more until enough sample was obtained for wet chemical analysis. More recently the buildup of sulfate on a filter during a steady 64 km/h cruise was measured through changes in electrical resistance,[1] but no data was presented on changing emission rates during a variable speed test cycle. Therefore, it was not clear how changes in vehicle operating conditions affect exhaust sulfate concentration.

For this measurement the lasers were fabricated from crystals with the composition $Pb_{0.94}Sn_{0.006}Te$ which was known to have the right bandgap to produce emission in the 1250-1300 cm^{-1} region.[2] A schematic of the laser system is shown in Fig. 1. The beam from the laser is collected by a lens, imaged and collimated for multiple-pass transmission through the sample cell. After the cell, the beam passes through a monochromator to eliminate unwanted laser modes. After the monochromator, a cooled HgCdTe detector measures the transmitted intensity.

The design of the sample handling system was dictated by the need to maintain the chemical integrity of the sulfate in the form of H_2SO_4 vapor. The temperature had to be in a range from 160°C to 200°C to prevent both condensation on walls[3] and decomposition into SO_3.[4] The plumbing from the tailpipe to the sample cell and the cell itself were heated to approximately 180°C before the start of each test. Except for the optical components stainless steel was used throughout, since it demonstrated minimal reactivity with the H_2SO_4. The ability of the sample cell and connecting plumbing to transport H_2SO_4 without changing its concentration was tested on a vehicle. The H_2SO_4 concentration was measured at the tailpipe and at the outlet of the entire sample system by a condensation tube and subsequent chemical analysis of the condensate. The inlet and outlet concentrations were 14 ± 2 and 15 ± 2 ppm, respectively, confirming the transport capability of the system.

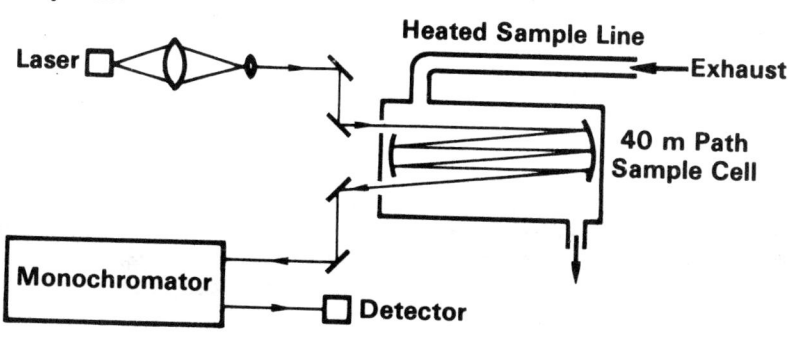

Fig. 1 Schematic of laser system.

The sample cell was a redesigned version of a commercial, multiple-pass White cell. Special attention was given to the two mirrors between which the beam passes. Their mounts were designed to maximize their stability against vibration or changes in temperature as the exhaust flow rate varied. In practice, it was found that the mirrors did not need adjustment during the course of a vehicle test. There was also a substantial amount of baffling to assure uniform distribution of the exhaust stream as it passed through the cell.

The installation of the equipment in a vehicle emission laboratory is shown in Fig. 2. The laser system was mounted on an optical table with air supports and one section of stainless steel bellows isolated it from motion of the vehicle on the dynamometer. These were the only provisions required for satisfactory operation.

Sulfate emissions were measured[5] during a Highway Fuel Economy Test (Fig. 3). Starting from idle, the vehicle speed reaches about 80 kph during the first minute. After a dip at 5 min it rises to an average of approximately 90 kph until the vehicle stops. The prolonged high speed rasied the exhaust system temperature by 200°C.

The measured H_2SO_4 concentration as a function of time into the test is shown in Fig. 4. The 100% conversion level (all the sulfur in the fuel converted to acid) is indicated. At the beginning of the test the H_2SO_4 concentration was unobservable, but it began to rise after about 2 min. The acid concentration generally increases until near the end of the test when the vehicle speed dropped again. The very slow manner in which the sulfate emission rate changes suggests that it is controlled by something which also changes slowly. As shown in Fig. 4, the temperature of the catalytic converter varied in approximately the same manner. At the beginning of a HWFET (after a vehicle has been idling) the catalyst temperature was typically 240°C, but it consistently peaked at $\sim$450°C at the same time the H_2SO_4 concentration peaked. This suggests that to first order sulfate emission depends on catalyst temperature, which is consistent with a model developed by Hegedus.[6] Furthermore, the Hegedus model predicts that significant sulfate formation (greater than 2-3% conversion) will not occur until the catalyst temperature reaches $\sim$350°C. This is reasonably consistent with the appearance of H_2SO_4 at 300°C.

From Fig. 4 it is evident that the sulfate emissions can be greater than that corresponding to 100% conversion of the fuel sulfur. The variation from negligible conversion to sulfate at the beginning of the test to more than 100% conversion is consistent with proposed models of storage and release of sulfur on a catalyst. It appears that a cool catalyst stores sulfur, then releases it as SO_3 when the catalyst temperature rises.

The results above represent the first time that vehicle sulfate emissions were resolved as a function of time. Filter or condensation tube measurements which require a minimum of 10 min. would obliterate the time dependence observed above. This was the fist demonstration of the ability of tunable diode lasers to track vehicle emissions durinmg a test procedure.

85

Fig. 2 Installation of laser spectrometer in a vehicle emission laboratory. John Hill, Daniel Hayden and Richard Majkowski conduct the experiment.

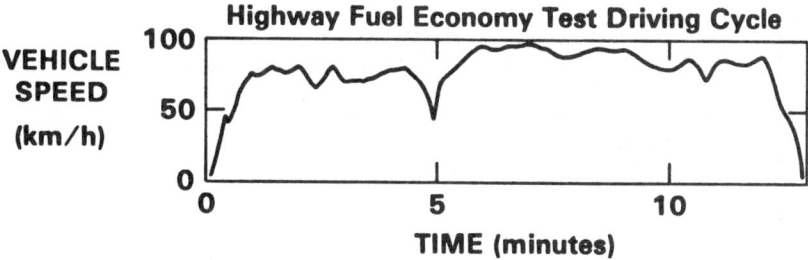

Fig. 3 Vehicle speed vs. time during a Highway Fuel Economy Test.

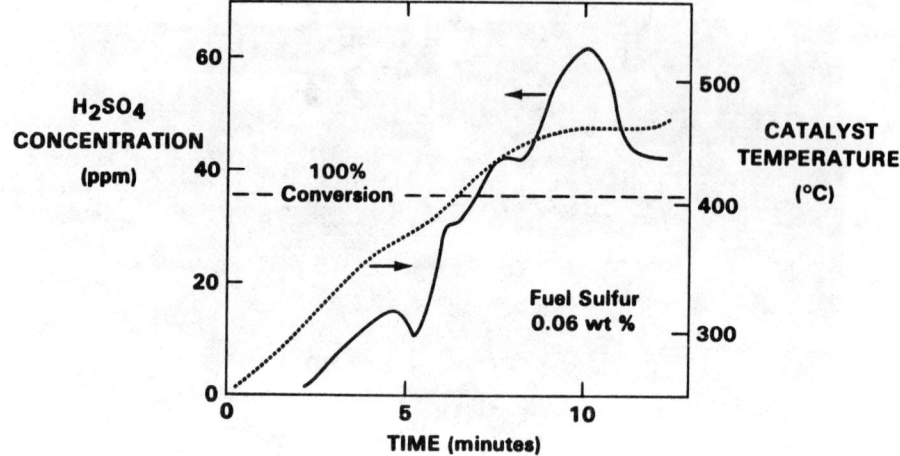

Fig. 4   Exhaust H_2SO_4 concentration (—) and catalyst temperature (---) during a HWFET.

CO Measurements

Analysis of the dynamics of computer-controlled engines and the associated catalytic converter systems is desirable because the performance of a converter at a given air-fuel ratio (A/F) setpoint is affected by the amplitude and frequency of the A/F fluctuations.[7-9] In order to analyze the dynamic response of catalytic converters, it is necessary to use techniques of gas concentration analysis that have a response time faster than characteristic fluctuations in the A/F, which occur at frequencies between 0.5 and 4 Hz.[10] The usual method of CO measurement uses nondispersive infrared spectroscopy. This method has a long response time (> 1s) since it requires condensation of water from a side stream of exhaust gas which is pumped from the main exhaust flow. The slow response of this method prevents its use in the analysis of catalytic converter dynamics in computer-controlled engine systems.

A block diagram of the apparatus is shown in Fig. 5.[11] Basically, a chopped infrared diode laser beam is tuned into the center of a CO absorption line and split into two components by a beam splitter. One component passes through windows in the exhaust line before the catalytic converter and the other component passes through windows in the exhaust line after the catalytic converter. The laser beams then impinge on infrared detectors whose signals are processed by lockin amplifiers and sent to a computer for data acquisition. A zirconia oxygen sensor indicated whether the exhaust was lean or rich.

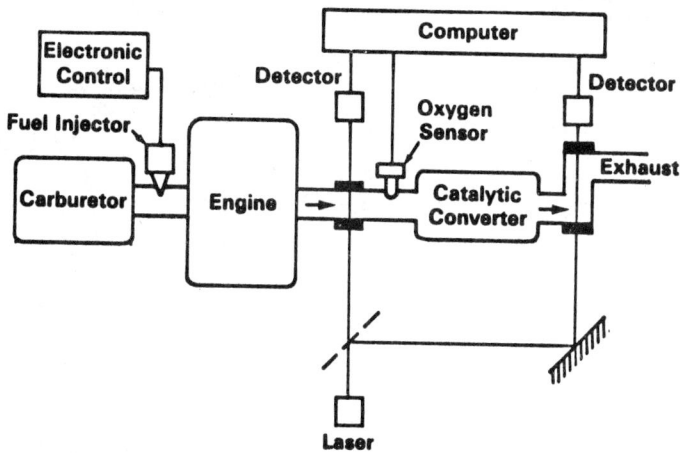

Fig. 5 Schematic of laser system for detection of CO.

The engine used in this study was a 1978 Chevrolet 5.7 ℓ V-8 with exhaust gas recirculation. Standard engine operating conditions were 1700 RPM and 54 kPa vacuum. The exhaust gas temperature varied between 400°C and 470°C as measured by thermocouples in the exhaust line before and after the converter. The exhaust gas flow rate was about 35 ℓ/s at NTP (0°C, 1 atm).

The air/fuel ratio (A/F) was adjusted either manually or electronically. The manual adjustments were performed by changing the setting on the partial throttle adjustment screw on the carburetor. The electronic adjustments were accomplished by varying the duty cycle on a fuel injector mounted between the carburetor and the intake plenum. The fuel injector was pulsed at a 16.7 Hz frequency. The percent of each cycle which the injector was open (the duty cycle) was adjustable from 0 to 100%. The fuel injector control unit allowed the injector to be operated in two modes. It could be operated at 0% duty cycle (off) then switched to a predetermined duty cycle giving a step change in A/F. It could also be switched automatically between two selectable duty cycles giving a square wave oscillation in A/F.

The response time of the system was measured by injecting a known, additional concentration of CO into exhaust as it flowed through one of the sample cells (Fig. 6a). As shown in Fig. 6b, the measured concentration rose from 10 to 90% of its final value in 25 ms. Since the actual speed of the injector is unknown, this represents an upper limit on the actual response time.

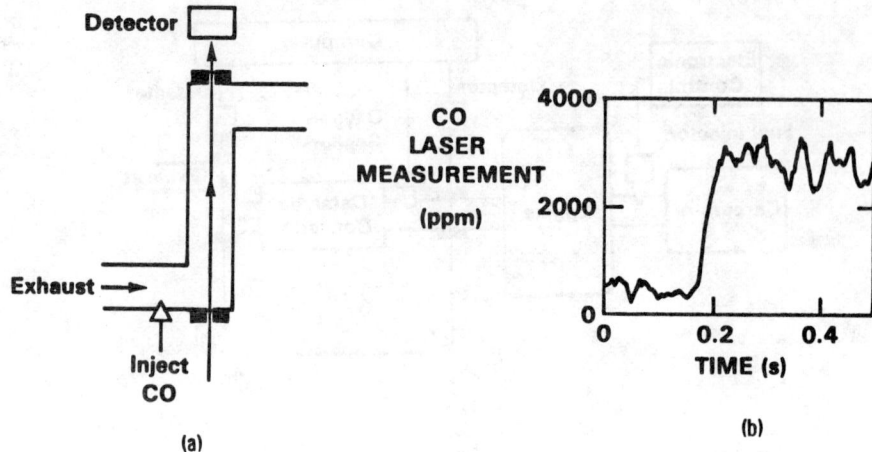

Fig. 6   Response time of laser system.

Figure 7 shows how the engine out and converter out CO concentrations change as the fuel injector is switched between rich and lean conditions. During a rich-to-lean step the two concentrations change almost simultaneously. However, after a lean-to-rich change the converter out CO stays relatively low for a matter of seconds. This lag depends on the magnitude, as well as the direction, of an A/F change.

In actual operation the A/F ratio for a computer-controlled engine oscillates between rich and lean conditions at frequencies of a few Hz. Typical results at 0.5 Hz are shown in Fig. 8. The output of the oxygen sensor clearly registers the oscillation in A/F ratio, and the CO out of the engine and converter does also. Similar results were obtained at 2.5 Hz (Fig. 9), except that the oxygen sensor output does not change as much as at the lower frequency. In both cases it should be noted that the lag in converter out CO following lean-to-rich transitions is clearly visible. This is the first time that the dynamic variation of CO from a computer-controlled engine and catalytic converter has been measured.

Summary

We have shown that infrared diode lasers can selectively detect species such as H_2SO_4 and CO without interference from other molecules in vehicle exhaust. The relatively intense output of these lasers allows detection of concentrations down to the ppm

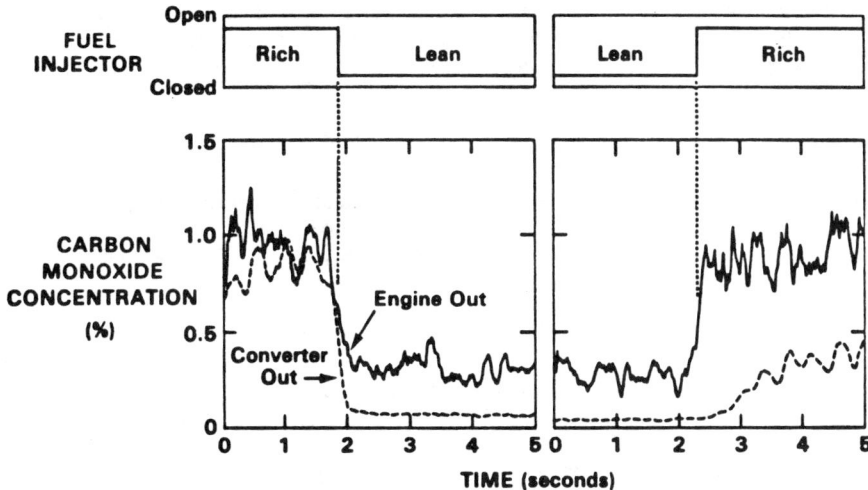

Fig. 7 CO concentration during step changes in A/F ratio.

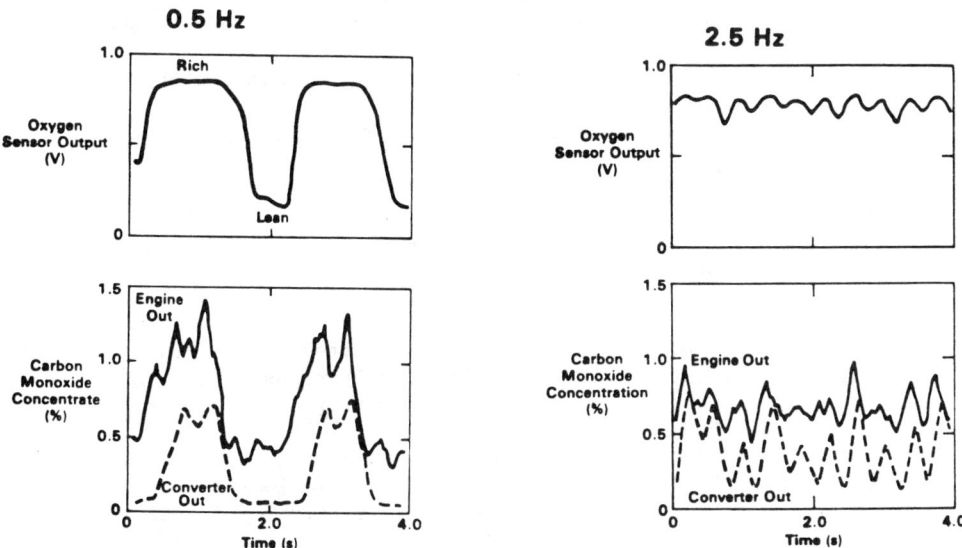

Fig. 8 Oxygen sensor output and CO concentration during a 0.5 Hz oscillation of A/F ratio.

Fig. 9 Oxygen sensor output and CO concentration during a 2.5 Hz oscillation of A/F ratio.

level. They are also fast, with system response time as fast as 25 ms. With this new tool we have begun to measure dynamic emissions from vehicles with the latest generation of control systems.

Acknowledgments

Many colleagues at the General Motors Research Laboratories contributed to the results reported here. Special thanks are due W. Lo, R. F. Majkowski, J. A. Sell, R. K. Herz, D. K. Monroe and L. L. Hegedus.

References

1. M. Beltzer, "Real-Time, Continuous Measurement of Automotive Sulfuric Acid Emissions," J. Air. Poll. Control Assoc. 29, 57 (1979).
2. W. Lo, "Homojunction Lead-Tin-Telluride Diode Lasers with Increased Frequency Tuning Range," IEEE J. Quan. Elecs. QE-13, 591 (1977).
3. F. H. Verhoff and J. T. Banchero, "Evaluation and Interpretation of Vapor Pressure Data of Sulfuric Acid Aqueous Solutions with Application to Flue Gas Dewpoints," Chem. Eng. Prog. 70, 71 (1974).
4. W. R. Leppard, "Sulfate Control Technology Assessment Phase I, Literature Search and Analysis," Exxon Research and Engineering Company report to EPA, No. EPA-460/3-75-002-a, November 1974.
5. J. C. Hill and R. F. Majkowski, "Time-Resolved Measurement of Vehicle Sulfate and Methane Emissions with Durable Diode Lasers," Paper 800510, SAE Automotive Engineering Congress and Exposition, Detroit, Michigan, 1980.
6. L. L. Hegedus, General Motors Research Laboratories, private communication.
7. L. L. Hegedus, J. C. Summers, J. C. Schlatter, and K. Baron, "Poison-Resistant Catalysts for the Simultaneous Control of Hydrocarbon, Carbon Monoxide and Nitrogen Oxide Emissions," J. Catalysis 56, 321 (1979).
8. Y. Kaneko, H. Kobayashi, R. Komagome, O. Hirako, and O. Nakayama, "Effect of Air-Fuel Ratio Modulation on Conversion Efficiency of Three-Way Catalysts," Paper 780607, SAE Automotive Engineering Congress and Exposition, Detroit, Michigan, 1978.
9. H. S. Gandhi, A. G. Piken, M. Shelef, and R. G. Delosh, "Laboratory Evaluation of Three-Way Catalysts," Paper 760201, SAE Automotive Engineering Congress and Exposition, Detroit, Michigan, 1976.
10. R. P. Canale, S. R. Winegarden, C. R. Carlson, and D. L. Miles, "General Motors Phase II Catalyst System," Paper 780205, SAE Automotive Engineering Congress and Exposition, Detroit, Michigan, 1978.

11. J. A. Sell, K. K. Herz and D. R. Monroe, "Dynamic Measurement of Carbon Monoxide Concentrations in Automotive Exhaust Using Infrared Diode Laser Spectroscopy," Paper 800463, SAE Automotive Engineering Congress and Exposition, Detroit, Michigan, 1980.

ADVANCED BATTERIES FOR ELECTRIC VEHICLES - A STATUS REPORT

William J. Walsh
Energy and Environmental Systems Division
Argonne National Laboratory
9700 South Cass Avenue
Argonne, Illinois 60439

ABSTRACT

The candidate battery systems for electric vehicles have been evaluated on a common basis. The batteries with the highest probability of successful development and commercialization appear to be lead-acid, nickel-iron, nickel-zinc, zinc-chlorine, lithium-metal sulfide, and sodium sulfur. The relative development risk was assessed and compared to the desirability of the corresponding batteries.

No clear-cut "winner" can be projected since each advanced battery has less than 50% probability of successful development. The overall probability that at least one of the batteries will be successfully developed by 2000 AD is judged greater than 75%.

INTRODUCTION

The very real possibility of an immense electric vehicle market has created a technological "race" to develop a suitable battery. Dozens of industrial developers in the USA, Western Europe, and Japan have entered this competition, and the net result is a world-wide "renaissance" in battery technology. The urgency of these R&D efforts is underscored by recent announcements by GM and Ford that they intend to market electric vehicles during the 1980's.

THE BATTERY CANDIDATES

A multitude of battery systems are potential candidates for the electric vehicle application.[1] Figure 1 shows the batteries most often suggested for this end use. Several of these battery candidates can be ruled out because they require large quantities of rare or expensive materials. The remaining 15 to 20 batteries each possess a group of loyal advocates who insist that their system is clearly the best, and that successful development and commercialization is nearly certain. In reality, each of these battery development efforts is a high-risk enterprise with major electrical performance, cycle life, or cost barriers.

ISSN:0094-243X/81/660092-15$1.50 Copyright 1981 American Institute of Physics

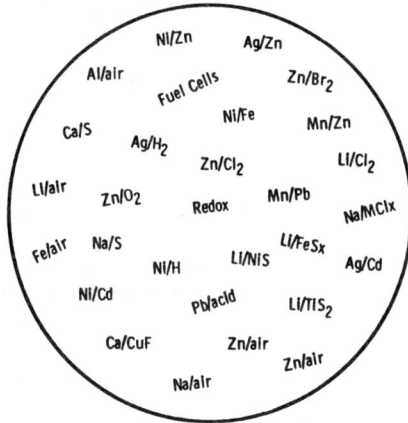

Fig. 1. The Battery Candidates

THE LEADING CONTENDERS

Only a few of the battery candidates have promise for successful development and penetration of large transportation markets before the year 2000.[2] These "leading contenders" are listed in Table I and are described below.

Table I. Most Promising Electric-Vehicle Batteries

Near-Term	Lead-Acid Nickel-Iron Nickel-Zinc Zinc-Chlorine
Intermediate-Term	Lithium-Metal Sulfide Sodium-Sulfur (Ceramic Electrolyte)

<u>Lead-Acid Batteries</u>. The lead-acid battery is the most widely used electrochemical system. Lead-acid cells consist of positive and negative electrodes that are immersed in an electrolyte solution of sulfuric acid. When the cell is fully charged, the active material of the positive electrode is lead dioxide (PbO_2), and the active material of the negative is lead (Pb). As the cell is discharged, the lead dioxide of the positive electrodes and the lead of the negative electrodes are converted to lead sulfate by the following reactions:

Positive: $PbO_2 + 4H^+ + SO_4^{--} + 2e^- \rightleftarrows PbSO_4 + 2H_2O$

Negative: $Pb + SO_4^{--} \rightleftarrows PbSO_4 + 2e^-$

Adding these two equations yields the overall cell reaction:

$$Pb + PbO_2 + 2H_2SO_4 \rightleftarrows 2PbSO_4 + 2H_2O$$

That is, lead, lead dioxide, and sulfuric acid are converted to lead sulfate and water. During the process, the electrodes remain solid since lead, lead dioxide, and lead sulfate are all relatively insoluble in sulfuric acid. The reactions are reversible, and the cell may be recharged to its initial state.

There are two types of electrode structures in lead/acid batteries used for motive power applications: flat plate (pasted) and tubular. The flat plate electrode has a center skeleton (grid) made of Pb alloy that has been coated with a paste-like mixture of active material. In the tubular electrode, powdered active material is loaded in a tubular envelope usually of woven glass-fiber or polyester material. Tubular electrode batteries have somewhat higher volumetric energy density but are more costly and somewhat more difficult to fabricate. The majority of current U.S. lead-acid batteries for traction use are of the flat plate type.

Work on lead-acid batteries is being carried out on two fronts, (1) development of improved state-of-art batteries (ISOA) and (2) development of "advanced" lead-acid systems capable of about 50% higher performance. These two development efforts represent very different technologies and are discussed separately below.

ISOA Lead-Acid Batteries. Much progress has been made in the development of ISOA lead-acid batteries for transportation end-uses. Within the next 18 months, these batteries should be capable of 45-45 W-hr/kg and lifetimes of 500-800 cycles. However, this performance level is still quite inadequate for many transportation applications.

ISOA lead-acid batteries are not very well suited for use in electric automobiles. The low specific energy (less than 50 W-hr/kg) generally results in an excessive battery weight unless range and EV performance are severely compromised. Vehicle range and performance can be enhanced through the use of clever designs which allow more batteries to be stuffed into the vehicle; however, these battery packs tend to become excessively expensive and energy conservation suffers since more and more energy is required to propel the battery itself. Peak power of ISOA batteries is quite marginal, especially late in the discharge and at low temperatures. This limits acceleration and other performance characteristics, especially in the case of intermediate and compact automobiles. In addition, ISOA batteries are quite bulky (less than 100 W-hr/liter) and thus are difficult to package into an electric vehicle.

On the positive side, ISOA batteries can be produced using existing production facilities, and will be the only EV battery available at less than $100/kW-hr by 1982. Eventual costs of about $45/kW-hr are projected assuming the present cost of lead. Environmental and safety problems associated with lead mining and battery manufacture are becoming of increasing concern; resolution of these problems could result in a cost penalty for the ISOA battery. The lead-acid battery seems most attractive for electric vehicle applications in which limited range (less than 100 miles) is acceptable. The principal vehicle markets for lead-acid vehicles are expected to be commercial fleets, especially vans, trucks and buses. At present, the lead-acid battery is the only alternative available for any type of electric vehicle.

Advanced Lead-Acid Batteries. Whereas the ISOA battery is a natural extension of existing technology, the "advanced" lead-acid battery will require one or more major breakthroughs. Attainment of the technical goals of 60 W-hr/kg and 1000 deep cycles will be very difficult. This technology is quite exploratory and challenging, similar to the high-temperature battery technologies. A dramatic technical improvement such as the successful development of a practical bipolar cell, will be needed for lead-acid batteries to approach satisfactory performance levels for widespread use in electric vehicles. Several promising approaches are under development, including (1) use of layered negative plates, (2) bipolar systems (3) circulating electrolyte batteries, and (4) attempts to greatly improve lead utilitization. Much of this advanced work is underway in Europe and Japan.

The development of a low cost lead-acid battery capable of 60 W-hr/kg and 1000 cycles would have a major impact on the emerging electric vehicle market. Unfortunately, the probability that this will occur by 1990 appears to be less than 10%.

Nickel-Zinc Batteries. Prospects for commercialization of Ni/Zn batteries have improved greatly during the past few years, and the battery has emerged as a leading candidate for near-term transportation applications. However, a major improvement in cycle life must be attained before significant penetration of a major market will be possible. This appears to be the only remaining barrier to successful development. The electrode reactions are given below:

Positive: $NiOOH + H_2O + e^- \rightleftarrows Ni(OH)_2 + OH^-$

Negative: $Zn + 2OH^- \rightleftarrows ZnO + H_2O + 2e^-$

The complete cell reaction is:

$$2NiOOH + H_2O + Zn \rightleftarrows 2Ni(OH)_2 + ZnO$$

One of the inherent problems with this system is that ZnO is partly soluble in the electrolyte (30-45% KOH solution) leading to shape change, dendrite formation, and densification during cycling, and subsequent abbreviated battery life. A wide variety of potential solutions to this lifetime problem are under development including (A) electroporous and other advanced separators, (B) additives to the electrolyte and zinc electrode, (C) techniques for homogenization of ion currents and reaction rates within the cells, and (D) the use of advanced designs. Successful resolution of the

Ni/Zn lifetime problem is far from certain, although the present cycle life capability of 200-300 deep cycles may be extended to 300-500 cycles within a few years. Moreover, most vehicle end-uses would require a mix of deep and shallow discharges, which should extend the practical life of the battery. For example, personal automobiles in the United States are typically driven hundreds of short trips and only a few dozen long trips per year. In this case, a ten-year, 100,000-mile electric vehicle may require thousands of shallow cycles, but only a few hundred deep cycles. The lifetime of Ni/Zn batteries for this type of service is very poorly known, but will definitely be superior to that achievable with repeated deep cycling.

The specific energy attainable with today's technology is about 65 W-hr/kg, with an additional 25% improvement expected by the year 2000. Peak power and sustained power characteristics are excellent, with about 175 W/kg attainable throughout the discharge. Volumetric energy density is excellent (about 120 W-hr/liter) and steadily improving with time. The Ni/Zn battery is well suited for the transportation application and easily adaptable into a wide variety of EV designs. General Motors has announced their intention to develop a Ni/Zn electric vehicle for sale to the public in the mid-1980's. However, General Motors has assumed an early resolution of the battery lifetime problem, which is far from certain.

The cost of Ni/Zn batteries will be in excess of $100/kW-hr until a major market is penetrated and automated mass-production facilities are in place. Eventual mass-production costs of $50-60/kW-hr are projected, assuming the present nickel price of $2.50/lb. Each additional dollar per pound of nickel would add about $7/kW-hr to this cost.

Production and reserves of nickel in the U.S.A. are insignificant when compared with the world production of nickel, which is dominated by Canada. It is clear that efficient battery recycling (>90% nickel recovery) will be mandatory if the future U.S.A. vehicle fleet is to include a meaningful percentage of Ni/Zn vehicles. However, unlike gasoline which is totally consumed in automobiles, nickel imports will represent a resource which can be reused many times. The nickel required for one million passenger automobiles (25 kW-hr size) corresponds to about 10% of the 1975 world production of nickel.

<u>Nickel-Iron Batteries</u>. The nickel-iron battery was developed by Thomas Edison in 1901 and was the most prominent secondary battery in industrial usage until the 1920's. Although still widely used by the Russians, the Ni/Fe battery has been displaced almost entirely from the market by the Pb/acid battery in this country. Recent advances in Russia, the U.S., Japan, Sweden, and Bulgaria, especially improvements in sintered-iron technology, have revived interest in this battery system.

The active materials in a Ni/Fe battery consist of finely divided hydrated nickel peroxide for the positive plate and finely divided iron for the negative plate. Nickel electrode technology, which has generally been developed for other systems such as Ni/H_2, Ni/Cd, and Ni/Zn, is directly applicable to the Ni/Fe system. The iron electrode operates on two voltage plateaus since the negative electrode reaction takes place in two steps: Fe $\to$ Fe^{++} followed by Fe^{++} $\to$ Fe^{+++}. The negative electrode reactions are the following:

Negative electrode (upper plateau) $Fe + 2\,(OH)^- \rightleftarrows Fe(OH)_2 + 2e^-$

Negative electrode (lower plateau) $Fe(OH)_2 + (OH)^- \rightleftarrows Fe(OH)_3 + e^-$

In recent years, there has been less emphasis on the use of the lower plateau reaction. Most Ni/Fe developers have designed their battery to utilize the upper plateau reaction only.

An inherent problem with the Ni/Fe battery is that during charging, the voltage for H_2 evolution and iron reduction from $Fe(OH)_2$ are similar. This gas generation is, of course, undesirable. A number of additives and design techniques have been proposed to reduce the gassing. In general, trace quantities of a sulfur-bearing anion appear to decrease the gas evolution to a more manageable rate; however, many of these "advances" are untested in large-scale batteries. The principal ill effects of the gassing reaction are reduced energy efficiency, the need for gas and electrolyte maintenance systems, and safety problems related to hydrogen management.

Ni/Fe batteries appear to be highly underrated at present in the U.S.A. Ni/Fe is the only battery system among the major contenders with demonstrated ruggedness and long life. This battery is in a relatively mature state of development with specific energies of 50 to 55 W-hr/kg presently attainable. There appears to be no major technical barrier to increasing the specific energy to about 60 W-hr/kg.

The major problem associated with Ni/Fe batteries is the high <u>initial cost</u> of the system. However, <u>life-cycle costs</u> may be competitive because of the excellent cycle life. Ni/Fe batteries are especially attractive for commercial fleet operation (buses, light trucks, etc.). The use of Ni/Fe batteries in personal automobiles is less attractive, because of the bulkiness of the battery and the high initial cost.

Because of its lower cell voltage, the Ni/Fe battery may ultimately require about 20-40% more nickel per kW-hr of capacity than the Ni/Zn battery. As a result, Ni/Fe batteries are particularly sensitive to the cost of nickel, and the nickel availability problem is somewhat more serious than in the case of Ni/Zn batteries.

In summary, the Ni/Fe battery is a leading contender for the near-term electric bus and electric truck markets. However, it is not well suited for automobiles.

<u>Lithium/Iron Sulfide Batteries</u>: U.S. developers have actively investigated the lithium/iron sulfide battery since the system was conceived in 1973. Earlier work on Li/S cells has been largely abandoned due to irreversible sulfur transfer mechanisms and to ma-

terials and containment problems with liquid lithium. In 1973 it was found that the above problems could be avoided by the use of Li-Al alloys and iron sulfides instead of the molten elements. Both FeS_2 and FeS have been studied as positive-electrode active materials for transportation applications. The electrode and cell reactions for the Li-Al/FeS_2 system are the following:

Negative electrode: $Li \rightarrow Li^+ + e^-$

Positive electrode: $4Li^+ + 4e^- + FeS_2 \rightarrow 2Li_2S + Fe$

Overall reaction: $4Li + FeS_2 \rightarrow 2Li_2S + Fe$

The electrolyte is a LiCl/KCl eutectic (molten salt) with a melting point of 352°C. This necessitates battery operation above 400°C since the battery becomes inoperable as the freezing point is approached. Although Li-Al/FeS_x batteries appear to be capable of surviving multiple temperature cycles through the melting point, most applications will require battery temperatures to be continuously maintained above 400°C through the use of a well-engineered, thermal-insulation jacket. The energy losses associated with this high-temperature operation may be very small in batteries that are used several times per week, since the normal energy dissipation (which occurs in all batteries) may equal or exceed the energy passing through the insulation.

This battery technology has made impressive progress since 1973, but many difficult problems must be overcome before the Li/Al/FeS_x battery is a practical reality. Although lifetimes of over two years have been achieved in low-performance cells (50 to 75 W·h/kg), specific energies of 100 W·h/kg have never been achieved after 200 cycles of operation. An intensive effort to determine the causes of the lifetime problem is underway. The fabric, boron-nitride separators presently in use appear to have excellent compatibility in the cell environment. However, the separator cost must be reduced by more than an order of magnitude. Efforts are underway to develop thin boron-nitride felts, to reduce the amount of boron-nitride required and to produce a better filtering action for electrode particles. However, electrode expansion forces are large, and separator durability may be a serious problem.

Rapid progress has been made since the conception of Li-Al/FeS_x batteries in 1973. A large commercial development program involving Gould, Eagle-Picher, and other manufacturers has been underway for over three years, and hundreds of 100- to 400-W·h cells have been fabricated by industrial firms. However, practical hardware units will not be possible until the separator and lifetime problems are resolved. Prospects for overcoming the technical barriers appear to be fairly good, but successful development of the system is not expected until the mid-1980's.

Lithium demand and production are quite low at present; world production of lithium will have to be increased by a factor of 10 to allow a meaningful number of Li-Al/FeS_x vehicles. For example, the 1975 world production of lithium corresponds to only 300,000 Li-Al/FeS$_x$ vehicles (25-kW·h size). On the positive side, lithium producers are optimistic about the feasibility of rapidly expanding lithium production to meet this possible need. The U.S. Geological Survey has pointed out that although sufficient lithium resources exist for the electric-vehicle application, proven reserves are grossly inadequate, and extensive geological exploration efforts will be required to meet future needs.

The Li-Al/FeS$_x$ battery is very well suited for use in electric vehicles. This battery will probably be the most compact battery by 1990 with volumetric energy densitites expected to exceed 200 W-hr/liter. The specific energy is expected to be about 20 to 40% higher than that of Ni/Zn systems and peak power should be satisfactory.

Safety appears to be a strong point. The Budd Company has performed safety tests in which engineering-scale cells were crushed. The results were encouraging in that no reaction or combustion of cell materials was observed, and the cells were able to absorb the energy of a 30 mph barrier crash.

Li-Al/FeS$_x$ batteries have been very difficult to assess because of the absence of meaningful multi-cell battery tests. The first full-scale Li-Al/FeS battery was built in 1979 and slated for road testing. However, this early battery failed by short circuit and became inoperable because of excessive internal temperatures. One to two years of battery engineering work may be required before such a test is attempted again.

The future cost of Li-Al/FeS$_x$ batteries is very difficult to project. Mass-production costs of about 60 $/kW-hr may be possible provided that a low-cost separator is developed, and the price of lithium does not escalate.

The cycle life and cost barriers are quite difficult and successful development of this battery system is far from certain. However, the Li-Al/FeS$_x$ battery has emerged as the most promising "advanced-stage" (or intermediate term) battery for electric vehicles.

Zinc-Chlorine Batteries. Until recently, the zinc-chlorine couple, long recognized as offering high energy and low cost, was not exploited because of problems associated with chlorine management. Recent development of the chlorine-hydrate storage method has transformed the system into a viable secondary battery that is approaching the engineering stage of development. Energy Development Associates (EDA) appears to be the only significant developer of Zn/Cl$_2$ batteries.

The EDA Zn/Cl$_2$ battery represents a unique and very complex system involving a circulating (pumped) electrolyte and a refrigeration system for storage of frozen chlorine hydrate. The electrolyte is an aqueous solution of zinc chloride, and the operating temperature is near ambient (40-50°C). During charge, zinc is plated out of the solution onto graphite substrates in the individual cells that make up the battery stack, while chlorine gas is liberated into a common gas space between the stack and the chlorine store. Since the reaction product $ZnCl_2$ must be stored in dissolved form in the electrolyte when the battery is in the discharged state, a high concentration (initially 40 wt% Zn/Cl_2) is needed to minimize volume. The liberated chlorine is contacted with a small element of cooled electrolyte to form the chlorine hydrate, which is filtered out and retained in the hydrate store. The charge is generally terminated when the $ZnCl_2$ concentration drops to about 10 wt%. For discharge, warm electrolyte from the electrode stack will circulate through the hydrate store causing decomposition of chlorine hydrate and liberating the chlorine into the gas space. Chlorine is then dissolved in the electrolyte via the chlorine adsorber and circulated through the battery stack for reaction of the cells. Hydrogen liberated during the charge/discharge cycle is reacted with chlorine to form hydrochloric acid and then returned to the sump.

The present specific energy capability of Zn/Cl_2 batteries is about 75-85 W·hr/kg. EDA recently lowered its specific energy goal from 130 W·hr/kg to about 80-100 W·hr/kg, not including the refrigeration system. Energy efficiency may be an inherent problem as a result of energy losses associated with the refrigeration and pumping systems, together with coulombic efficiencies that are well below 100%. However, the developers are optimistic about their ability to attain 65% energy efficiency in vehicle end uses.

The Zn/Cl_2 battery is a major contender for future use as an off-peak energy storage device for electric utility systems. A strong point is the absence of a resource availability problem; in addition none of the basic raw materials are intrinsically expensive. The Zn/Cl_2 battery will probably be the first advanced battery developed for the electric utility-storage application, and it has high promise for this use. There is little doubt that Zn/Cl_2 batteries with impressive specific energy (80-100 W·hr/kg) and lifetime (possibly greater than five years service life) will be developed. Unfortunately, this battery is not well-suited for electric vehicles and suffers from a safety stigmata. Zn/Cl_2 batteries are intrinsically bulky and present a serious packaging problem for use in electric vehicles. In addition, this battery does not "scale-down" well because of the multiple auxiliary systems, and use would probably be restricted to buses and trucks. It is highly unlikely that Zn/Cl_2 batteries will ever be successfully developed for passenger automobiles.

The developers (Energy Development Associates) make a very persuasive case that the probability of serious chlorine releases to the environment can be made very small, through clever engineering and design. The most serious questions center around the consequences of the occasional improbable accident which could result in the sudden release of over 50 kg of chlorine. Years of testing and some very favorable safety test results will be required before the Zn/Cl_2 battery can be considered a serious contender for the electric vehicle application. It appears that the probability of overcoming the electrical performance, lifetime, and safety barriers by 1990 is less than 20%. However, the Zn/Cl battery has progressed into the vehicle-testing stage, and early road tests are underway.

Sodium/Sulfur Batteries (β-Al_2O_3 Electrolyte): The sodium/sulfur battery has been under intensive development with large programs under way in the U.S., the United Kingdom, France, and Japan for more than 10 years. The essential feature of this battery system is the use of a ceramic electrolyte called "beta alumina" ($Na_2O \cdot 11\ Al_2O_3$). The material is ionically conductive at 300-350°C, with the charge carrier being sodium ions. The active materials, sodium and sulfur, are both liquid at the temperature of operation, and the solid electrolyte serves as the separator. The electrode and cell reactions are the following:

Negative electrode: $Na \rightleftarrows Na^+ + e^-$

Positive electrode: $Na_xS + Na^+ + e^- \rightleftarrows Na_{x+1}S$

Overall reaction: $Na_xS + Na \rightleftarrows Na_{x+1}S$

Typically, Na/S cells involve a central beta-alumina tube containing liquid sodium; this tube is surrounded by a layer of graphite felt loaded with liquid sulfur/polysulfide. This cell assembly is encased in a metal housing that also acts as the positive current collector. Corrosion of the positive current collector is a serious problem, especially for the electric vehicle application. British researchers have developed an "inside-out" design, in which the sulfur is contained within the beta-alumina tube with the sodium contacting the exterior surface of the tube; this approach appears to result in reduced electrical performance, but may possess life and cost advantages. Ford has taken the position that the "inside-out" design is not promising for high-performance vehicle batteries because of heat transfer problems in the positive electrode.

The reaction mechanism of the sulfur electrode is quite complex. Because elemental sulfur is an electronic insulator, a conductive material such as graphite felt is added to assist current collection. The sodium polysulfide formed during discharge is not soluble in sulfur. Thus, the sulfur electrode contains two liquid phases throughout about 60% of the discharge. Beyond this point, essentially no elemental sulfur remains, and all the polysulfides are miscible, forming one phase. To keep this phase liquid throughout its compositional range (Na_2S_5 to Na_2S_3), it is necessary to operate above 270°C, with typical operating temperatures falling in the range of 300-375°C. For transportation applications involving a high peak-to-average-power ratio, sodium/sulfur batteries must operate in the single-phase region (Na_2S_3 to Na_2S_5), which limits energy density significantly. The present goals for Na/S electric vehicle batteries (>110 W·h/l and >130 W·h/kg) may be very difficult to achieve for this reason.

The prospects for successful commercialization of Na/S batteries (ceramic electrolyte) for electric vehicles appear to be declining. These batteries are far better suited for bulk energy storage on electric-utility networks and remain as a leading contender for this application.

The major technical problems are (1) marginal durability of the ceramic electrolyte tubes, (2) corrosion of current collectors in the positive electrode, (3) design inflexibility and packaging problems, and (4) safety. The probability of solving these problems by 1990 appears to be less than 10%.

Even if the electrical performance and ruggedness problems were overcome extensive safety testing would be required before Na/S batteries could be introduced for public use. A crashworthy battery casing may be necessary to minimize the likelihood of sodium fires, sodium-water explosions, and runaway sodium-sulfur reactions. The cost and weight of these safety systems may represent a significant performance and economic penalty.

A major plus for the Na/S battery is the absence of a serious resource-availability problem. Also, none of the raw materials used in the battery are likely to become expensive in future years. Nevertheless, world-wide interest in this battery system seems to be declining.

Other Battery Systems: The other battery candidates are judged to be far less likely to be successfully commercialized by the year 2000. However, it must be recognized that a major breakthrough or technical advance could radically improve these prospects. The most promising exploratory battery systems include Na/S (glass electrolyte), Zn/Br_2, Fe/Air, Al/Air, Li/TiS_2, and various special-purpose batteries for hybrid vehicles.

Impressive advances have been made during the past 12 months by Dow Chemical with respect to the Na/S (glass electrolyte) battery. They have developed and demonstrated a metal cased, hermetically-sealed cell. In addition, Dow has built several 40 A-hr versions of this cell, which they believe to represent full-scale for the EV application. These cells are expected to attain about 145 W-hr/kg and 175 W-hr/liter within about 12 months. Dow plans to build a pilot plant in 1980 to produce the 40 A-hr cells. A flow regulator has been developed to prevent excessive contact of Na with sulfur, which previously had produced a "roman candle" effect in some of their test cells. Important advances in lifetime have been made by developing helium-tight tube sheet seals and rigid reservoir cups. The cells have demonstrated good overcharge capability. Major problems that remain unsolved include freeze/thaw failure, failure propagation mechanisms, life-time in full-scale cells, and the need for an improved tube-sheet composition and fabrication method.

The aluminum-air battery has made good progress during the past 12 months, with demonstration of the cell chemistry and development of working cell stacks accomplished. An important advance has been the development of improved power capability which could make Al/air batteries suitable for use in compact automobiles. The principle problems relate to the "chemical engineering" of the system (rather than the cell stack itself) and a very poor energy efficiency (20-35%). However, the specific energy and mechanical recharge capability are expected to make the Al/air battery the only electrochemical system with realistic prospects for achieving performance equivalent to gasoline-fueled vehicles. This battery system is especially difficult to evaluate because of uncertain costs, and lack of experience with fully-integrated battery systems.

Development of Li-Al/TiS$_2$ batteries by EXXON has been stalled by the lack of a suitable electrolyte for the high-rate EV application. EXXON has selected Li-Al alloy as the negative electrode material, instead of liquid lithium. The battery appears to have high promise, if a suitable electrolyte is developed.

Work on the Ca/FeS$_2$ battery system at Argonne has progressed to exploratory work with 300 A-hr cells. The battery system represents an attempt to avoid the use of lithium in metal sulfide cells, since lithium is relatively expensive and produced in limited quantities. A major advance for the Ca/FeS$_2$ cells has been the discovery that high-solubility sulfur species are not formed in the electrochemical reactions at the positive electrode. Consequently, these cells may have the capability of much higher lifetimes that the lithium battery counterpart. Present efforts have centered on developing a reliable, long lifetime cell. Major improvements in specific power capabilty will be required for this battery to become an EV candidate. This work is still very exploratory.

RISK/REWARD RELATIONSHIPS

A Bayesian decision analysis technique has been developed for evaluating electric vehicle batteries.[3] The principal features of this system are (A) sub-division of batteries into groups of comparable technical maturity, (B) assessment of technical risk, including methods for coping with poor quality or distorted inputs from "experts", (C) a Bayesian interrogation technique for quantifying subjective judgements, and (D) direct comparison of development risk and the benefits of successful development.

<u>Technical Risk</u>. The assessment of technical risk is the most important and most difficult task in the comparative evaluation of batteries. The Bayesian decision-analysis method consisted of a two-step procedure:

1. Identification of the "key" technical barriers (those which could potentially disqualify the battery)

2. Estimation of the probability of overcoming each key barrier.

Table II summarizes the development risk findings for the most promising battery systems. A wide variation in the number and relative difficulty of technical barriers can be seen in Table II.

Table II Development Risks

Battery System	Number of Technical Barriers	Average Difficulty of Barriers
Ni/Fe	1	Medium
Pb/Acid	2	Medium
Ni/Zn	2	Difficult
Zn/Cl_2	5	Difficult
$Li-Al/FeS_x$	7	Difficult
Na/S (ceramic)	8	Difficult
Na/S (glass)	10	Difficult

Consequences of Successful Development: The consequences of successful development were evaluated by selecting eight "battery desirability factors" which were judged to be the most important characteristics in defining the suitability of a battery for electric vehicles. Table III gives the list of battery desirability factors; each battery candidate was rated with respect to each factor, and an overall "battery desirability" rating obtained.

Table III Relative Desirability Summary[a]

	Pb/Acid	Ni/Zn	Ni/Fe	Zn/Cl_2	$Li-Al/FeS_x$	Na/S (Ceramic)	Na/S (Glass)
Specific Energy	3	5	4	6	8	8	8
Volumetric Energy Density	3	6	4	4	8	5	5
Peak Power[b]	2	8	4	4	5	5	9
Sustained Power	3	7	5	8	5	5	9
Cost	7	(5)	3	(5)	(5)	(5)	(8)
Cycle Life	(5)	(5)	10	(5)	(5)	(5)	(5)
Safety	7	7	7	2	8	2	3
Resource Availability	4	3	3	9	(4)	9	9
OVERALL DESIRABILITY RATING[c]	3.5	7.5	4.5	6.0	8.0	6.0	8.5

[a] Parentheses denote relatively uncertain assessment.
[b] At 80% state-of-discharge.
[c] The values have no meaning except to illustrate the "overall relative desirability" for the automobile application on a linear scale (obtained using Bayesian interrogation).

Comparison of Risk and Reward: In general it was found that a rough proportionality exists between the difficulty of development and the desirability of the resulting battery. This relationship is shown graphically in Fig. 2 for the case of urban electric-vehicle batteries. Since all of the batteries lie within an approximately linear envelope in Fig. 2, it was inferred that the ratio of relative reward to risk was not greatly different for these battery systems. Recent trends in the various battery technologies are indicated by the arrows in Fig. 2. Not shown in the figure are the points for 23 battery systems judged to be relatively unpromising for the transportation application: Each of the 23 points fall well below the linear envelope in Fig. 2.

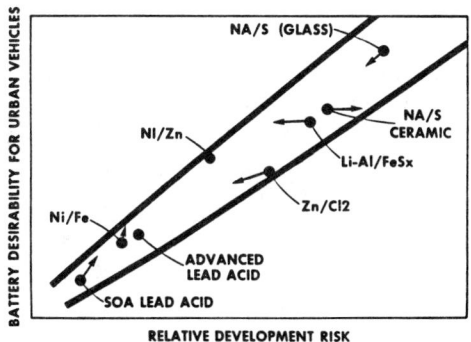

Fig. 2. Risk/Reward Relationship for Advanced Batteries

CONCLUSION

The overall conclusions obtained in this comparative evaluation are shown in Table IV. Each individual battery system was found to have less than 50% probability of successful development and commercialization; however, the cumulative probability that at least one of the batteries would be successfully developed was judged to be greater than 75%. No clear-cut battery "winner" can be projected at this time.

Table IV General Conclusions

No clear-cut battery "Winner" at present.

Each advanced battery has less than 50% probability of successful development.

Overall probability that at least one of the advanced batteries will be successfully developed is judged greater than 75%.

It is clear that vastly-improved electric vehicles will be developed by 1985. However, the gasoline-powered vehicle will probably continue to predominate until gasoline becomes scarce or much more expensive. Market penetrations of millions of electric vehicles are likely by 2000 A.D. The magnitude of this market penetration will depend on the severity of future liquid fuel shortages along with the cost and quality of the advanced batteries.

REFERENCES

1. W.J. Walsh, "Advanced Batteries for Electric Vehicles - A Look At the Future," Physics Today, Pages 34-41 (June 1980).

2. E. Behrin, W.J. Walsh, et al, "Energy Storage Systems for Automobile Propulsion," Volumes 1 and 2, Lawrence Livermore Laboratory, UCRL-52303 (1977).

3. W.J. Walsh, "A Bayesian Approach to Forecasting Technical Success," University of Chicago Conference on the Economics of Research and Development Policy (April 1979).

THE ROLE OF EXOELECTRONS AND OXIDE FILMS IN FATIGUE DETECTION

William J. Baxter
Physics Department
General Motors Research Laboratories, Warren, MI 48090

ABSTRACT

Most approaches to the assessment of fatigue damage have been aimed at detecting fatigue cracks in the metal. This paper describes techniques for measuring the early accumulation of surface deformation prior to the initiation of a crack. These techniques have stemmed from our investigations of exoelectron emission (i.e. enhanced photoemission), which occurs when the surface deformation produces microcracks in the natural surface oxide film. Direct observations in a photoelectron microscope have shown that the oxide is ruptured by crystallographic slip in the underlying metal, so that the intensity of exoelectron emission is intimately related to the amount of fatigue deformation. An ultraviolet laser scanning system provides quantitative information on the distribution and extent of the deformation. The remaining fatigue life may be predicted from a quantitative assessment of damage.

An electrochemical method, now being developed, provides a simpler means of measuring the development of microcracks in the surface oxide. The basic principle is to measure the flow of charge during electrochemical reoxidation of these microcracks. The distribution of the fatigue damage is again revealed by a simple scanning procedure. Fatigue cracks only ~ 50 µm in length have been detected in aluminum and the electrochemical reoxidation currents again provide a method of predicting fatigue life.

INTRODUCTION

The engineering structures required for all forms of transportation contain components that experience repetitive cyclic loading during operation. Although the maximum stresses involved may be well within the range of elastic behavior, the phenomenon of metal fatigue can still occur, and limit the useful service life. In the case of an automobile, the avoidance of premature failure due to metal fatigue is a primary consideration in the design of many components of the suspension system, steering mechanism, engine and drive train. This assurance of adequate fatigue performance is a difficult design problem. Numerous uncertainties arise due to such factors as complex geometries, complicated sequences of service loads of various magnitudes, localized stress raisers, surface condition, retained stresses, material variability, and the service environment. Therefore the design engineer must ultimately rely upon testing of actual components under simulated service conditions, and/or prior experience with similar components in service. This approach has been, and continues to be, very successful, but is particularly time consuming.

The crux of the problem is that a fatigue failure can occur after apparently satisfactory operation for 10^6 or even 10^8 cyclic loadings. Thus, the determination of the fatigue performance requires at least days, but more often weeks or months. Furthermore, such tests yield only one, albeit vital, piece of information, namely the number of cyclic loadings to cause failure. Thus the desirability of a quantitative measure of the development of fatigue in metals has long been recognized, since it could provide the basis of an abbreviated testing technique for the prediction of fatigue life. Such a tool would permit rapid design iterations, with the present prolonged testing techniques being reserved for final validation.

The quantitative measurement of metal fatigue damage is an old problem, which has resisted the efforts of many investigators employing a variety of techniques.[1] The difficulty lies in the complexity of the fatigue process, which for convenience can be regarded as consisting of two stages: (i) the initiation, and (ii) the propagation of very fine cracks. Neither of these stages are completely understood, but they are both known to involve plastic deformation, often referred to as damage, within very localized regions of the metal. This deformation is very inhomogeneous, and during the crack initiation stage is distinguished by the formation of localized regions of more severe deformation known as persistent slip bands. These slip bands have an irregular surface profile, produced by the extrusion and intrusion of metal, and it is within these bands that cracks eventually develop in the metal itself. As these cracks grow, they become increasingly important stress concentrators, so that the cyclic load produces severe deformation around the crack tip - the so-called plastic zone. Thus, while it is conventional to regard fatigue as a two stage process, it is important to remember that throughout there is a continual generation of surface deformation.

Previous attempts to measure the accumulation of fatigue damage have been aimed at detecting the initial fatigue crack in the metal, and success was measured in terms of the smallest crack which was detected. Unfortunately this often does not occur until more than half the fatigue life has been expended. This paper describes the development of a quite different approach: the detection of the much earlier development of persistent slip bands.

The cornerstone of this research has been the exploitation of the phenomenon of exoelectron emission,[2,3] i.e. the enhanced photoelectron emission from a metal after it has been plastically deformed. Our research revealed that the enhanced photoemission is due to microcracks which develop in the surface oxide at the sites of plastic strain in the underlying metal during the very early stages of fatigue. Exoelectron emission measurements provided the first quantitative measurements of the accumulation of fatigue damage.[4,5] The capabilities and requirements of the exoelectron method are detailed in Section II. A much simpler electrochemical method,[6] which can also detect the sites of oxide rupture, is described in Section III. This technique is still under development, but the present status is summarized and compared with the exoelectron method.

II. THE EXOELECTRON METHOD

A. Mechanism of Exoelectron Emission

When a ductile metal is plastically deformed, the brittle surface layers of naturally-occurring oxide develop microcracks revealing microscopic regions of bare metal. Under ultraviolet illumination, photoelectrons are able to escape more easily from the freshly revealed metal surfaces in the oxide cracks where the photoelectric work function is smaller than that for the surrounding oxide coated material. In this way surface deformation results in a pronounced increase of the photoelectron emission rate often referred to as exoelectron emission. Under normal atmospheric conditions, of course, the microcracks are healed in a few minutes as the bare metal surfaces reoxidize. Thus in general these subtle microscopic events pass virtually unnoticed. However if the metal is deformed in a vacuum, reoxidaton is prevented and the exoelectron emission is quite stable.

Unequivocal evidence for this mechanism was provided by direct imaging of the exoelectrons emitted from a specimen during deformation in the vacuum chamber of a photoelectron microscope (PEM).[7,8] The example shown in Fig. 1 is a photoelectron micrograph of a specimen of 1100 aluminum after 8,000 fatigue cycles. The exoelectron emission appears as white lines in this micrograph, and defines the locations where slip band extrusions have ruptured the natural surface oxide film.

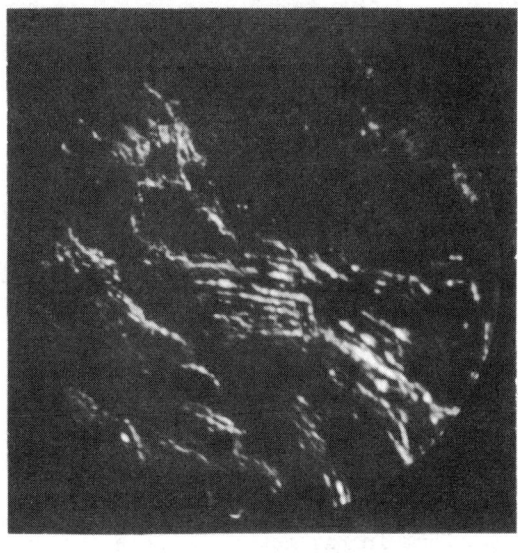

Fig. 1. Photoelectron micrograph of specimen of 1100 aluminum, showing sources of exoelectron emission after 8000 fatigue cycles.

As fatigue cycling continues, some of the sources of exoelectron emission become very intense, and their detailed surface structure is beyond the resolution of the PEM. However, previously identified sources of intense emission have been examined in the scanning electron microscope, and found to consist of local regions of very severe surface deformation.[4] The example in Fig. 2 shows the deformation structure on a sample of SAE 1018 steel after 70,000 fatigue cycles (∿6% of the fatigue life). The cyclic deformation has in this case generated a "honeycomb" structure of very large surface area. A series of experiments of this type showed in fact that, during the crack initiation stage in SAE 1018 steel, there is a continual increase in the area of fresh metal created in these very localized regions.[4] It is this process that results in the very large increases of intensity of exoelectron emission described in section IIc.

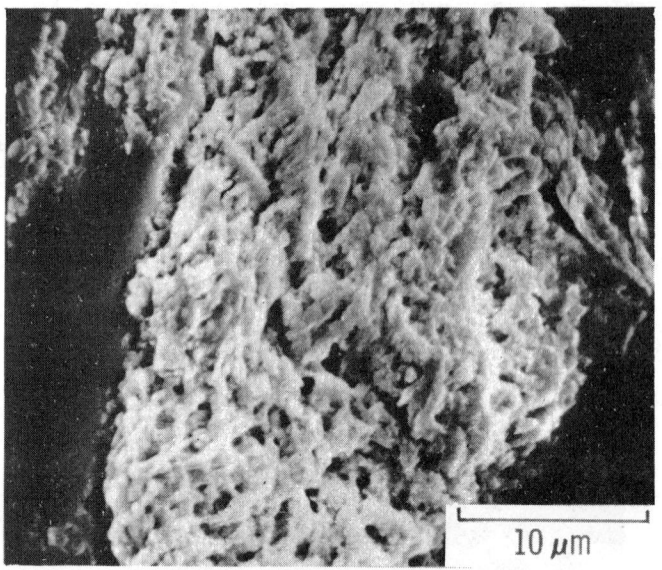

Fig. 2. Scanning electron micrograph of the severe localized surface deformation produced on SAE 1018 steel after 70,000 fatigue cycles (6% of fatigue life).

Eventually cracks form in the metal in these regions of severe damage. As mentioned above, the growth of these cracks continues to generate further deformation nearby in a region known as the plastic zone. Both the crack and its associated wake of plasticity are strong sources of exoelectron emission.[9]

B. Laser Scanning System

Since the deformation produced during metal fatigue is distributed very inhomogeneously, quantitative measurements of the intensity of exoelectron emission are more meaningful if performed as a function of position. For this reason a scanning spot system was developed, as shown schematically in Fig. 3. An ultraviolet (λ = 257 nm) laser beam was focused to form a spot diameter of 15 μm and scanned over the entire surface of the specimen. The electrons photoemitted from the specimen are detected by an electron multiplier, and the electron emission rate can be displayed on a pen recorder, or used to control the beam intensity of an oscilloscope. The beam of the oscilloscope is synchronized with the scanning of the laser beam, so that a photoelectron image of the surface of the sample is formed on the oscilloscope. This display identifies the locations of the sources of exoelectron emission, where the fatigue deformation has ruptured the surface oxide. More detailed quantitative information is then obtained with the pen recorder by allowing the laser beam to scan slowly through these regions.

Two modes of scanning are depicted in Fig. 3. In Mode 1, the laser beam is scanned on an X-Y raster while the specimen is stationary. This is ideal for flat specimens, such as in bending

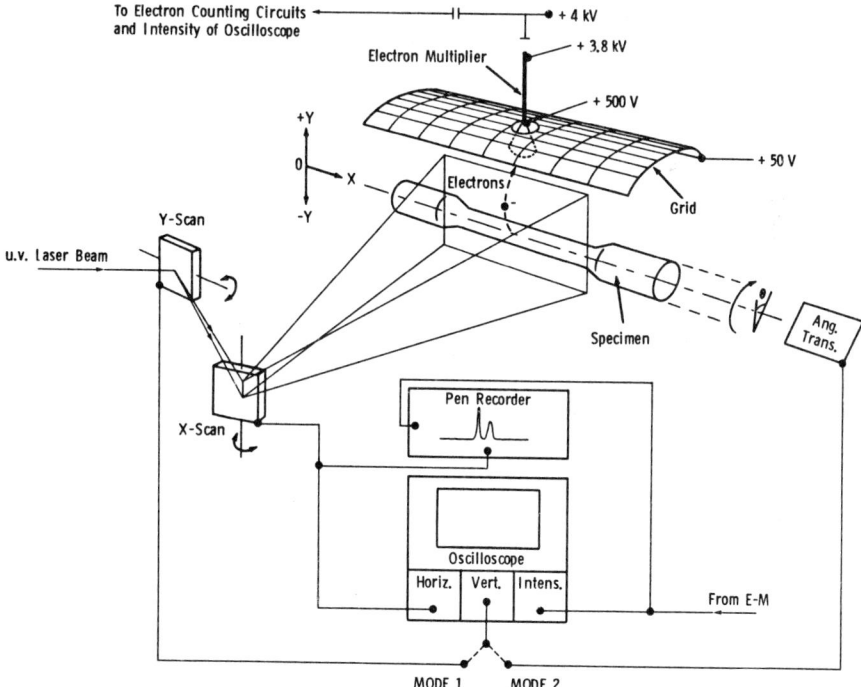

Fig. 3 Schematic diagram of the laser scanning and electron emission recording system.

fatigue experiments. However, in the case of cylindrical torsion specimens as depicted in the figure, it is more difficult to collect electrons from the lower portion of the specimen surface than from the upper portion. In this case (Mode 2), the specimen is rotated slowly about its axis while scanning the laser beam continuously back and forth along its centerline. The angular position of the specimen is monitored by an angular transducer which now controls the Y-axis of the oscilloscope. In this way an electron emission map of the entire cylindrical surface is unfolded onto the oscilloscope screen. To scan a specimen in Mode 2, it is of course necessary to unclamp one end. This is done at intervals during a fatigue test: after scanning, the sample is carefully reclamped without perturbing the vacuum and the test continued.

C. Quantitative Measurements of Fatigue

An example of the quantitative measurements obtained with the pen recorder is shown in Fig. 4, where the rate of electron emission is displayed as a function of the position of the focused laser beam, as it scans along the gauge length of a torsional fatigue specimen. The material in this case was SAE 1144 steel which had been shot peened to improve its fatigue properties.

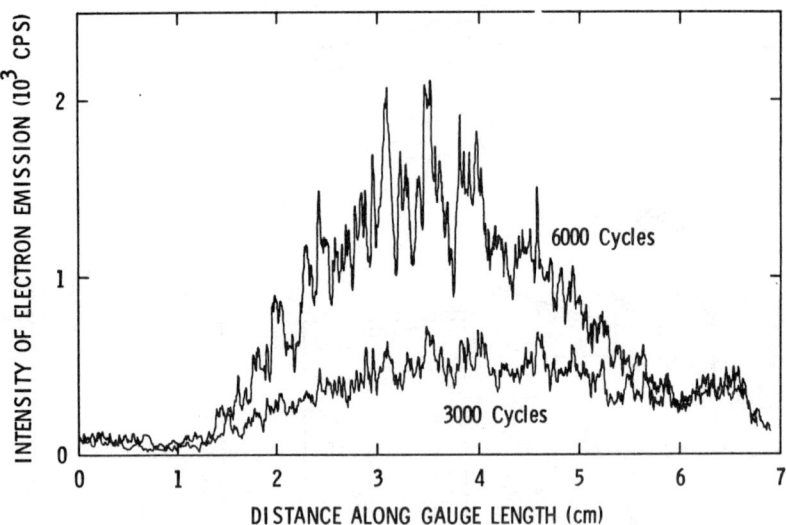

Fig. 4   Distribution of intensity of electron emission along the length of a shot peened specimen of 1144 steel after 3,000 cycles (0.26% life) and 6,000 cycles (0.52% life).

After only 3000 cycles, or 0.26% of the fatigue life, a large number of emission peaks (exoelectrons) have developed, and after 6000 cycles they have grown considerably larger. Each of these peaks corresponds to a localized region where the natural surface oxide has developed microcracks. Note that the low intensity of electron emission near the ends of the sample was essentially unchanged by the fatigue cycling. This weak background emission is escaping through the still intact surface oxide, and no appreciable damage has developed in these regions. This distribution of exoelectron emission reflects the distribution of surface fatigue damage.

Similar traces, with different arrays of emission peaks, may be obtained by scanning the sample along parallel paths at different azimuthal angles. However, with the aid of the oscilloscope display, at any point during a fatigue test, the magnitude and location of the largest exoelectron emission peak is readily identified. This maximum value is then taken as a measure of the most severe fatigue deformation in an apparently critical, localized region of the specimen.

This procedure is summarized by results such as shown in Fig. 5, where for each specimen only the largest emission peak is plotted regardless of its location. The two sets of data were obtained from several samples of two quite different types of steel: martensitic 1541 and shot peened 1144. The intensity of

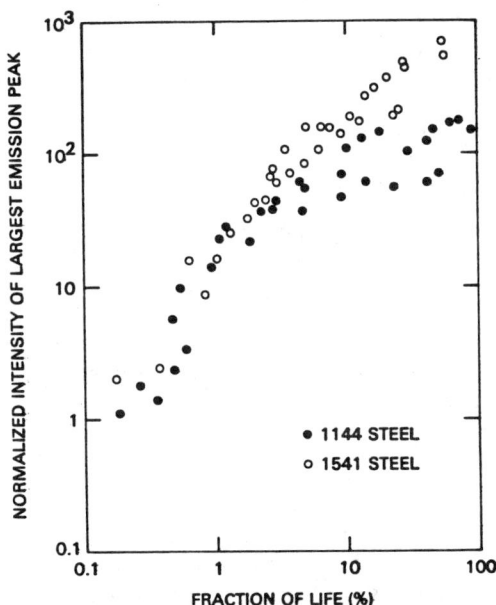

Fig. 5 Normalized intensity of largest emission peak as a function of the fraction of fatigue life.

the largest emission peak (I) has been normalized with respect to the initial background emission (I_o). Each sample was fatigued to failure, their fatigue lives spanning the range from 3×10^5 to 2×10^6 cycles. In order to normalize fatigue life, the number of fatigue cycles at any point during a test was plotted on the abscissa as a percent of total life for that specimen. From these results, it is evident that the development of localized sources of exoelectron emission, reveals the presence of fatigue deformation after only $\sim 1\%$ of the fatigue life. Furthermore the intensity of the localized emission increases with continued fatigue cycling in a very systematic manner, particularly during the early stages.

Similar results were also obtained for a lower strength steel (SAE 1018) fatigued by reverse bending,[4] suggesting that the same fatigue process is operative and that it occurs in a systematic manner when viewed on this localized basis. This finding stimulated a separate series of experiments, in which it was found that the crack initiation stage accounts for the initial one-hundredfold increase of emission, due to the generation of extruded surface structures of the type shown in Fig. 2. Thus it is the crack initiation process which is systematic and reproducible, even between materials of substantially different microstructures. In the crack propagation stage (>10% of life) the intensity data tends to diverge.

Thus, to summarize this section: 1) The development of plastic deformation in the metallic surface was shown to occur very early in life and to proceed in a systematic manner, 2) microcracks in the surface oxide accompanied the fatigue damage and thus the intensity of the exoelectron emission provided quantitative measurements of the severity of the surface fatigue damage which could be expressed in terms of the fraction of life expended, and 3) results such as those illustrated in Fig. 5 provide a calibration for a very abbreviated fatigue test.

III. THE ELECTROCHEMICAL METHOD

A. Basic Principle

This method also relies upon the detection of fatigue induced microcracks in a surface oxide film but the requirements differ from those of the exoelectron technique in two respects.

(i) It is not necessary to perform the fatigue test in a vacuum chamber.
(ii) The microcracks must be produced, not in the very thin natural oxide film, but, in a previously formed slightly thicker oxide.

The procedure is to grow electrochemically a layer (~ 10 nm) of strongly adherent surface oxide on the metal prior to the application of the cyclic fatigue loading. During the fatigue test microcracks are created in this oxide revealing fresh metal surfaces, just as in the exoelectron method. Under normal atmospheric conditions these fresh surfaces reoxide rapidly, but only a very thin layer (~ 3 nm) of "natural" oxide is reformed. Thus these microcracks may be detected by measuring the flow of electric charge during subsequent electrochemical reoxidation.

B. Experimental

The incorporation of a simple scanning procedure is again an important feature of this method because of the localized nature of the fatigue damage. It is demonstrated here for 1100 aluminum, with oxide films formed by the well known anodization process.[10] The specimens were cleaned in a chromic acid solution at 70°C, then anodized in tartaric acid at a potential of +10 V to produce an oxide film thickness of 14 nm. After fatigue cycling, one end of the specimen was reanodized at the original voltage (10 V) to heal the oxide where it had been ruptured by the grips of the fatigue machine. The gauge section was then reanodized at a lower voltage (5 V), as it was slowly immersed into the tartaric acid. Thus whenever a region containing microcracks entered the electrolyte there was an immediate reanodization current transient of short duration. In this way a linear scan was obtained, as defined by the intersection of the specimen with the surface of the electrolyte.

The experimental arrangement for recording the reanodization transients is shown schematically in Fig. 6. As the sample was

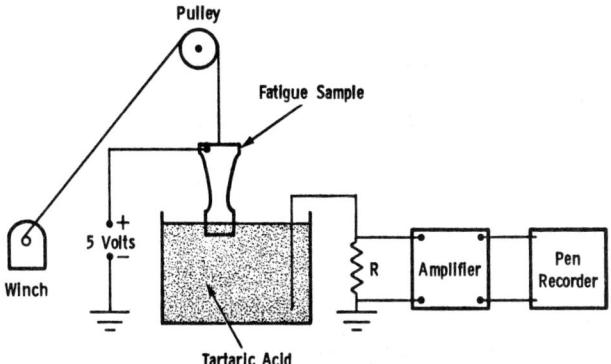

Fig. 6 Schematic diagram of experimental arrangement for immersion scanning and recording of reanodization currents.

lowered into the electrolyte (at $\sim$100 µm/sec) the flow of current was detected and continuously recorded. The recording system was evaluated in a separate series of experiments and shown to provide a simple quantitative measure of the flow of charge during rapid current transients, in a manner similar to the action of a ballistic galvanometer. Specifically, the recorded magnitude of a current spike (I_{max}) during a rapid current transient is related to the total flow of charge (Q) by

$$I_{max} = \frac{Q}{2T} \qquad (1)$$

where T, the response time of the pen recorder, is 0.3 s. Current transients, corresponding to a vertical spatial resolution on the sample of ∼50 μm, could be resolved with this system.

C. Measurements on Fatigued Aluminum

The current flow during an immersion scan of a sample after 10,000 fatigue cycles (∼10% of life) is shown in Fig. 7. The location of the primary fatigue damage is identified by two current spikes in close proximity to each other. Similar traces were obtained from many samples fatigued to different fractions of expected life. In general, after application of a larger number of fatigue cycles both the magnitude and number of current transients increased appreciably.

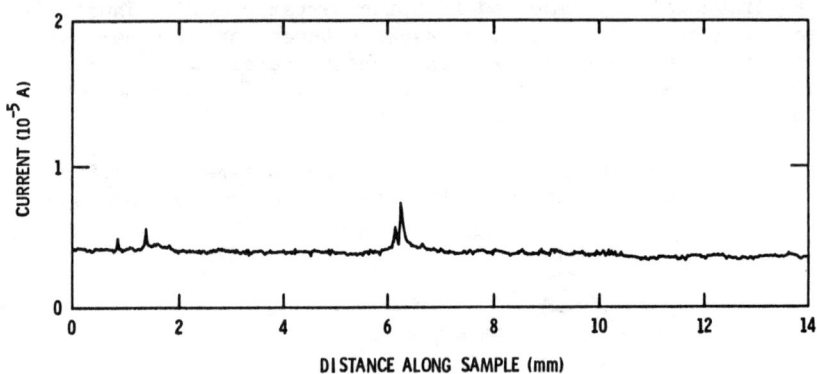

Fig. 7 Recording of current flow during slow immersion of a fatigue sample as a function of the location of the surface of the electrolyte. Sample fatigued for 10,000 cycles.

Such arrays of current peaks may be summarized in a manner similar to that employed in the exoelectron technique. Namely, the magnitude of the largest current peak is regarded as a measure of the most severe localized fatigue damage, which will lead to eventual failure. The results from a series of 30 samples are summarized in this way in Fig. 8, as a plot of the magnitude of the largest current peak (I_{max}) as a function of the number of fatigue cycles. (The additional ordinate scale shows the total flow of charge involved in these transients, as calculated from Eq. (1)).

There are two noteworthy features of these results:
1) Fatigue damage is detected as early as 10 percent of the fatigue life, and thereafter there is an enormous growth in the magnitude of these localized reanodization current transients.

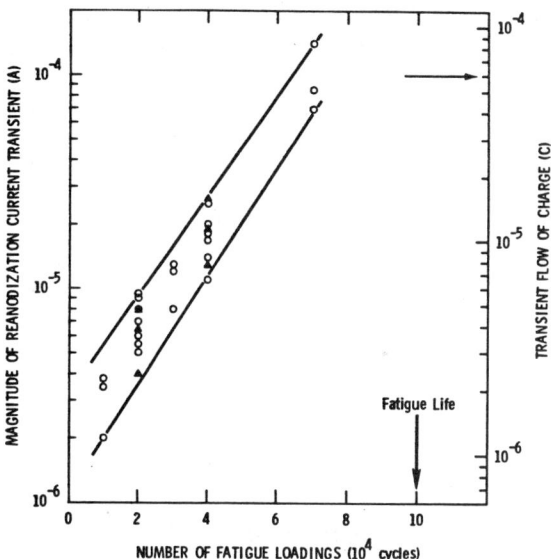

Fig. 8 The value of the largest localized current transient (I_{max}) observed during scanning of many samples as a function of the number of fatigue cycles. Each data point corresponds to a different sample.

2) Figure 8 provides a basis for the prediction of fatigue life. The accuracy is limited by the width of the scatter band in Fig. 8 to a factor of ± 50 percent, which is quite reasonable for fatigue life prediction.

Subsequent examination of several of the samples in a scanning electron microscope (SEM) showed that the scatter in Fig. 8 does not arise from inadequacies of the electrochemical scanning technique, but rather it is mainly due to actual variations in the fatigue damage sustained by different samples under identical conditions of cyclic loading. The SEM samples were selected to represent the extremes of the scatter band in Fig. 8. All were found to have developed extensive surface deformation, but the most severe damage consisted of small fatigue cracks which had propagated from the edges of the sample. The length of these cracks, as estimated from scanning electron micrographs, clearly correlated with the magnitude of the current peaks plotted in Fig. 8. This correlation is summarized in Fig. 9 which shows that there is a simple linear relationship between the transient flow of charge (Q) and the crack length (ℓ). The line drawn in Fig. 9 corresponds to

$$Q = 2.7 \times 10^{-5} \ell \qquad (2)$$

where Q is in coulombs, and ℓ is in mm.

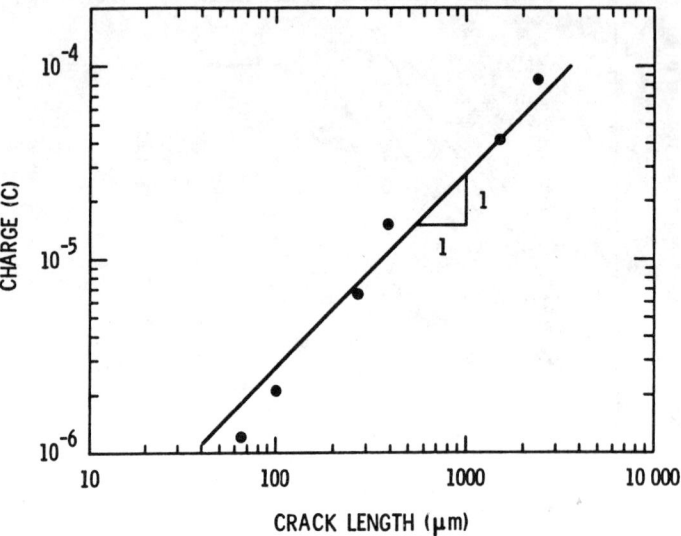

Fig. 9 Relationship between the flow of charge during the largest localized current transient to several samples, and the length of the largest fatigue crack as estimated from scanning electron micrographs.

This linear relationship merits comment since the flow of charge (Q) is known to be a measure of the surface <u>area</u> being reanodized. Therefore this result implies that the reanodization of the crack only occurs within a small constant distance from the surface, probably due to the inability of the electrolyte and/or applied potential to penetrate deeply into the fatigue cracks. In addition, some of the observed current flow may be associated with healing the oxide ruptured by the deformation in the plastic zone surrounding the crack.[9] However the important point is that this significantly improved correlation (Fig. 9) demonstrates that the technique is inherently capable of greater accuracy than that shown in Fig. 8.

Finally it is noteworthy that the trend line in Fig. 8 is of the form

$$Q = Ae^{\beta N} \qquad (3)$$

where Q is the flow of charge measured after N fatigue cycles. Substituting for Q from Eq. (2) and differentiating we obtain an expression for the rate of crack propagation

$$\frac{d\ell}{dN} = \beta \ell \qquad (4)$$

where ß is a constant. Since this type of fatigue crack growth law has been reported previously for a variety of materials,[11-13] this result adds further credence to the fundamental capabilities of the electrochemical scanning technique.

Thus, to summarize this section, in these preliminary experiments on aluminum, it is demonstrated that: 1) electrochemical reoxidation currents can detect fatigue damage as early as 10% of the fatigue life; 2) the damage at this fatigue level consists of cracks as short as ~50 μm; and 3) the magnitude of the current transient is an accurate measure of the crack length and can predict the total fatigue life within ±50%.

IV. SUMMARY

Both the exoelectron and the electrochemical techniques provide quantitative measures of the accumulation of damage during fatigue in metals. At the preent time the exoelectron method offers better sensitivity; it can detect and quantitatively assess the accumulation of fatigue deformation as early as 1% of the fatigue life, i.e. during the crack initiation stage of fatigue. However the fatigue test must be performed <u>in vacuo</u>. The electrochemical method is simpler and the fatigue test can be performed with conventional equipment under normal atmospheric conditions. It can detect and measure the length of fatigue cracks in the metal, as short as ~50 μm, which in this investigation developed at ~10% of the fatigue life. Both techniques provide a basis for an abbreviated fatigue test.

REFERENCES

1. J. R. Barton and F. N. Kusenberger, "Metal Fatigue Damage - Mechanism, Detection, Avoidance and Repair," STP 495, ASTM, Philadelphia (1971), p. 123.
2. W. J. Baxter, "Research Techniques in Nondestructive Testing," Academic Press, London, 1977, $\underline{3}$, 395 (1977).
3. W. J. Baxter, "Electron and Positron Spectroscopies in Materials Science and Engineering," Academic Press, N.Y., 1979), p. 35.
4. W. J. Baxter, Met. Trans. $\underline{6A}$, 749 (1975).
5. W. J. Baxter, Met. Trans. $\underline{8A}$, 899 (1977).
6. W. J. Baxter, submitted to Met. Trans.
7. W. J. Baxter and S. R. Rouze, J. Appl. Phys. $\underline{44}$, 4400 (1973).
8. W. J. Baxter and S. R. Rouze, J. Appl. Phys. $\underline{46}$, 2429 (1975).
9. W. J. Baxter and S. R. Rouze, Met. Trans. $\underline{7A}$, 647 (1976).
10. S. Tajima, Adv. Corrosion Science and Technology $\underline{1}$, 229 (1970).
11. N. E. Frost and D. S. Dugdale, J. Mech. Phys. Solids $\underline{6}$, 92 (1958).
12. J. C. Grosskreutz, J. Appl. Phys. $\underline{33}$, 1787 (1962).
13. H. W. Liu, Trans. ASME Section D. J. Basic Eng. $\underline{83}$, 23 (1961).

PANEL DISCUSSION AND QUESTION PERIOD

MODERATOR: Richard H. Sands, University of Michigan

PARTICIPANTS: George A. Ball, Chrysler Corporation
Roger I. George, American Motors Corporation
Frank E. Jamerson, General Motors Corporation
Patrick N. Keating, Bendix Corporation
John R. Reitz, Ford Motor Company

SUMMARIZED BY: Daniel R. Gustafson, Wayne State University

Sands:

To start the discussion, I would like to ask each member of the panel to discuss relations between the industry and the colleges and universities. Are there specific areas in student training that could be improved? Are there research areas where universities could be of particular help?

Reitz:

Ford has very good relations with universities and we expect them to continue. We don't expect to find physics graduates already working in the exact area we are interested in; we realize physicists should be and are fundamental in their thinking. What we want are good students with a demonstrated ability to solve problems and a willingness to look into applied areas. In the area of research we do have cooperative projects with Wayne State University and the University of Michigan.

George:

Recently, we have been in a unique position at AMC, we have been making money lately (laughter). Traditionally, research at AMC has been short-range and oriented toward applications, we try to keep current with the work in other automotive research labs. When we hire new people, we look for people who can tackle immediate problems and solve them.

Ball:

Chrysler has had cooperative research arrangements with MIT and the University of Michigan. Right now Chrysler is having serious difficulties so research has been scaled down. Nearly all of our work is concentrated on applications. I would support the idea that the industry needs problem solvers, but we also want self-motivated people often typical of the PhD physicist. In research, we would like to see more work on controls and sensors.

The operating parameters of an automobile are often difficult to measure — we need reasonably inexpensive, reliable sensors for a wide range of things from fuel and air flow to exhaust characteristics.

Jamerson:

I would like to suggest three areas of research that have particular promise for innovation in the industry. (1) New Materials — A wide range of new materials should be studied at the basic level. For example, there are some real opportunities for solid-state physicists to conduct research on magnetic alloys. Higher performance magnetic alloys are needed to reduce the weight of electric motors used in accessories such as heaters and air conditioners as well as for future electric vehicle traction motors. We have found some promising materials, but the raw material costs have been too high to use them in automobiles. In addition, fundamental studies in traditional materials, such as steel and aluminum, are needed. There is a need to improve properties and quality for lighter weight, stronger automotive structures. Also, new composite materials offer unique material research opportunities. (2) Energy — New energy sources and energy conversion methods deserve more research. Electrochemical systems, important in batteries and fuel cells, could be studied by physicists; the subject of the liquid-metal interface is a particularly important region that physicists have only just begun to investigate. (3) Sensors — I agree with Dr. Ball that the development of dependable, inexpensive sensors is a key step in the introduction of engine control by computer in the automobile.

We need people in particular subdisciplines of physics that are of interest, but who are also broadly trained so as to be flexible in the future. Flexibility is important as most physicists at GM are involved in a multitude of projects over the course of their careers.

Communication skills are especially important, not only for communication with colleagues but also with management and production personnel. Far too many new graduates cannot write and speak effectively.

GM is involved with several universities in research projects. We are also involved in the APS Visiting Physicists Program which arranges one or two day visits by industrial physicists at colleges and universities.

Keating:

I discussed the concerns of the automotive supply industry with several other physicists and two things about the role of universities emerged. (1) We would like to see engineers taught to think in the same flexible way physicists think. Too many new engineers tend to look for a textbook solution to a problem and when none exists they don't know how to look for another approach. (2) At the last conference on Physics in the Automotive Industry in 1938, C. F. Kettering compared technological progress to dragging a heavy load across the ground with a block and tackle. He said that in order to pull the load, stakes must be driven into the ground ahead of the load. In industrial development, discoveries in physics were the stakes from which technology was pulled ahead. Those of us in the supply industry agree with Kettering and would like to see more "stakes" being driven by the university research community. I might add that Bendix does give grants and contracts to universities to support the type of research that leads to the placement of new "stakes".

I also agree that sensor development is very important.

Question:

What sort of sensors are needed?

Ball:

First of all, ones that work in actual cars. We need knock indicators, air flow and fuel flow sensors, and almost anything to do with engine operation. We also need better sensors for the standard physical quantities such as pressure, position, acceleration, and temperature. Of course by "better" I mean more reliable, less expensive, and lighter as well as more accurate; that is, I mean better in the practical engineering sense of the word.

Question:

How can universities approach the communication skills problem at an early stage in a student's development? I would suggest that industrial recruiters emphasize the need for such skills when they visit universities.

Jamerson:

The use of English proficiency tests should certainly be encouraged. I would suggest working closely with the English departments on this problem. Also, the message that this problem must be solved has to go down from the universities to the junior colleges, high schools, and elementary schools.

Sands:

Universities are certainly becoming aware of this problem and are starting to do something about it. For instance, at the University of Michigan there is now a writing proficiency requirement. If the students fail that they must take a course to improve themselves until they can pass it. In addition, all departments have started required courses in communication for their majors to supplement the broader courses in the English and Speech departments.

Comment:

As an industrial physicist who often recruits at universities, I have found that seminar participation is essential in communications skills training. I think that graduate students should give at least six oral presentations during their academic careers. Those students who have never given an oral presentation are usually not ready to begin an industrial career. I rarely recommend such applicants as they simply don't have the communications skills we need.

Ball:

Science Fair participation is very helpful both in science and in learning how to explain your work to others.

Comment:

Lab reports are one of the best places for students to sharpen their writing. We should grade them carefully to help the students improve both their laboratory skills and their writing.

Question:

Students often ask, "What formula do I use?" What can be done to improve the student's attitude toward problem solving? Could recruiters stress that they would like to see a better attitude toward problem solving?

Keating:

Does this problem start at the high school level?

Reply:

Yes

Sands:

Some improvements can be expected as higher university proficiency requirements gradually force high schools to improve their training.

Question:

The industry has a real problem producing enough small cars. Do physicists get involved in speeding up production?

Reitz:

They do occasionally, in a peripheral way, but the basic problem is the very long lead time needed to change models.

Ball:

Changing a plant to produce an entirely new line of cars simply takes a long time.

George:

And a lot of money. Plant replacement requires huge capital investments.

Question:

How long will it take to have totally flexible assembly lines; lines which can be changed to a new product by changing the instructions in a computer?

George:

Thirty or more years. Programmable robots are still in a fairly primitive state and they are still costly.

Ball:

It should be mentioned that there are long lead-times that are established by law to meet various government standards, such as emissions, so that "total flexibility" is really not possible today. After a design is selected, fleets of cars must be built and subjected to comprehensive test programs. At Chrysler's Chelsea Proving Ground, chassis roll dynamometers are computer operated around the clock to accumulate the miles legally required. In spite of such automation, emissions certification can easily consume a whole year's elapsed time. There are, of course, other requirements such as crashworthiness that also consume time in order to meet government standards.

Question:

I know that most of the physics research in the automotive industry is done by PhD's. I wondered if there was any need for BS level physicists in the industry?

George:

Certainly, AMC wants BS level people - but we don't do any research.

Ball:

Bachelor level graduates have been very successful at Chrysler.

Question:

A well-known physicist once remarked that the energy crisis would be solved if the physicists would get out and the inventors would come in. What does the panel think of that approach?

Reitz:

Good inventors can be very innovative certainly, but they are even harder to find than good physicists. We need people with a wide range of skills and backgrounds to solve problems posed by the energy crisis.

Jamerson:

The problems of today are more complicated than ever before. Basic research will continue to be a necessary forerunner to technical innovation.

Question:

University researchers often don't realize that industry is in need of their ideas. How can industry let the university researcher know what is needed?

Jamerson:

The automotive industry is receptive to new ideas from outside its own organization. One of the purposes of this conference is to let academic physicists know what goes on in the automotive industry. The conference proceedings will be published and hopefully serve as a reference for the current, and future, research topics of interest to the industry.

Question:

Most of the talks and the tours have presented basic research projects. What are some of the other things physicists do in the automotive industry?

Reitz:

We use BS/MS physicists primarily as research support personnel at the Ford Scientific Labs. In other parts of the Corporation BS/MS physicists often work in engineering. Here their flexibility is particularly appreciated. There are a number of very successful BS and MS physicists in the Corporation, many of whom started in the Scientific Labs and then moved to engineering and production departments as part of our efforts to use new basic research discoveries in the production of automobiles and other products. At Ford, physicists run the full gambit — basic research, applied research, engineering, production, and management.

George:

At AMC there are a huge number of physicists — six or so (laughter). All six are involved in management because of their good problem-solving skills. Although this does not advance basic research, it is encouraging for physics as a profession.

Jamerson:

GM has a large number of physicists in engineering and manufacturing departments throughout many production divisions of the Corporation. In addition, physicists are employed in departments other than the Physics Department at GMR; Engine Research, Computer Science and Societal Analysis Departments, to name a few. Dr. Lawrence R. Hafstad, a physicist, was Vice President of GMR from 1955-1969 and currently Dr. Betsy Ancker-Johnson is Vice President of Environmental Activities Staff and Dr. David S. Potter is Vice President of GM Public Affairs.

Question:

Does the BS physicist suffer a financial disadvantage compared to the engineering graduate?

George:

No. There is no monetary disadvantage (or advantage) for the BS physicist. Nor is there any culture shock for the physicist coming to the industry. I feel the BS physicist does the job equally as well as the engineering grad.

Ball:

I agree.

Question:

What improvements should be made in the physics curriculum?

Keating:

I would like to see an improvement in communications skills. Almost all new graduates have room for improvement. Foreign-born students are often a special problem; many need extra training in communication before they can function outside of the laboratory.

Question:

Does the Master's graduate suffer compared to the PhD or BS graduate?

Jamerson:

It is true that there are not as many opportunities for the MS graduate in research where PhD's are typically sought for research scientist positions. However, there are many opportunities for them at production divisions in engineering or manufacturing positions. MS physicists do extremely well in product development such as in microelectronics at Delco Electronics Division. There is a growing need for electronics expertise in the automobile industry.

Comment:

Coming from a small college, I would like to make the point that we also train physicists; recruiters should visit us too.

LASER SPECTROSCOPY IN COMBUSTION

J. H. Bechtel
Physics Department
General Motors Research Laboratories, Warren, Michigan 48090

ABSTRACT

An important challenge to the automotive industry is to develop a detailed understanding of the combustion of a wide variety of fuels. The development of accurate theories for combustion demands that the predictions of these theories be compared in detail to experiments. Recent advances in laser technology now permit one to measure accurately and nonintrusively both temperatures and species concentrations in combustion systems. An application of these measurements is given here to obtain a systematic comparison between a recent laminar methane-air flame theory and measured temperature and species concentration profiles. These measurements are obtained by both laser Raman spectroscopy and laser induced fluorescence spectroscopy. The results show a good agreement between the theoretical predictions and the measured concentrations of CH_4, O_2, H_2O, CO_2 and OH in several CH_4-air flames. An application of a sensitivity analysis to the kinetic reaction mechanism in the burned gas region of one of these flames allows a new value of the rate constant for the $H + O_2 + M \rightarrow HO_2 + M$ reaction to be inferred from the spectroscopic data.

INTRODUCTION

More than forty years ago at the first Symposium on Physics in the Automotive Industry, Lloyd Withrow and Gerald Rassweiler[1] employed various optical methods including spectroscopy to glean new insights into combustion in the internal combustion engine. Withrow and Rassweiler recognized at that time that optical methods of combustion diagnostics do not interfere with either the fluid motion or the chemistry of the combustion process. They were capable of using high speed cinematography to measure flame motion, sodium line reversal to measure temperature, and emission and absorption spectroscopy to obtain qualitative measurements of flame composition. An example of their photographs of flame motion in an L-head engine is exhibited in Figure 1.

In the intervening forty-two years there have been two very significant technological advances that now allow combustion experiments that could not have been done then or even twenty years ago. These technological developments are the high-speed digital computer and the laser.

These devices are now playing an ever increasing role in helping to unravel the complexities of combustion. The computer, for example, allows one to numerically solve systems of coupled differential equations that reflect the conservation of total mass, species mass, momentum, and energy that are subject to the initial

ISSN:0094-243X/81/660127-13$1.50 Copyright 1981 American Institute of Physics

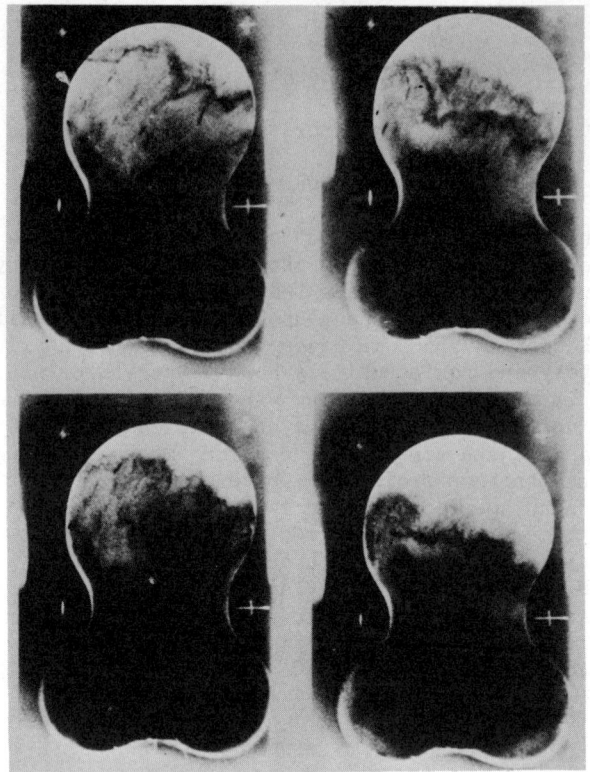

Fig. 1 High-speed photographs of flame propagation in an L-head engine. The valves are beside the engine cylinder rather than above it. The photographs are from the Withrow-Rassweiler era[1].

and boundary conditions of various combustion systems. The solution to these equations provides theoretical predictions for such variables as temperature, composition, burning velocity, and fluid motion.

The laser permits accurate measurements of temperature, species concentrations, and fluid motion in combustion systems. These laser measurement techniques do not disturb the processes occurring in the sampled volume, a region that can be very small due to the excellent focusing properties of the laser radiation. Some of these methods include laser-induced fluorescence, laser Raman spectroscopy, coherent Raman spectroscopy, and laser velocimetry. One application of these devices is the understanding of the combustion process in special laboratory flames. Here careful measurements of the flame structure and comparisons with the numerical results of available theories are giving new insights into the importance of chemistry, heat transfer and mass transport in these special combustion systems. A principal reason for choosing these flames is that much of our detailed knowledge of combustion has been derived from the study of laboratory flames.[2,3] One of the few hydrocarbon fuels for which a detailed reaction mechanism with air has been postulated is methane. The flame theories for methane combustion include both species diffusion and thermal conduction.[4-7] Most previous measurements of flame structure have been done on low pressure flames (a few kPa). These flames are much thicker than near stoichiometric atmospheric pressure flames. Temperatures have usually been measured with thermocouples and species profiles have been measured with sonic microprobes[3] or supersonic molecular beam sampling with mass spectrometer detection.[8-11]

As mentioned previously one of the important attributes of laser scattering methods is the very high spatial resolution that can be achieved by focusing the laser. The primary reaction zone has a thickness t given by $t \simeq \kappa/S$.[12] Here κ is a diffusivity and S is a burning velocity. For an atmospheric pressure hydrocarbon-air flame t is typically only a fraction of a mm thick. Since the laser beams used for the experiments reported here are a few tens of microns in diameter, an accurate profile of the primary reaction zone may be determined.

The reaction mechanism for CH_4-air combustion may be schematically represented as a sequence of steps for carbon evolution: $CH_4 \rightarrow CH_3 \rightarrow CH_2O \rightarrow CHO \rightarrow CO \rightarrow CO_2$. These steps involve various parallel reactions and a specific reaction scheme[4] is exhibited in Table I. Other possible schemes may be found elsewhere.[5-7] One realizes the complexity of methane combustion when one notes that there are still many unresolved problems associated with methane-air flames. These include the importance of HO_2, CH_3O, and CH_2; the fates CH_2O and CH_3; accurate rate constants for many of the reactions and accurate high temperature species diffusivities. In spite of these many uncertainties one can theoretically predict the structure of premixed CH_4-air laminar flames and the accuracy of this predicted structure may be tested by laser spectroscopy.

EXPERIMENTAL METHODS AND APPARATUS

To examine the primary reaction zone of these premixed laminar flames it is necessary to stabilize the flame with a burner that allows accurate probing of the flame. A schematic diagram of such a burner is given in Figure 2. The geometry of the flame is such that the focused laser beam can probe the center of the flame where the flame geometry is approximately one-dimensional. To maintain a stable flame the unburned gases were flowed through critical flow orifices and were premixed before combustion. The entire burner was affixed to a two-dimensionally translatable stage that allowed positioning the burner with a precision of 10 μm.

The Raman scattering experiment used a frequency doubled Nd:YAG (neodymium doped yttrium aluminum garnet) laser that was Q-switched at 2 kHz. To obtain the desired spatial resolution the laser beam was focused to a spot size that contained 90% of the laser power within a diameter of 40 μm even in the region of maximum index of refraction gradients. The typical average laser power was 0.25 W.

TABLE I Postulated mechanism for a methane-air flame.[4]

No.	Reaction	Forward Rate Constant (cgs units)*		
		A	n	C
				cal/g mol
A1	$CH_4+OH \rightleftarrows CH_3+H_2O$	3×10^{13}	0	5,000
A2	$CH_4+H \rightleftarrows CH_3+H_2$	2×10^{14}	0	11,900
A3	$CH_4+O \rightleftarrows CH_3+OH$	2×10^{13}	0	6,900
B1	$CH_3+O \rightleftarrows CH_2O+H$	7×10^{13}	0	1,000
B2	$CH_3+O_2 \rightleftarrows CH_2O+OH$	3×10^{13}	0	17,500
C1	$CH_2O+M \rightleftarrows CO+H_2+M$	2×10^{16}	0	35,000
C2	$CH_2O+OH \rightleftarrows CHO+H_2O$	2.5×10^{13}	0	1,000
C3	$CH_2O+O \rightleftarrows CHO+OH$	3×10^{13}	0	0
C4	$CH_2O+H \rightleftarrows CHO+H_2$	1.7×10^{13}	0	3,000
D1	$CHO+O_2 \rightleftarrows CO+HO_2$	3×10^{13}	0	0
D2	$CHO+OH \rightleftarrows CO+H_2O$	1×10^{14}	0	0
D3	$CHO+O \rightleftarrows CO+OH$	5.4×10^{11}	1/2	0
D4	$CHO+M \rightleftarrows CO+H+M$	2×10^{12}	1/2	28,800
E1	$CO+OH \rightleftarrows CO_2+H$	5.5×10^{11}	0	1,080
E2	$CO+O+M \rightleftarrows CO_2+M$	3.6×10^{18}	-1	2,500
F1	$HO_2+O \rightleftarrows O_2+OH$	2.5×10^{13}	0	0
F2	$HO_2+OH \rightleftarrows O_2+H_2O$	2.5×10^{13}	0	0
F3	$HO_2+H \rightleftarrows OH+OH$	2×10^{14}	0	2,000
F4	$HO_2+H \rightleftarrows O_2+H_2$	6×10^{13}	0	2,000
F5	$H+O_2+M \rightleftarrows HO_2+M$	1.4×10^{16}	0	-1,000
G1	$H+O_2 \rightleftarrows OH+O$	2.2×10^{14}	0	16,800
G2	$O+H_2 \rightleftarrows OH+H$	1.7×10^{13}	0	9,460
G3	$OH+H_2 \rightleftarrows H_2O+H$	2.2×10^{13}	0	5,200
G4	$OH+OH \rightleftarrows H_2O+O$	6×10^{12}	0	780
H1	$H+OH+M \rightleftarrows OH+M$	7×10^{19}	-1	0
H2	$O+H+M \rightleftarrows OH+M$	4×10^{18}	-1	0
H3	$H+H+M \rightleftarrows H_2+M$	2×10^{19}	-1	0
H4	$O+O+M \rightleftarrows O_2+M$	4×10^{18}	-1	0

*$K=AT^n \exp(-E/RT)$ g-mol, sec, K units

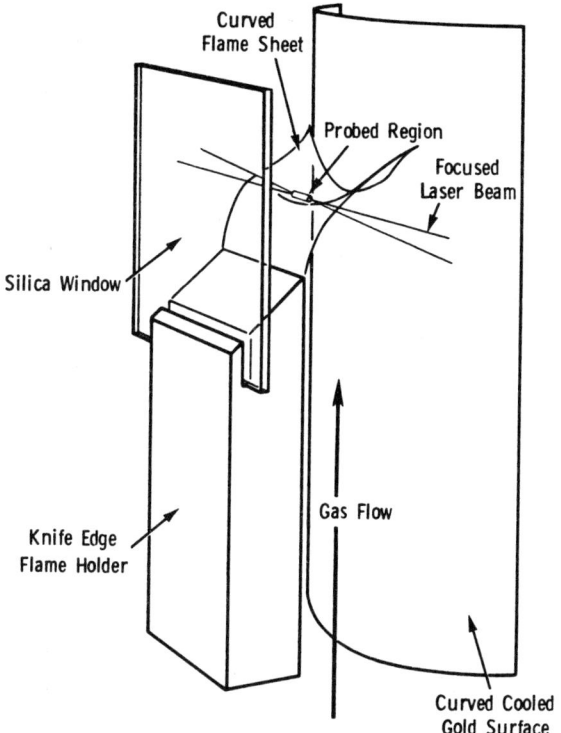

Fig. 2. Schematic diagram of the slot burner used in this experiment.

The spectral shape and intensity of the Raman scattering from the flame molecules were processed by a central computer to derive both temperature and species concentration.[13-15] Absolute concentrations of fuel, O_2, CO, H_2, CO_2 and H_2O in the flame were determined by flowing known calibration concentrations of these gases through the burner and measuring the Raman scattering signals.

Hydroxyl temperatures and concentrations were measured in these flames by both laser absorption and laser-induced fluorescence. These experiments were conducted with a frequency-doubled, tunable dye laser. The fluorescence from the laser excited electronic excited state was scaled to an absolute hydroxyl concentration by laser absorption measurements of the hydroxyl concentration along a homogeneous concentration path length in the burned gas region of the flames. The collisional deactivation of the laser excited state was determined throughout the flame by measuring the concentration of the major quenching species by using literature values of the quenching cross sections[16] and by determining the relative collision velocities of hydroxyl with the other species.

The rotational temperature of the electronic ground state was also measured by laser fluoresence spectroscopy. The laser was scanned across several P and Q branch transitions of the $^2\Pi(v" = 0) \rightarrow {}^2\Sigma^+ (v' = 0)$ spectrum. The spectrometer, however,

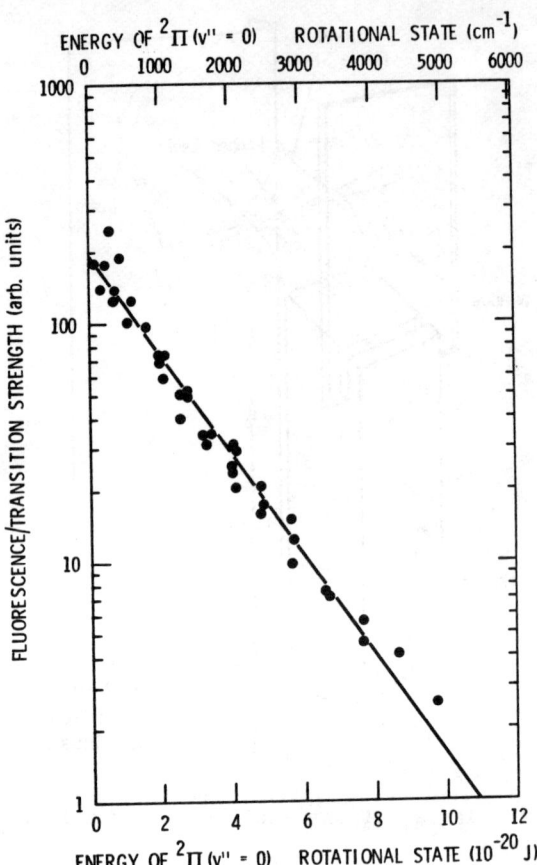

Fig. 3. Plot of the laser-induced fluorescence intensity per transition strength versus energy of the initial rotational state in $^2\Pi$ (v" = o) electronic state. The slope of the line gives the OH rotational temperature.

detected only the fluorescence of a large number of lines in the R_1 and R_2 branches. The temperature is determined by plotting the fluorescence intensities of a given laser-excited transition divided by the transiion strength of the absorption versus the energy of the absorbing rotational state in the $^2\Pi$ (v" = 0) electronic ground state. A requirement for the validity of this method is that the laser beam is not significantly attenuated before it reaches the scattering region. An example of this type of plot is given in Figure 3. The temperature is determined by the slope of the line through the data. In fact this type of plot demonstrates that the $^2\Pi$ (v" = 0) state exhibits a Boltzmann distribution in the population of rotational energy levels. Additional details of the experiment are given in Ref. 17.

THEORY

The theoretical procedure for calculating flame temperature and concentration profiles is described in detail in Ref. 4. The general method consists of solving the differential equations that specify the conservation of total mass, individual special mass, momentum and energy. The coupled differential equations are solved by finite difference methods with the space derivatives treated explicitly and the kinetic terms treated implicitly. The coupled conservation equations are solved subject to several assumptions. These include the following: laminar flow, one dimensional, constant static pressure, negligible viscous dissipation, negligible external forces, negligible radiative heat transfer, negligible heat lost to the surroundings, and no Soret or Dufour effects.[12] The coupled conservation equations are solved in a transformed coordinate system by the method described by Smoot.[4] The initial temperature and the composition of each species are specified at the unburned boundary. At the burned boundary the diffusive flux of each species is zero. Moreover, the computer program requires thermal conductivity, species diffusivity, reaction rate constants, equilibrium constants, and heat capacities. The program for solving the finite difference equations typically contains 50 grid points in the direction of the flame and requires approximately 600 time iterations for convergence to a steady-state.

RESULTS

The theoretical and experimental results for a fuel-lean methane-air flame are given in Figures 4 and 5. These results include temperature and major species concentrations. The experimental and theoretical results are compared by matching the abscissas of the respective temperature profiles. The results demonstrate that the theory very accurately predicts the slope of the temperature profile but predicts a larger final flame temperature than is measured. This is a consequence of heat lost to the cooled, gold coated burner wall that is 1.5 mm away from the positions where data were taken.

If one compares the composition profiles in Figures 4 and 5, one finds that the agreement between experiment and theory is very good. Any differences between them may be attributed to experimental scatter in the data.

The hydroxyl concentration profile for a fuel-lean CH_4-air flame is presented in Figure 6. There the maximum concentration observed and the predicted concentration agree to within 20%. The abscissas of the theoretical and the experimental results were matched by setting the theoretically predicted temperature equal to the measured hydroxyl rotational temperature. At all positions in the flame the hydroxyl $^2\Pi$ ($v'' = 0$) state exhibited a Boltzmann distribution of rotational states. The rotational temperature is equal to the N_2 vibrational temperature to within the $\pm$ 100 K precision of the laser-induced fluorescence and laser Raman scattering experiments. A comparison of these temperatures is given in Figure 7.

If one looks at the OH concentration beyond the flame front one observes the OH concentration to decrease in this so-called recombination zone of burned gases. One can also model this

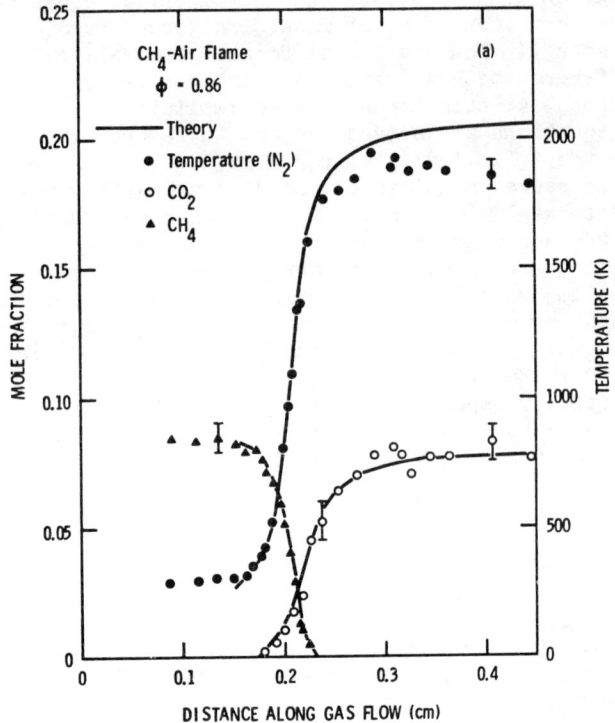

Fig. 4. Temperature, CH_4, and CO_2 profiles for a fuel-lean
($\phi = 0.86$) atmospheric pressure, premixed, laminar
CH_4-air flame. The experimental data are from laser
Raman scattering and the theoretical predictions are from
the computer code of Ref. 4.

recombination zone by neglecting the hydrocarbon reactions in Table I. The concentration profile of hydroxyl as well as the other species such as O, H, O_2, H_2, H_2O, CO, CO_2 and HO_2 may be determined from the measured temperature and the initial concentrations.[17] The predicted OH concentration, the measured concentration as well as the equilibrium concentration are exhibited in Figure 8. Although the OH concentration is well above the equilibrium concentration for the measured temperature, the experimental result agrees well with the theoretical prediction. Moreover, a sensitivity analysis of the theory shows what reactions have the most important influence on the rate of hydroxyl destruction.

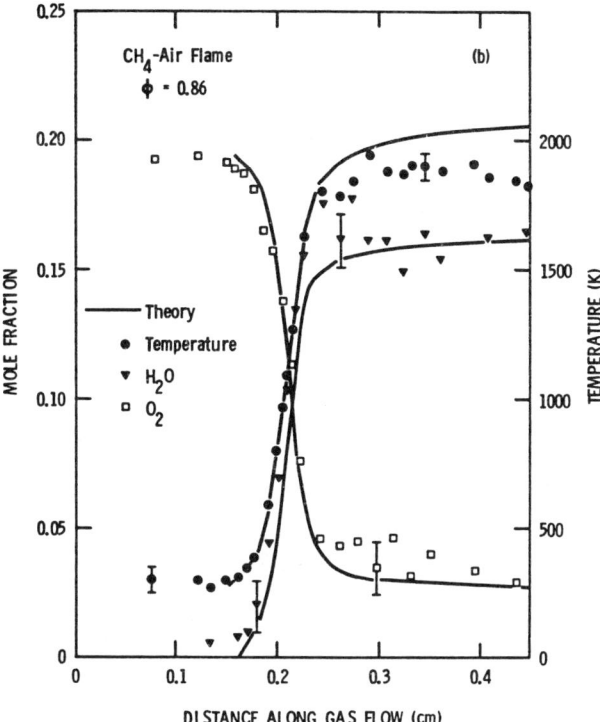

Fig. 5. Temperature, H_2O, and O_2 profiles for a fuel-lean ($\phi = 0.86$) atmospheric pressure, premixed laminar CH_4-air flame. The experimental data are from laser Raman scattering and the theoretical predictions are from the comptuer code of Ref. 4.

Many reactions destroy OH such as

$$HO_2 + OH \rightarrow O_2 + H_2O$$

or $\quad H + OH + M \rightarrow H_2O + M$

(M is any third body such as N_2, O_2, CO_2 or H_2O.). For the fuel-lean flame, however, the sensitivity analysis shows that the rate limiting reaction for OH destruction is

$$H + O_2 + M \rightarrow HO_2 + M.$$

This reaction is important because it creates HO_2 which destroys OH in other reactions. The theory of the recombination zone also shows that reactions G1-G3 are very fast. Thus a measurement of the OH concentration and temperature in the recombination zone

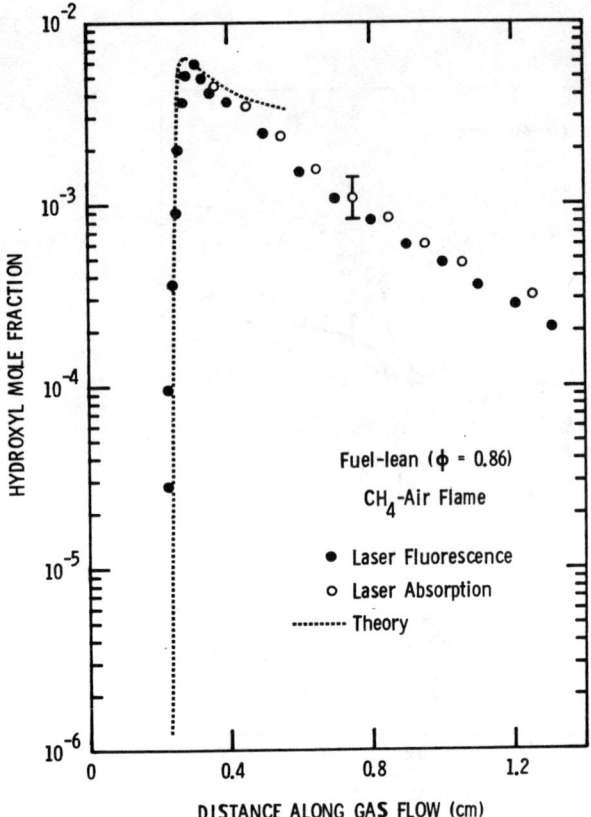

Fig. 6. Comparison of hydroxyl concentration as measured by laser-induced fluorescence, laser absorption and the theoretical predictions of Ref. 4.

provides a method of determining O atom and H atom concentrations as well. For example one finds

$$[O] = \frac{K_{G3}}{K_{G2}} \frac{[OH]^2}{[H_2O]} ,$$

and

$$[H] = \frac{K_{G3}}{K_{G1} K_{G2}} \frac{[OH]^3}{[H_2O][O_2]} .$$

Here K_{G1}, K_{G2}, and K_{G3} are the temperature dependent equilibrium constants for reactions G1, G2, and G3, respectively. For fuel-lean flames $[H_2O]$ and $[O_2]$ would be nearly constant in the recombination zone and would be known from calculated equilibrium values or measurements such as Raman scattering.

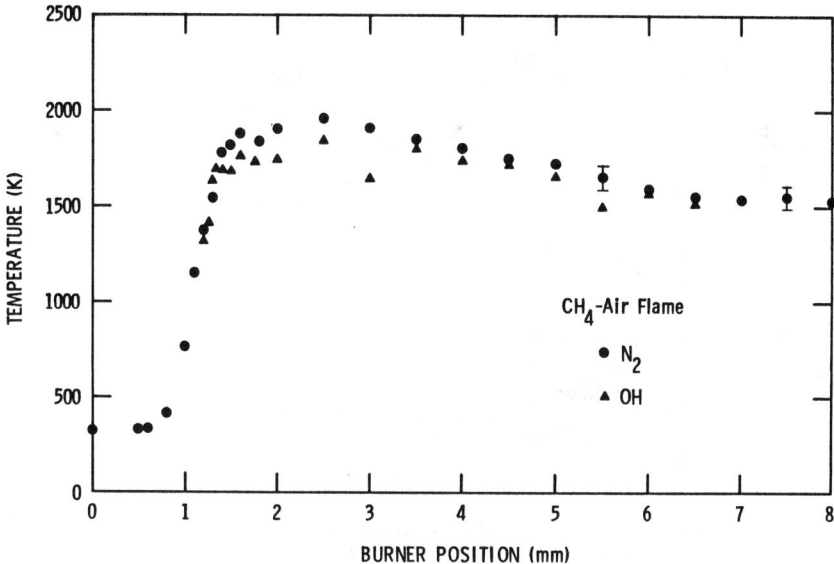

Fig. 7. Comparison of OH and N_2 temperatures in both primary reaction zone and recombination zone. The fuel-air equivalence ratio was $\phi = 0.93$. The probed region was 1.5 mm from the curved wall. The uncertainty in the hydroxyl temperature is ± 100 K.

If one fits the experimental data of Figure 8 to a rate constant for the $H + O_2 + M \xrightarrow{k_f} HO_2 + M$ reaction such that the best fit is obtained, one finds $k_f = 4 \times 10^{-29} \exp(-140/T)/T$ for the flame.

CONCLUSIONS AND FUTURE APPLICATIONS

In conclusion, the laser spectroscopic methods that have been described here are useful for giving new insights into a number of fundamental problems of combustion. These experiments demonsrate, for example, that comparison of temperature and species concentrations show a good agreement with recent laminar flame theories for methane-air flames. A sensitivity analysis of the reaction mechanism for the recombination zone of a fuel-lean flame shows that the rate limiting reaction for OH as well as H and O decay can be determined.

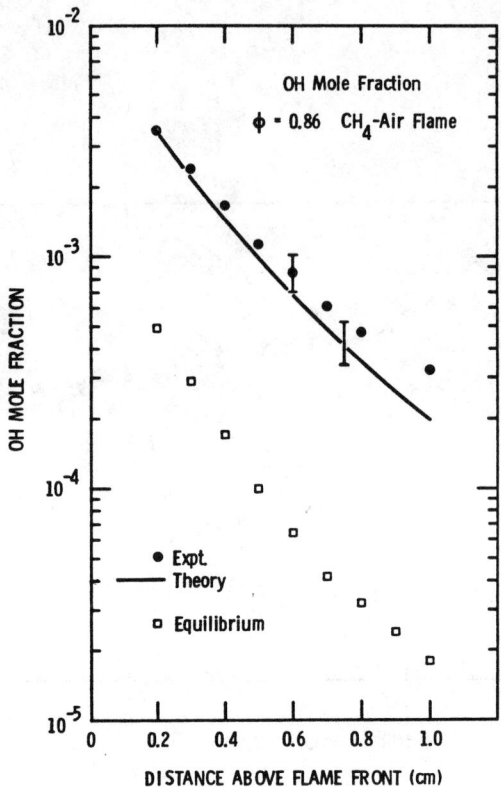

Fig. 8. Hydroxyl concentration expressed as a mole fraction above a $\phi = 0.86$ methane-air flame.

There are many future applications of laser spectroscopy for combustion research. These include the detection of other important combustion species such as CH_2O, CH_3O, NH, NH_2, and NO. These molecules are important in the combustion of hydrocarbon fuels or in fuels that contain nitrogen.

Finally these same spectroscopic methods have recently been used to make initial measurements of fuel air ratios in special motored stratified charge engines[19,20] as well as time resolved temperature and density measurements in firing homogeneous charge engines.[21] It is clear that laser spectroscopy will play an increasingly important role in understanding many facets of the combustion process and selected combustion devices.

ACKNOWLEDGMENTS

The author would like to acknowledge his close collaboration with his colleagues R. J. Blint, C. J. Dasch, and R. E. Teets in much of the research reviewed here. He would like to acknowledge the technical assistance of Louis Green and the support and encouragement of A. D. Gara and J. C. Tracy.

REFERENCES

1. L. Withrow and G. M. Rassweiler, J. Appl. Phys. $\underline{9}$, 362 (1938).
2. C. P. Fenimore, Chemistry in Premixed Flames (MacMillan, N.Y., 1964).
3. R. M. Fristrom and A. A. Westenberg, Flame Structure (McGraw Hill, N.Y., 1965).
4. L. D. Smoot, W. C. Hecker, and G. A. Williams, Combust. Flame $\underline{26}$, 323 (1976).
5. G. Tsatsaronis, Combust. Flame $\underline{33}$, 217 (1978).
6. J. T. Kelly and R. M. Kendall, Proceedings of the Second Stationary Source Combustion Symposium Vol. IV. EPA-600/7-77-073d (1977) p. 311.
7. J. R. Creighton and C. M. Lund, in Characterization of High Temperature Vapors and Gases, J. W. Hastie, Editor, Natl. Bur. Stds. Spec. Pub. No. 561 (U.S. GPO, Washington, D. C., 1979) p. 1223.
8. S. N. Foner and R. L. Hudson, J. Chem. Phys. $\underline{21}$, 1374 (1953).
9. C. P. Lazzara, J. C. Biordi and J. F. Papp, Combust. Flame $\underline{21}$, 371 (1973).
10. J. C. Biordi, Prog. Energy Combust. Sci. $\underline{3}$, 151 (1977).
11. J. Peters and G. Mahnen, Fourteenth Symposium (International) on Combustion (The Combustion Institute, Pittsburgh, 1973) p. 133.
12. F. A. Williams, Combustion Theory (Addison-Wesley, Reading, 1965) p. 99.
13. D. A. Stephenson and R. J. Blint, Appl. Spectrosc. $\underline{33}$, 41 (1979).
14. R. J. Blint, D. A. Stephenson, and J. H. Bechtel, J. Quant. Spectrosc. Radiat. Transfer, $\underline{23}$, 89 (1980).
15. J. H. Bechtel, R. J. Blint, C. J. Dasch, and D. A. Weinberger, General Motors Research Laboratories Publication GMR-3058 (1979), Combust. Flame (to be published).
16. J. H. Bechtel and R. E. Teets, Appl. Opt. $\underline{18}$, 4138 (1979).
17. J. H. Bechtel, Appl. Opt. $\underline{18}$, 2100 (1979).
18. R. E. Teets and J. H. Bechtel, General Motors Research Laboratories Publication GMR-3109 (1979). Eighteenth Symposium (International) on Combustion (to be published).
19. S. C. Johnston, SAE paper 790433 (1979).
20. S. C. Johnston, SAE paper 800136 (1980).
21. J. R. Smith, SAE paper 800137 (1980).

EXHAUST GAS OXYGEN SENSORS

Robert E. Hetrick, D. K. Hohnke and E. M. Logothetis
Engineering and Research Staff, Research, Ford Motor Company
Dearborn, Michigan 48121

ABSTRACT

Ceramic ZrO_2, TiO_2 and related oxides with suitable O_2-sensitive electrical properties have found important applications in devices for measuring exhaust-gas O_2 concentration. For example, such devices are key components in feedback control systems that would maintain the intake air-to-fuel ratio near the stoichiometric value where regulated emissions can be minimized. The physical principles underlying the operation of ZrO_2 based O_2-concentration cells and TiO_2-based resistive devices for the stoichiometric application are described. Finally, a device based on electrochemical O_2 pumping is discussed which may be useful for A/F control in the fuel-efficient lean region.

The control and adjustment of the intake air-to-fuel ratio (A/F = mass of air/mass of fuel) is a key factor simultaneously influencing fuel economy, driveability and regulated emissions (HC, CO, NO_x). For laboratory development and testing, steady-state A/F can be determined from quantitative measurements of the major exhaust gas constituents. It has become desirable in some cases to have a fast and inexpensive sensor of A/F for on-board control purposes. As an example, to enable an exhaust-gas catalyst to simultaneously convert the emissions to their minimum values, the average A/F must not be allowed to vary too lean (air excess) or too rich (fuel excess) of the stoichiometric A/F (A/F_{stoich}).[1] This value ($\sim$ 14.6 for gasoline) is the ratio where there is just enough O_2 in the intake air to react with each HC molecule in the fuel charge. To achieve the required precision in A/F control, it is advantageous in some cases, to employ a closed-loop feedback system. For two reasons exhaust-gas O_2 partial pressure, P_{EX}, is the quantity which recommends itself as the useful parameter for on-board A/F measurements. First, high temperature, O_2-sensitive ceramic materials are available to measure P_{EX} in the exhaust environment. Second, the variation of P_{EX} with A/F is distinctive and particularly advantageous for the stoichiometric application. Figure 1 shows a typical plot of $\log(P_{EX})$ vs A/F. The dashed curve represents the variation that results from the combustion processes occurring at a combustion temperature of approximately 1300°C. As would be expected, P_{EX} falls monotonically on going from lean to rich conditions with

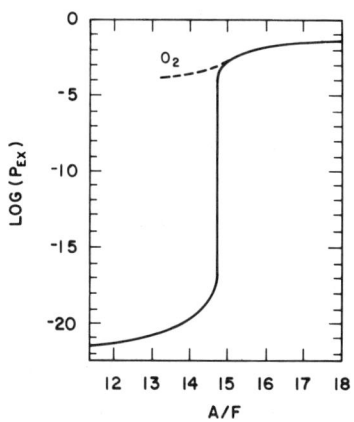

Fig. 1. Variation of O_2 partial pressure in the exhaust with A/F.

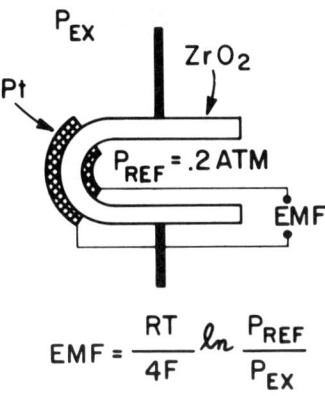

Fig. 2. Schematic of ZrO_2 based O_2-concentration cell.

the sharpest drop occurring near A/F_{stoich}. As the gas cools on emerging from the cylinders, a highly non-equilibrium state may develop. If the constituents are fully reacted to thermal equilibrium at a typical exhaust temperature of 700°C, the variation shown by the full curve is observed. The precipitous drop in P_{EX} by over twenty orders of magnitude clearly marks A/F_{stoich}. The reason for the abrupt drop is, of course, due to the fact that the hydrocarbon oxidation reaction is so strongly favored.

Two main types of O_2-sensitive devices, the semiconducting resistive type[2,3] and O_2-concentration cells, have been used in the exhaust gas both to equilibrate the constituents and sense the resulting value of P_{EX}. Figure 2 shows a schematic drawing of a solid electrolyte, concentration cell now enjoying significant usage in the stoichiometric application.[4] The electrolyte in the form of a cylinder closed at one end is composed of ceramic ZrO_2 strongly doped with Y_2O_3. This well-known material is an excellent oxygen ion conductor at elevated temperature ($\sigma(800°C) \sim 2 \times 10^{-2} \Omega$-cm) and well suited for use as a solid electrolyte. Thin Pt electrodes are attached to opposing faces of the electrolyte which are respectively exposed to the exhaust gas and a reference atmosphere (usually air) with an O_2 partial pressure P_{REF}. The emf that develops between the two electrodes is given by the familiar Nernst equation

$$\text{emf} = (RT/4F)\ln(P_{REF}/P_{EX}) \quad (1)$$

where R and F are the ideal gas and Faraday constants while T is the absolute temperature. The 4 arises because the overall electrochemical reaction step (Eq. (2)) at each

$$O_2(\text{gas}) + 4e^-(\text{electrode}) + 2V_o(\text{electrolyte}) \rightleftarrows 2O^=(\text{electrolyte}) \quad (2)$$

electrode involves the transfer of 4 electrons as O_2 is taken up or released by O_2 vacancies, V_o, in the electrolyte.

Besides providing electrical contacts, Pt electrodes are chosen for their ability to catalyze the local equilibration of the exhaust gas. If the activity is great enough, then despite the low sensitivity offered by the logarithmic function, a substantial emf step can be observed at A/F_{stoich} because of the enormous change in P_{EX}. Figure 3a shows a typical result where the emf rises sharply from about 50 meV to 1.0 V on passing from lean to rich conditions. Figure 3b sketches the use of the sensor for stoichiometric control. The sensor output is sent to a comparator whose other input is a reference voltage, V_R, with a value midway between the extremes of the output. The system is arranged so that a lean sensor output drives an electrically controllable fuel-metering system rich and vice versa. The result is a limit cycle oscillation (see Fig. 3c) in which A/F oscillates about A/F_{stoich}. The frequency of the oscillation (typically on the order of 1.0 Hz) is determined primarily by the time for exhaust gas to be transported between the engine and sensor.

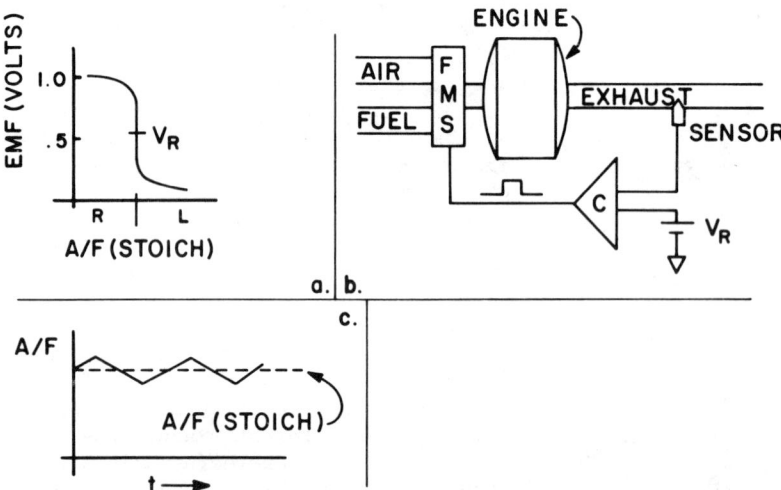

Fig. 3. (a) Sensor output vs A/F, (b) Schematic of closed-loop fuel metering system, (c) Limit-cycle oscillations of the A/F ratio.

An alternate approach to a stoichiometric sensor lies in the use of certain metal oxides whose resistivity at elevated temperatures is sensitive to the ambient O_2 partial pressure. A good example is TiO_2 where O_2 in the solid phase and an ambient gas come to equilibrium by means of surface reactions. A reasonable example of such a reaction is given by Eq. (3)

$$O_2(\text{gas}) + 2V_o(\text{oxide}) + 4e^-(\text{oxide}) \rightleftarrows 2O^=(\text{oxide}) \tag{3}$$

which is similar to Eq. (1) except that the 4 electrons in this case are available for n-type electronic conduction. Using a point defect model involving O_2-ion vacancies, one predicts a resistance with dependencies as shown in Eq. 4,

$$R \sim e^{E/kT} P_{EX}^{1/4} \tag{4}$$

where E is an activation energy that depends on both the formation energy of the relevant defects, and the specific carrier conduction process. The 1/4-power sensitivity to P_{EX} is the basis for sensor action. Figure 4 shows the resistance of a specimen of ceramic TiO_2 (rutile) plotted against P_{EX}. The resistance variation in the low-pressure region (established using calibrated mixtures of CO and CO_2) indeed shows a near 1/4-power dependence. However, at the higher values of P_{EX}, the resistance peaks and actually decreases at lower temperatures. This behavior is interpreted as the onset of p-type conductivity at the higher partial pressures. For the sensor application, the main feature is a resistance decrease of some three to four orders of magnitude on passing from lean to rich P_{EX} values. These variations are shown again in Fig. 5 where the resistance of a typical TiO_2 sensor is plotted versus A/F for a high and low-temperature case. As with the concentration cell, the step-like change in response at A/F_{stoich} can be "read out" electrically to provide a feedback signal for stoichiometric control.

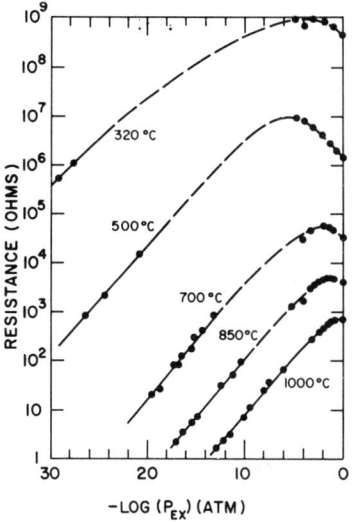

Fig. 4. Resistance of TiO_2 (rutile) specimen versus P_{EX} at various temperatures.

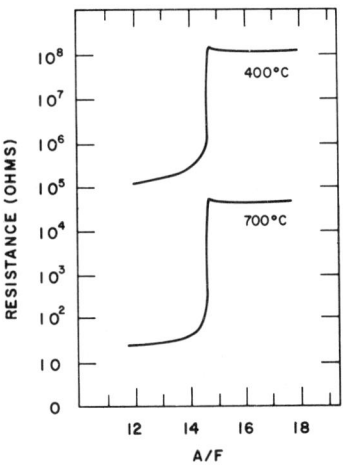

Fig. 5. Resistance of TiO_2 sensor versus A/F.

Important technical considerations for TiO_2 sensors (as for other exhaust gas sensors) are response time, catalytic activity and temperature dependence. To minimize response time, the ceramic is made both fine-grained and porous. The latter feature promotes the rapid exposure of the material to changes in exhaust-gas composition while the former reduces the influence of bulk defect diffusion processes on the equilibration time between the solid and gas phases. To enhance the intrinsic catalytic activity of TiO_2, sensors are treated with a fine dispersion of Pt particles. This is found not only to improve the activity but also has a salutory effect on the response time which can be as small as a few milliseconds. A principal advantage of resistive sensors is that they do not require a reference atmosphere. Thus a small size and simplicity of structure are possible. A disadvantage, however, is a strong temperature dependence as is clearly illustrated in Fig. 5. In practice the effect of temperature must be reduced with either an auxiliary heater or a temperature compensating resistor.

Although stoichiometric sensors are in production usage, they are still the subject of active research interest.[4] The reasons include cost reduction, extension of operating conditions especially with regard to low temperature operation and improvements in durability without compromising performance.

Ideally one would like an on-board device which could monitor A/F across the entire range of interest. Such a device would permit the accuracy of feedback control to be coupled with a more variable A/F strategy designed to optimize different aspects of performance under different driving conditons. Such flexibility should become increasingly desirable in the future with mounting pressure for engines or engine strategies which operate in the fuel efficient lean region.

P_{EX} is a well characterized function of A/F in the lean region and could be employed as the measured quantity in a lean-burn sensor. However, perusal of Fig. 1 shows that the variation of P_{EX} with A/F is weak in the lean region compared to the changes occurring near stoichiometry. This fact argues for a sensor with a sensitivity to P_{EX} which is stronger than the logarithmic or 1/4-power dependencies of the previous devices. A device which shows some promise for achieving at least a first power sensitivity is based on O_2 pumping[5] with ZrO_2 cells. A side view of a pumping device[6] is shown in Fig. 6a. Here two cells, a pump cell and a sensor cell, composed of ZrO_2 platelets and attached Pt electrodes are separated by a hollow ceramic spacer in order to define an enclosed volume. A leak aperture is introduced so that the exhaust gas in which the device is immersed can establish itself within the volume. Operation of the device is illustrated in Fig. 6b where a bias is applied to the pump cell with proper polarity to electrochemically pump O_2 from the volume and return it to the surrounding ambient. As expressed by Eq. 5, a steady state is eventually reached

$$I_p(\text{amps}) = 4e\, I_L (O_2 \text{ molecules/sec}) \quad (5)$$

where the rate at which O_2 is pumped (measured by the pump cell current Ip) equals the rate at which O_2 leaks into the volume (I_L) by means of the aperture. The factor 4e converts the leakage flux in O_2 molecules/sec to an equivalent number of amps. Characterizing the steady state is a reduced value of the O_2-partial pressure in the volume, $P_V < P_{EX}$. As a result, an emf (which shall be termed V_S) is induced on the sensor cell as given by Eq. 6

$$V_S = (RT/4F)\ln(P_{EX}/P_V) . \quad (6)$$

A further steady-state condition quantifies the relation of Eq. (5). Using calibrated gases to fix P_{EX}, and using Eq. (6) to determine P_V from measured values of V_S, one can empirically establish the relation given in Eq. (7).

$$I_p = \sigma_L (P_{EX} - P_V) \quad (7)$$

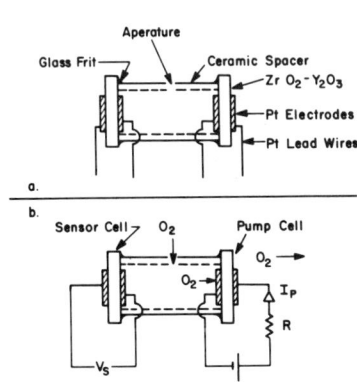

Fig. 6. (a) Pumping-cell construction; (b) Electrical hook-up.

The right-hand term, which characterizes the steady-state leakage mechanism, indicates that leakage is accomplished by O_2 diffusion in its carrier gas and is driven by the pump-induced difference between P_{EX} and P_V. σ_L can be thought of as a leak conductance for the diffusion process and is proportional to aperture area, temperature, and the O_2-diffusion coefficient while being inversely proportional to the absolute pressure P. Using Eq. (6) to substitute for P_V in Eq. (7), one finds the important result that

$$I_p = \sigma_L P_{EX}[1 - \exp(-\frac{4F V_S}{RT})] \quad (8)$$

Thus if V_S can be held constant, Ip provides a first power measure of O_2 concentration through the $\sigma_L P_{EX}$ product. Qualitatively Eq. 8 quantifies the reasonable expectation that as P_{EX} increases, O_2 must be removed from the leaky enclosure at a greater rate to establish the necessary (to keep V_S constant) reduced partial pressure within the volume. Since σ_L and P_{EX} have inverse dependencies on the absolute pressure, the $\sigma_L P_{EX}$ product and hence Ip is in fact proportional to the percentage of O_2 in the ambient rather than the partial pressure. In practice the device can be operated with a feedback amplifier whose output drives the pump cell just hard enough to maintain V_S equal to some preset reference voltage. Alternate modes of operation are also possible for such a device.

In summary, several metal oxides with gas-phase sensitive electrical properties have found important applications as exhaust gas oxygen sensors. New devices or materials which can refine these measurements, or with the potential for measuring other exhaust gas constituents, should be a significant focus for research in the years ahead.

REFERENCES

1. H. S. Gandhi, R. G. Delosh, A. G. Piken and M. Shelef, Paper No. 760201, SAE Automotive Engineering Congress, Detroit, February 1976.
2. T. Y. Tien, H. L. Stadler, E. F. Gibbons and P. J. Zacmanidis, J. Amer. Ceramic Soc. 54, 280 (1975).
3. E. M. Logothetis, K. Park, A. H. Meitzler and K. R. Laud, Appl. Phys. Lett. 26, 209 (1975).
4. H. Dietz, W. Haecker and H. Jahnke, in Advances in Electrochemistry and Electrochemical Engineering, edited by H. Gerischer and C. Tobias (Wiley, New York, 1977), Vol. 10, p. 1.
5. D. Yuan and F. A. Kröger, J. Electrochem. Soc., 116, 594 (1969).
6. R. E. Hetrick and W. A. Fate, to be published.

TRANSITION METAL SURFACE ELECTRONIC STRUCTURE

J. R. Smith, F. J. Arlinghaus and J. G. Gay
Physics Department
General Motors Research Laboratory, Warren, MI 48090

ABSTRACT

In the automotive industry, solid surface effects are encountered in areas such as exhaust gas catalysis and sensing, corrosion, adhesion, friction and wear. Transition metals are involved in all of these types of interfaces. Our surface and interface physics programs are designed to characterize relevant physical phenomena in the atomistic sense. Transition metals are characterized in large part by their d-electron behavior. The localized nature of the d-orbitals has necessitated the formulation of a self-consistent local orbital method in order to compute surface electronic structure. Results for the (100) surfaces on palladium, silver, copper, and nickel will be presented. Electron work functions agree well with experiment. We found a surprisingly large density of surface states, i.e., localized to the surface region), on palladium, copper, and silver. One-fifth to one-fourth of the electrons in the surface layer are in surface states on these metals. A prominent surface state band found theoretically on copper has subsequently been observed by Heimann et al., and Kevan and Shirley via angular photoemission. It is clear that henceforth surface states will have to be considered in the analysis of physical and chemical processes on transition metal surfaces.

INTRODUCTION

Transition metal surfaces enter into automotive technology in a number of areas. For example, the catalytic converter, which is designed to control the emissions of hydrocarbons, carbon monoxide, and nitrogen oxides in engine exhaust, contains an alloy of platinum, palladium and rhodium as the catalyst. Chromium alloys are used to provide a decorative coating for metal or plastic trim components. Automobile bodies and parts are made primarily of alloys of the transition metal iron. Catalytic efficiency, paint and metal film adhesion, corrosion, friction and wear are all related to surface and interfacial phenomena.

We would like to gain a fundamental understanding of the electronic structure of transition metal surfaces -- both clean and containing chemisorbed adlayers of atoms and molecules in order to predict material behavior. At the moment, we are in a very rudimentary stage in this field (for a recent review, see Ref. 1). While experiment is perhaps somewhat ahead of theory, there is not enough experimental information to perform reliable, semiempirical calculations of surface electronic structure.

First-principles calculations on transition metal surfaces have been inhibited by two properties, both of which are exhibited in Fig. 1. That figure shows the computed conduction electronic charge density contours plotted on a plane perpendicular to the Cu (100) surface. First, note that the charge density varies by a factor of 100 in a distance of roughly an Angstrom. That is because copper has a large number of d-electrons in its conduction bands which are highly localized around each atomic core. Because of these localized d-orbitals, jellium models or plane wave bases, which are useful for simple metals and semiconductors respectively, cannot be applied to transition metals. The second property that has inhibited progress in transition metal surfaces is the extensive charge rearrangement that takes place at the surface. Note that the charge contours are bulk-like for the second and deeper layers. This is the result of short metallic screening lengths. However, there is significant rearrangement in the surface layer. This rearrangement must be computed self-consistently, i.e., the potential used in the Schrödinger equation must be consistent with the wave functions computed from it. It has only been in the last two or three years that self-consistent solutions have been obtained for transition metal surfaces.

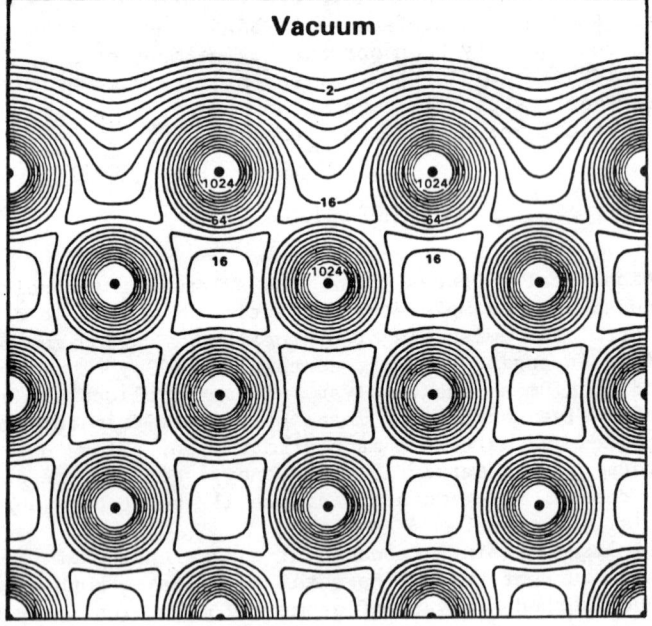

Fig. 1 Self-consistent conduction band electronic charge density for a nine-layer Cu(100) film plotted on a plane perpendicular to the surface and passing through a line connecting a surface atom with one of its near neighbors in the second plane of atoms. The units of charge density are 2.44×10^{-3} a.u. Charge densities on successive contours are in the ratio $\sqrt{2}$.

COPPER(100)

The first ab initio, self-consistent surface calculation for a transition metal was done[3] for a three atomic-layer-thick crystal of Cu(100). We used what is now called the self-consistent local orbital (SCLO) method. In the SCLO method, we first solve the atomic problem, and then use the atomic wave functions as basis functions for the solid state wave functions. This minimum basis set is augmented by additional orbitals so that the basis has much of the flexibility of the quantum chemist's double-zeta-plus-polarization basis sets.[4] The Kohn-Sham[5] equations are then solved self-consistently and to numerical accuracy within the aforementioned basis set.

The density of electronic states for the Cu(100) crystal with a monolayer of nitrogen adsorbed on it shows changes[6] relative to the clean Cu(100) surface which reproduce the changes observed[7] in photoemission spectra when N is chemisorbed on Cu (100). The changes were seen to be due to the presence of the N 2p-bands, and to significant alteration of the surface Cu 3d-bands by the chemisorption of N. The chemisorption bond was found to be essentially localized to the surface Cu(100) atomic layer. Full self-consistency was demonstrated to be essential for these calculations.

The three layer thickness was not sufficient to study surface states, however. An electron in a surface state is essentially localized in the surface. While surface states were thought to exist on metals, they were not considered to be as important or as prevalent as on semiconductor surfaces.[8] Nevertheless, we thickened the crystal to 9 atomic layers to allow for surface states.

We were quite surprised by the results, in that we found a large density of electrons which had 80% or more of their charge density localized in the surface layer or in the layer just beneath it. We use that criterion to define a surface state. As such, our definition includes strong surface resonances. In fact, 26% of the electrons in the surface atomic layer are in such states. The surface state charge density is plotted in Fig. 2 on same plane as that in Fig. 1. The contours are shown in the left panel, and the amplitudes going with those contours are shown in the right panel. It is quite obvious from the amplitude plot that the surface states are indeed well localized. Incidentally, these states are of primarily d-type symmetry, as can be inferred from their localization around the atomic cores as shown in Fig. 2.

Alternatively, one could look at the density of electronic states (DOS) as a function of energy. The difference between the bulk (central layer) DOS and that of the surface layer is shown in the upper panel of Fig. 3. The large negative peaks at -6 to -7 eV are due primarily to the large density of surface states we have been discussing. Because these surface state electrons are so localized in the surface region, one might expect that gas atoms or molecules which interact chemically or chemisorb, on the surface would interact relatively strongly with surface states. To look for this, one could take a photoemission spectrum of the clean

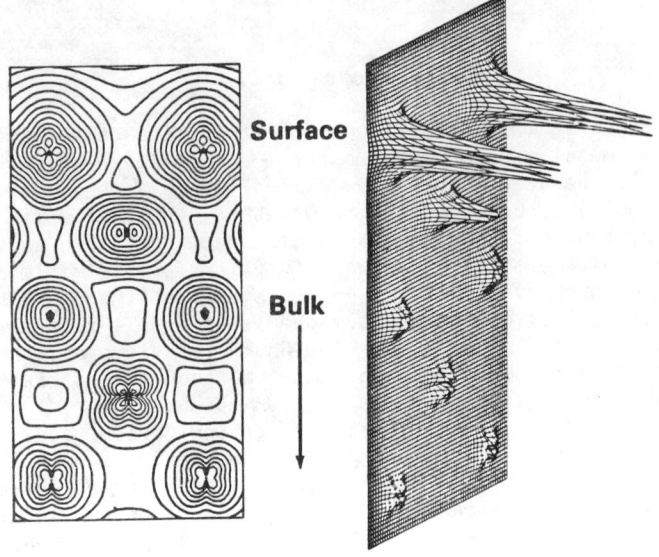

Fig. 2 Surface-state charge density for nine-layer Cu(100) crystal. Only those states with energies above -6.5 eV are included. The left panel shows the charge contours and the right panel shows the corresponding amplitudes. The plot is made along the same plane used in Fig. 1. The units of charge density are 2.44×10^{-4} a.u., and successive contours are in the ratio 2.

surface and subtract it from a spectrum of the gas covered surface. Such photoemission difference spectra for fractional monolayers of N, O, and S on Cu(100) are shown[7] in the bottom panel of the figure. All three spectra show a large negative peak in the -6 to -7 eV region, which has approximately the same shape as the large negative surface state peak in the upper panel. Thus, we contend that these perhaps dominant features in the difference spectra are due to the perturbing of a very large density of surface states via chemisorption.

One would have to conclude that surface states can play an important role in chemisorption on metals. This conclusion is not generally recognized nor agreed upon within the scientific community as yet.

Subsequently, the computed surface state band that was split off furthest from the low binding energy edge of the d-band was seen experimentally by Heimann[9] et al. These authors, using angular photoemission, found an energy dispersion for the band which is very similar to that which we reported.

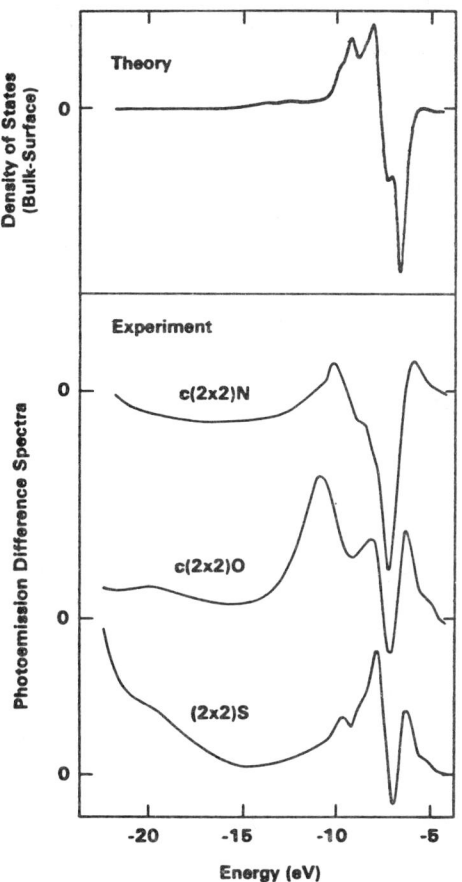

Fig. 3 Top panel: theoretical density of states difference between central and surface planes; bottom panel: experimental difference spectra for Cu(100) covered with partial monolayers of various adsorbates (taken from Ref. 7).

SURFACE STATES ON TRANSITION METALS

One is left with the question, "How common is the large density of surface states we found on Cu(100)?" The best way to answer that is to investigate other metals. If such a phenomenon were to have some generality, then one might expect to see it on other noble metals. Thus, we decided to do a calculation on Ag(100).

Silver, while in the same column of the periodic table as copper, is a 4d metal. The 3d metal next to copper is nickel. Nickel, having an unfilled d-band and hence not being a noble metal, may have different surface state characteristics than copper. Palladium is the 4d counterpart of nickel and also has an unfilled d-band.

One of the most difficult quantities to compute accurately is the electron work function, i.e., the work or energy necessary to remove the most weakly bound electrons (those at the Fermi level), from the metal. Full self-consistency is required if one wishes to be within volts of the experimental value, although experimentally the accuracy is usually ±0.1 eV. Our results for the four metals are given in Table I. One can see that the work function varies by almost one eV over the four metals. The agreement between theory and experiment is quite good.

Table I   Electron Work Functions

Metal Surface	Theory	Experiment
Ni(100)	5.1 eV	5.2[a] 4.95[b]
Pd(100)	5.0	5.3[c]
Cu(100)	4.5	4.58[d] 4.76[e] 4.59[f]
Ag(100)	4.2	4.2[g] 4.6[h]

[a] Reference 10
[b] Reference 11
[c] Reference 12
[d] Reference 13
[e] Reference 7
[f] Reference 14
[g] Reference 15
[h] Reference 16

The densities of states results for Ni(100) are very similar to those for Cu(100), with the exception that the nickel Fermi level lies within the d-band. However, the surface state peak which is so strong in Cu(100) (see Fig. 3) is much weaker in Ni(100). In fact, while there is a substantial density of surface states in the Ni(100) surface layer, 12%, it is much smaller than the 26% we found for Cu(100). The reader is referred to Ref. 17 for more information on Ni(100).

If the high density of surface states found on Cu(100) should exist anywhere else, it should be found on another noble metal, say Ag(100). In Fig. 4 we show the DOS results for Ag (100). The top panel shows the DOS for the entire (7 atomic layer thick), crystal. This contains both bulk and surface contributions.

The next panel down has the bulk DOS as computed by Moruzzi,[18] et al. The next two panels show the DOS projected on the central and surface atomic layers respectively. Note that the total, bulk, and central plane DOS are quite similar. This is consistent with the short screening lengths of metals we discussed in connection with Fig. 1. That is, all but the surface atomic layers are quite bulk-like. However, the surface DOS is much narrower than that of the central plane. This is to be expected, since the number of near neighbors of atoms in the surface layer is eight, whereas bulk atoms have twelve near neighbors. There is a peak in the surface DOS near the upper d-band edge ($\sim$-8 eV), not unlike that found for Cu(100). It turns out that 23% of the electrons in the Ag(100) surface layer are surface states. In fact, there is somewhat detailed resemblance of the surface state band structure on Ag(100) and Cu(100).

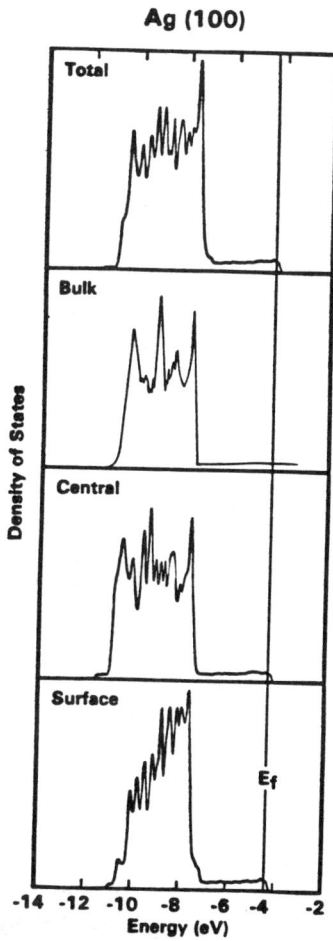

Fig. 4 Density-of-states curves for 7-plane Ag(100) crystal. The bulk density of states is taken from Ref. 18.

Having found such large densities of surface states on Ag(100) and Cu(100), and a smaller density on Ni(100), one might well wonder if the very large surface state densities are limited to noble metals. Palladium, having an unfilled d-band, will be a test of this.

The Pd(100) DOS for a 7 atomic layer crystal are shown in Fig. 5. The top panel contains the bulk results of Moruzzi[18] et al, which looks very much like the total and central-plane-projected

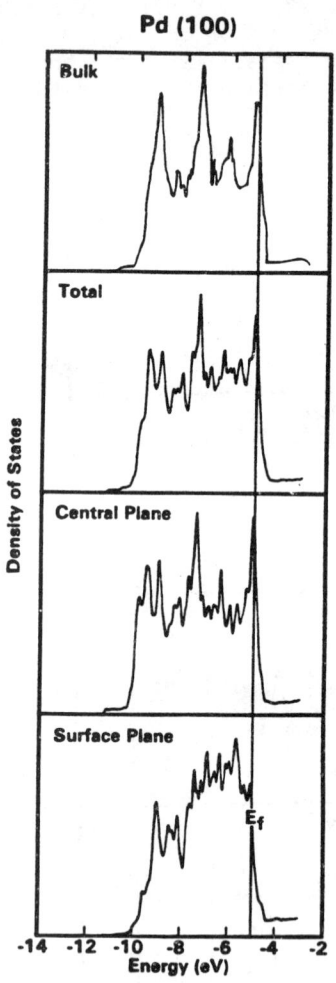

Fig. 5 Density-of-state curves for the 7-plane Pd(100) crystal. The bulk density-of-states was taken from Ref. 18.

DOS computed for our thin film. The surface plane DOS is again narrower, as is to be expected. Note, however, that it does not contain the large peak at the upper d-band edge that we found for both Ag(100) and Cu(100). The surface DOS does show a broad peak from -5 eV to ~-7 eV, about 1/3 of which is due to surface states. In fact 19% of the surface plane charge density is contributed by surface states. Thus, Pd(100) is intermediate between Ni(100) and Cu(100) in terms of surface site concentrations. These results are summarized in Table II.

Table II. Surface State Concentrations

Metal Surface	Percent of Surface Layer Electrons in Surface States
Cu(100)	26
Ag(100)	23
Pd(100)	19
Ni(100)	12

CONCLUSION

What we have found, then, is that four transition metals all show relatively large densities of surface states. As was mentioned earlier, surface states had not been considered to be of importance on metal surfaces. From now on, however, surface states will have to be considered in analyzing physical and chemical processes on transition metal surfaces.

REFERENCES

1. *Topics in Current Physics, Theory of Chemisorption*, edited by J. R. Smith (Springer, New York, 1980), Vol. 19.
2. J. R. Smith, J. G. Gay, and F. J. Arlinghaus, Phys. Rev. B $\underline{21}$, 2201 (1980); ibid, Phys. Rev. Lett. $\underline{42}$, 332 (1979).
3. J. G. Gay, J. R. Smith, and F. J. Arlinghaus, Phys. Rev. Lett. $\underline{38}$, 561 (1977).
4. *The Electronic Structure of Atoms and Molecules*, edited by Henry F. Schaefer III. (Addison-Wesley, Reading, Mass., 1972), p. 74.
5. W. Kohn and L. Sham, Phys. Rev. $\underline{140}$, A1133 (1965).
6. J. R. Smith, F. J. Arlinghaus and J. G. Gay, Solid State Commun. $\underline{24}$, 279 (1977).
7. G. G. Tibbetts, J. M. Burkstrand, and J. C. Tracy, Phys. Rev. B $\underline{15}$, 3652 (1977).
8. S. G. Davisson and J. D. Levine, Solid State Physics $\underline{25}$, 1 (1970).

9. P. Heimann, J. Hermanson, H. Miosga and H. Neddermeyer, Phys. Rev. B 20, 3059 (1979). See also S. D. Kevan and D. A. Shirley (to be published).
10. W. Eib and S. F. Alvarado, Phys. Rev. Lett. 37, 444 (1976).
11. C. A. Papageorgopoulos and J. M. Chen, Surf. Sci. 52, 40 (1975).
12. A. M. Bradshaw, private communication.
13. G. A. Haas and R. E. Thomas, J. Appl. Phys. 48, 86 (1977).
14. P. O. Gartland, S. Berge, and B. J. Slagsvold, Phys. Rev. Lett. 28, 738 (1972).
15. As determined from the cutoffs of the photoemission energy distribution curves of G. V. Hanson and S. A. Flodström, Phys. Rev. B 17, 473 (1978).
16. A. W. Dweydari and C. H. B. Mee, Phys. Stat. Sol. 27, 223 (1975).
17. F. J. Arlinghaus, J. G. Gay and J. R. Smith, Phys. Rev. B 21, 2055 (1980).
18. V. L. Moruzzi, J. F. Janak, and A. R. Williams, Calculated Electronic Properties of Metals (Pergamon Press, New York, 1978).

THIN-FILM LIGHT EMITTING DISPLAY DEVICES

S. L. McCarthy and John Lambe
Engineering and Research Staff, Research, Ford Motor Company
Dearborn, Michigan 48121

ABSTRACT

A review article is presented of the authors' work on light emission from electron tunneling junctions. The light emission arises from the radiative decay of junction surface plasmon modes excited by tunneling electrons. The coupling out of the light is assisted by roughness and resonant particle scattering schemes. As a consequence of the quantum nature of the light generation process, there is a fundamental relation between the applied voltage and the observed emission spectrum. Because of the limited tunneling electron-surface plasmon coupling, these thin-film light sources have photometric brightnesses of only a few foot-Lamberts. Other avenues of research for brighter thin-film light sources are: development of metal electrodes having a lower surface plasmon frequency and fabrication of devices exhibiting light emission from direct excitation of electronic transitions.

INTRODUCTION

With the trend toward smaller automobiles in the last few years space and weight reduction have become important aspects in structural and component design. One component being considered by the industry is the replacement of the instrument dashboard panel with a more compact and lightweight assembly with increased graphic flexibility. This would take the form of an electronic display incorporating digital, alphanumeric and analog systems. The electronic display offers the opportunity for presentation of operational and diagnostic information concerning the status of the engine and emission controls through a dashboard message center.

A large variety of display technologies exist in the marketplace. Currently, the vacuum fluorescent display appears in certain car lines. These displays are essentially flat facuum tubes where electrons from a hot filament bombard a powder phosphor coating on segments forming the elements of the display. In the future, however, only a display technology based on thin-films promise the highest graphic flexibility at lowest unit cost. The use of photolithographic patterning techniques used in the microelectronics industry enables the achievement of high pattern density and design freedom.

In this paper we will discuss our work on thin-film light emitting devices and their prospects for display applications.

THE LEIT EFFECT

Our research on thin-film display devices began with the discovery[1] by the authors of a new way of generating light. It was found that electron tunnel junctions when prepared in a certain manner could be made to emit visible light over a wide spectrum having the unique property that the maximum photon frequency, ν_{co}, is related to the externally applied voltage, V_o, through a fundamental relation

$$h\nu_{co} = e|V_o| \quad (1)$$

where h is Planck's constant and e is the electron charge. The absolute magnitude sign on the voltage reflects the independence of the frequency cutoff on the current direction. The most direct visual consequence of this effect is that by changing the voltage across the junction, color changes can be seen as the frequency equivalent voltages of the visual spectrum are applied to the device. The emission appears red when V_o is 2 volts, yellow at 2.5 volts and becomes blue-white at 3 volts. Devices have been prepared which emit in the near uv at λ = 1920 Å (at 6 volts applied).

Figure 1 shows emission spectra from an Al-Al$_2$O$_3$-Ag and an Al-Al$_2$O$_3$-Au tunnel junction biased at different voltages. The emission frequency is plotted in units of photon energy (eV) to more effectively display the fundamental relationship (Eq. 1). The phenomenon of light emission from metal-insulator-metal tunnel junctions was later found by ourselves and other workers[2,3] to be

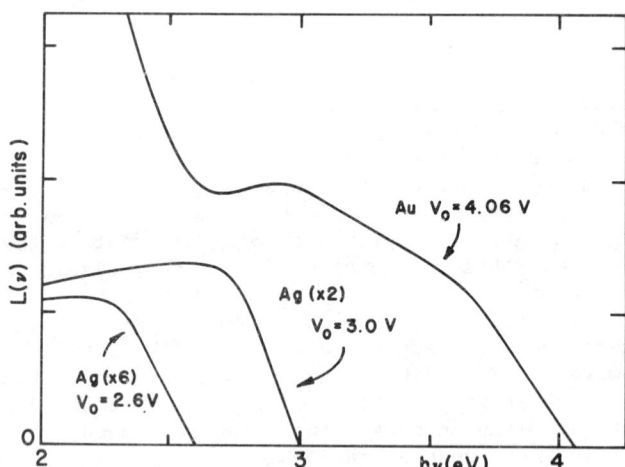

Fig. 1 A plot of $L(\nu)$, the photon flux per unit frequency bandwidth versus hν for an Au and an Ag junction at different junction bias voltages. The junction temperature was 77°K.

independent of the metals and oxides forming the junction. We have subsequently reported the occurrence of the effect in metal-insulator-semiconductor tunnel junctions[4] as well. For succinctness, we have termed this phenomena light emission via inelastic tunneling (LEIT). The light emission is interpreted as arising from the radiative decay of junction surface plasmon modes excited by the tunneling electrons.

When two metal film strips are separated by 30 Å of an insulator, the electrons can pass through the insulating layer by quantum mechanical tunneling when a voltage difference is applied. For the most part the electrons tunnel elastically, that is, energy is conserved in the tunneling process. If, however, mechanisms exist whereby the electrons can lose some of their energy in the tunneling process then an additional channel occurs for tunneling. This additional tunneling is refered to as inelastic electron tunneling. Using these ideas a sensitive spectroscopic tool has been developed[5] by placing organic molecules at the interface between the Al_2O_3 and a top electrode. The tunneling electrons couple to the vibrational modes of the organic molecules and analysis of the inelastic tunneling current can yield a vibrational mode spectra of the molecules.

In the absence of organic molecules there still remain sources of energy loss for the tunneling electrons. These sources are in the collective response of the conduction electrons in the metals to the tunneling electrons moving through the two metal interfaces adjoining the insulating layer.[6] One can think of these collective excitations at the metal surfaces as an attempt by the conduction electrons to screen the tunneling electron and its coulomb field in the insulating layer. The collective excitations of the conduction electrons at the metal surfaces are called surface plasmons. The spatial wavelength of the excitation along the surface is affected by the dielectric properties of the metal and the mode frequency through a dispersion relation obtained by solving Maxwell's Equations with the appropriate boundary conditions. Figure 2 gives an ω-k plot for surface plasmon modes associated with an $Al-Al_2O_3-Ag$ tunnel junction where ω is the frequency of the mode and k is the spatial wavevector projected along the surface. These modes have transverse magnetic fields in the junction with the electric fields decaying exponentially above and below the junction. The surface plasmon modes are characterized by asymptotic frequencies called the surface plasmon frequencies ω_{s_1} and ω_{s_3} of Ag and Al, respectively. ω_{p_1} corresponds to the bulk plasma frequency where the fields have longitudinal character in the interior of the films. The mode of principal concern is the lowest lying one called the "slow wave" mode. All other modes are lossy and not well defined for the tunnel junction configuration. The term "slow wave" arises from its relatively low phase velocity ($\omega/k \ll c$). For this mode the electric and magnetic fields are concentrated most strongly at the Al_2O_3-metal interfaces in the junction, with fields decaying exponentially on both sides of the junction region.

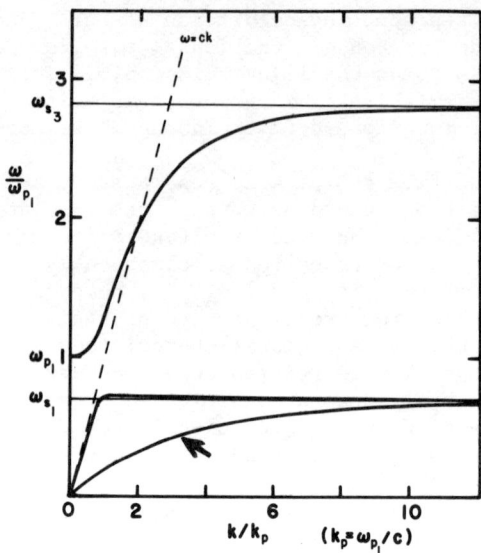

Fig. 2 Dispersion curves for a metal-insulator-metal tunneling junction. (Al-Al$_2$O$_3$-Ag for example). Arrow indicates "slow wave" branch of interest in present context.

In the inelastic tunneling process, when an electron tunnels from one metal film to the other through the oxide there is a finite probability that the electron will couple to the surface plasmon modes of the junction and lose an energy $\hbar\omega$ to a surface plasmon mode with wave vector k.[7,8] However, the excited plasmon modes will not be visible. All modes of the lower branch with $k > \frac{\omega}{c}$ have phase velocities less than that of light ($\omega = ck$) and, therefore, the electromagnetic energy of the surface plasmon mode will be trapped in the junction area. If, however, structural roughness of one or both films is introduced into the tunnel junction, by chemical etching for example, the electromagnetic fields will scatter and become visible. This is equivalent to saying that the Fourier components of the roughness of the surface of the junction essentially match the wavevector of the plasmon wave. In order for light to be observed

$$k_{plasmon} - k_{rough} < \frac{\omega}{c}.$$

In the experiment when a voltage is applied across a roughened tunnel junction light emission is observed arising from the out-coupled surface plasmon modes. From energetics, the highest energy surface plasmon generated by the tunneling electron can not exceed the maximum potential energy difference available, eV_o. The consequence of this limitation is the fundamental quantum relation relating the applied voltage to the maximum emission frequency.

Further insight into the nature of the quantum cutoff can be obtained by invoking a new spectroscopy.[1,9] In this case one uses a narrow band, fixed optical filter with a transmission function, $\Gamma(\nu)$, centered around a frequency ν_0. This filter is interposed between the emitting junction and a photomultiplier. The photomultiplier current, I_{pm}, and its second derivative, d^2I_{pm}/dV^2 are measured as the voltage, V, on the tunnel junction is varied. The results are shown in Figure 3 and show that I_{pm} "turns on" as V passes through the condition $|V| = h\nu_0/e$. Beyond this threshold I_{pm} increases linearly with voltage. $\frac{d^2I_{pm}}{dV^2}$ shows a peak when $|eV|=h\nu_0$. $\Gamma(\nu)$ is also plotted in Figure 3 for comparison, and it is clear that $\frac{d^2I_{pm}}{dV^2}$ as a function of voltage maps out the transmission function. The second derivative curve is somewhat broader than $\Gamma(\nu)$ due in part to thermal broadening of the Fermi levels. Figure 4 shows second derivative signals from a photomultiplier

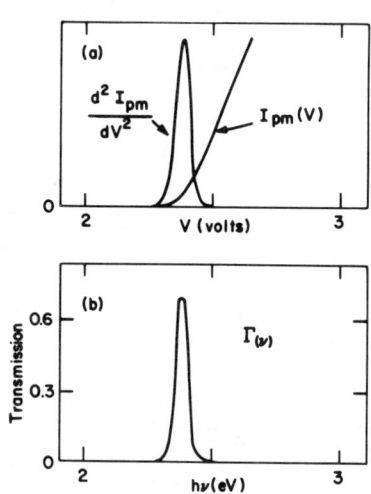
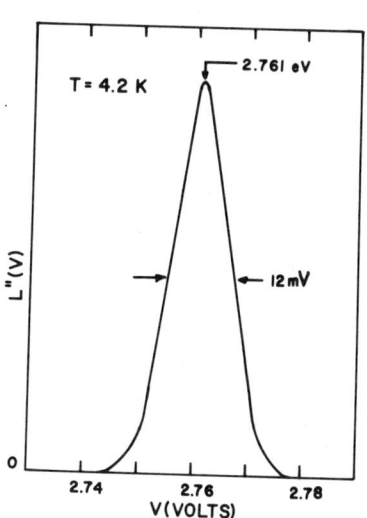
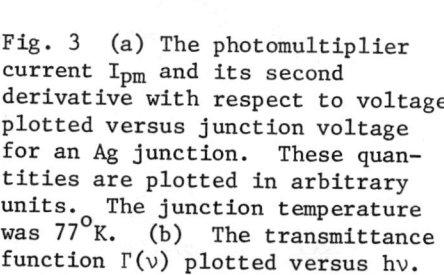

Fig. 3 (a) The photomultiplier current I_{pm} and its second derivative with respect to voltage plotted versus junction voltage for an Ag junction. These quantities are plotted in arbitrary units. The junction temperature was 77°K. (b) The transmittance function $\Gamma(\nu)$ plotted versus $h\nu$.

Fig. 4 Second derivative of light intensity through a fairly narrow optical filter. The junction was at 4.2°K.

opposite a junction at 4.2°K. The optical filter band width is
15Å (9 meV) and the width of the second derivative peak is 12 mV.
At these temperatures the theory of inelastic tunneling predicts
a second derivative peak width of 9.2 mV. We believe that the
additional width is due to the finite sheet resistance in the
electrodes. The result demonstrates that the fundamental cutoff
relation is precise to better than 1 part in 10^3 without utilizing
more sophisticated data processing and fitting techniques. It is
evident from these results that the LEIT devices can serve as
basic components in transmission or reflection spectroscopy when
used in a frequency modulation mode, since they incorporate both
source and monochromator functions in a single electrically
scanned unit.

The general shape of the emission spectrum from the LEIT devices
will depend on a number of factors: the electron tunneling probability, the surface plasmon-electron coupling, and character of the
output coupling mechanism. Influences of these factors are evident
in the results of our experiments. The linear cutoff at low
temperatures in $L(\nu)$ (see Figure 1) near ν_{co} follows from tunneling
theory.[5] The density of surface plasmon modes excited by tunneling
electrons will be dependent upon the dispersion relation. For
frequencies near the asymptotic surface plasmon values, the density
of states is large and this should be reflected in the emission
spectrum. Figure 5 gives the emission spectrum for an Al-Al$_2$O$_3$-Ag
tunnel junction with varying degrees of roughness outcoupling.[10]
Increasing the amplitude of roughness increases the outcoupling
efficiency and thereby the emission intensity. As the roughness
increases the coupling efficiency from the relatively large k values
of the roughness spectrum also increases. Thus, features associated
with high k-value plasmon modes will be apparent. The three curves
of increasing intensity reflect increasingly efficient outcoupling
schemes. In the most efficient method prominent features associated
with the asymptotic surface plasmon and the bulk plasmon frequencies
are evident. In this experiment the voltage bias extends beyond the
frequency range where well defined surface plasmons exist, so no
quantum cutoff is observed.

In addition to roughness scattering outcoupling schemes,
resonant antenna emission enhancement[10] was used on smooth Al-Al$_2$O$_3$-
Au tunnel junctions. Here a film of silver particles was placed just
above a smooth, low light-emitting tunnel junction separated by a
thin evaporated film of MgF$_2$. The Ag particles are formed in the
early stages of vacuum evaporated film growth and form oblate
spheroidal shapes with diameters of the order of a few hundred
angstroms. These aggregate silver particle films exhibit dipole
scattering resonances in the visible. If nonradiative optical
fields are present above the gold electrode surface, then the Ag
particles should scatter these fields, converting some of the energy
to visible light with peak emission frequencies near the scattering
resonances of assembly. Figure 6 gives the normalized spectrum of
an Al-Al$_2$O$_3$-Au tunnel junction before and after coating with a
MgF$_2$ spacer and Ag particle film. The strong emission enhancement
for the coated sample occurs at the scattering resonant frequency

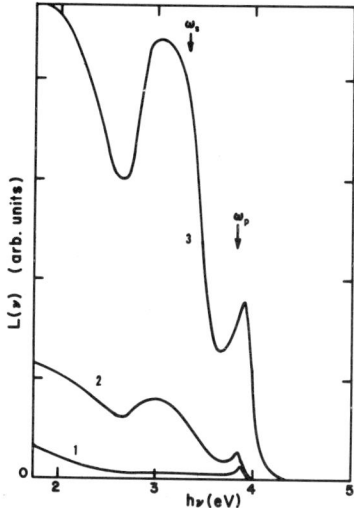

Fig. 5 A plot of L(ν) for an Al-Al$_2$O$_3$-Ag junction biased at 4.6 volts. Curves refer to different out-coupling schemes: (1) smooth junction, (2) chemical etching of Ag electrode, (3) emission from junction grown on micro-roughened substrate.[4]

of the particle assembly. This result establishes the existence of evanescent fields above the tunnel junction.

A series of samples was prepared with different MgF$_2$ spacer thicknesses in order to probe the plasmon field dependence away from the junction. An Ag particle layer was grown on the MgF$_2$ spacer. Figure 7 gives the light output at the emission peak frequency for these junctions plotted against spacer thickness. These results are in general agreement with the expected decay of plasmon fields away from these surfaces.[6]

Light emission has also been seen from metal-insulator-semiconductor (MIS) tunnel junctions.[4] These devices are Al-Al$_2$O$_3$-Sn doped indium oxide (ITO) junctions. ITO is an n-type degenerate semiconductor with a carrier concentration up to 10^{21}cm^{-3} (Ref. 11). A film of ITO is prepared by vacuum evaporation of a compressed pellet of 91% In$_2$O$_3$ and 9% SnO$_2$. The ITO film forms a nearly transparent but conducting top electrode to the tunnel junction. In the visible region of the spectrum the ITO has a positive dielectric constant and so there is only the free surface plasmon mode of the aluminum surface augmented by the presence of Al$_2$O$_3$ and the ITO film. The phase velocities of these modes are increased substantially by replacing the metal top electrode with a positive dielectric material. This result makes possible grating and prism monochromatic coupling schemes which contain only smaller k-values in their coupling spectrum, as opposed to what is encountered in chemically etched surfaces. Nevertheless, the reduced mode phase velocity of the MIS junction results in a lower plasmon density of states. It is not surprising, then, that the external quantum efficiency of the Al-Al$_2$O$_3$-ITO is about one-tenth that of an Al-Al$_2$O$_3$-Ag tunnel junction.

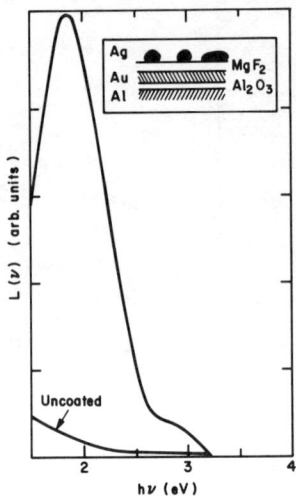

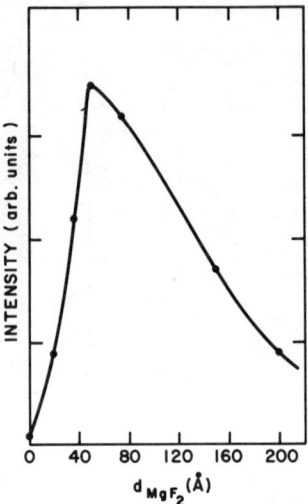

Fig. 6 A plot of L(ν) for an Al-Al$_2$O$_3$-Au tunnel junction. At one point the Au junction is coated with 50 Å MgF$_2$ followed by 100 Å particle film of Ag. The inset gives a sketch of the layer configuration of the coated junction. The junctions were biased at 3.22 V.

Fig. 7 The intensity of light emission from Ag-particle-coated Au junctions plotted against MgF$_2$ spacer thickness. The mass thickness of the particle layer was 100 Å.

PROSPECTS FOR AUTOMOTIVE APPLICATION

The LEIT device has an external quantum efficiency in the 10^{-5} range and produces a photometric surface brightness of 1-2 foot Lamberts (fL). A factor of 20-30 increase in intensity would be required for the automotive instrument panel application in order to preserve good readibility in high sunlight ambient lighting conditions. Nevertheless, the emission from the LEIT device is clearly visible in a dimly lit room or for nighttime viewing. Because of the low voltage operation, electronically controlled emission spectrum and thin-film processibility the LEIT device will find application as an active optoelectronic device compatible with silicon technology. Durability appears not to be a fundamental problem as an Al-Al$_2$O$_3$-ITO device biased at 3.6 volts operated over 1000 hours at room temperature before being turned off.

Since the LEIT effect is of a general nature other thin-film electrode materials might promise a brighter light source. Results of calculations by L. C. Davis[8] suggest that a top counterelectrode material with an asymptotic surface plasmon frequency in the visible probably would yield an increase of a factor of 10 in the intensity. For silver the maximum in the mode density occurs in the near ultraviolet with photon frequencies beyond 3 eV. Finding a material with an asymptotic surface plasmon frequency at a lower energy, such as at 2.25 eV (λ = 5500 A^o), would produce emission predominantly in the green, where the eye is most sensitive. At present there are no known materials with a well-defined plasmon frequency in this range.

Using chemical etching, micro-roughened substrates, and resonant particle antennas, outcoupling efficiencies encountered in our work have not exceeded 10%. This factor was estimated from optical reflectivity measurements on the in-coupling of light to the surface plasmon modes. In some cases increasing the scale of roughness appeared to produce too great a perturbation on the plasmon modes and the emission intensity was reduced.

As an alternative approach for brighter thin-film light sources, direct excitation of radiative mechanisms were considered. The internal quantum efficiency of the LEIT device is of order 10^{-4}. Yet allowed electronic transitions which could be excited by inelastic tunneling have large oscillator strengths of order 0.1. The system of interest would be rare earth ions (Eu^{+3} or Tb^{+3}) imbedded in an insulator in a tunnel junction. The 4-f electronic levels of the ion excited by the tunneling electrons would then decay radiatively with an emission spectrum characteristic of the ion. Attempts have been made in this laboratory and elsewhere[12] to observe the inelastic tunneling channel with these electronic transitions but no light emission has been reported.

Results of theoretical calculations[13] and experiments here suggest that when excited ions are placed within 30 Å of a metal surface the ion couples strongly to the collective excitations of the conduction electrons of the metal and very little of the excitation energy appears as free radiation.

Currently we are involved in studying the properties of metal-insulator-metal light emitting devices, where the insulator doped with rare earth impurities is substantially thicker than the 30 Å found in tunnel junctions. The rare earth ions are then placed far enough from the metal surface that surface plasmon quenching is not dominant. However, the electron transport through the thick insulator is not via quantum mechanical tunneling between the metal electrodes, but probably through a hopping conduction process[14] from one electron trap to the next. While preliminary devices demonstrate practical emission brightnesses, improvements in durability are required before automotive application is possible.

REFERENCES

1. John Lambe and S. L. McCarthy, Phys. Rev. Lett. $\underline{37}$, 923 (1976).
2. R. K. Jain, S. Wagner, and D. A. Olson, Appl. Phys. Lett. $\underline{32}$, 62 (1978).
3. P. K. Hansma and H. P. Broida, Appl. Phys. Lett. $\underline{32}$, 545 (1978).
4. S. L. McCarthy and John Lambe, Appl. Phys. Lett. $\underline{33}$, 858 (1978).
5. R. C. Jaklevic and J. Lambe, Phys. Rev. Lett. $\underline{17}$, 1139 (1966); J. Lambe and R. C. Jaklevic, Phys. Rev. $\underline{165}$, 821 (1968).
6. E. N. Economou, Phys. Rev. $\underline{182}$, 539 (1969).
7. K. L. Ngai and E. N. Economu, Phys. Rev. $\underline{B4}$, 2132 (1971).
8. L. C. Davis, Phys. Rev. $\underline{B16}$, 2482 (1977).
9. John Lambe and S. L. McCarthy, Solid State Sciences, Vol. 4 ("Inelastic Electron Tunneling Spectroscopy", Proc. Int. Conf. and Symp. on Electron Tunneling, Ed. T. Wolfram, Springer-Verlag, New York, 1978) p. 210.
10. S. L. McCarthy and John Lambe, Appl. Phys. Lett. $\underline{30}$, 427 (1977).
11. H. Kostlin, R. Jost, and W. Lems, Phys. Status Solidi A $\underline{29}$, 87 (1975).
12. S. de Cheveigné, J. Klein, and A. Léger, Solid State Sciences Vol. 4 ("Inelastic Electron Tunneling Spectroscopy", Proc. Int. Conf. and Sump. on Electron Tunneling, Ed. T. Wolfram, Springer-Verlag, New York, 1978) p. 202.
13. W. H. Weber and C. F. Eagen, Optics Lett. $\underline{4}$, 236 (1979).
14. J. G. Simmons, Phys. Rev. $\underline{155}$, 657 (1967).

A SYMPOSIUM
ON
PHYSICS IN THE AUTOMOTIVE INDUSTRY

March 14-15, 1938

UNDER THE JOINT SPONSORSHIP OF

American Institute of Physics

and

Department of Physics, University of Michigan

American Institute of Physics

New York

1938

A SYMPOSIUM ON PHYSICS IN THE AUTOMOTIVE INDUSTRY

Sponsored Jointly by

AMERICAN INSTITUTE OF PHYSICS

and

DEPARTMENT OF PHYSICS, UNIVERSITY OF MICHIGAN

CONTRIBUTORS TO THE SYMPOSIUM

F. K. RICHTMYER, *Cornell University*

CLIFTON G. FOUND, *General Electric Company*

LLOYD WITHROW, *General Motors Research Laboratory*

G. M. RASSWEILER, *General Motors Research Laboratory*

F. A. FIRESTONE, *University of Michigan*

M. MUSKAT, *Gulf Research Laboratories*

F. MORGAN, *Gulf Research Laboratories*

C. F. KETTERING, *General Motors Research Laboratories*

CARL BREER, *Chrysler Corporation*

W. F. BUSSE, *B. F. Goodrich Company*

PAUL HUBER, *General Motors Proving Grounds*

O. J. HORGER, *Timken Roller Bearing Company*

F. SEITZ, *General Electric Company*

E. J. MARTIN, *General Motors Research Laboratory*

J. S. THOMAS, *Chrysler School of Engineering*

A SYMPOSIUM ON PHYSICS IN THE AUTOMOTIVE INDUSTRY

CONTENTS

1. Applications of Physics in the Automotive Industry . . . . The Editor
   Journal of Applied Physics **9**, 349 (1938)
2. Physics and the Automotive Industry . . . . F. K. Richtmyer
   Journal of Applied Physics **9**, 350–351 (1938)
3. Contribution of the Physicist to Highway Illumination . . . . . . Clifton G. Found
   Journal of Applied Physics **9**, 354–361 (1938)
4. Studying Engine Combustion by Physical Methods . . . .
   . . . . Lloyd Withrow and Gerald M. Rassweiler
   Journal of Applied Physics **9**, 362–372 (1938)
5. Mobility Method of Computing the Vibration of Linear Mechanical
   and Acoustical Systems: Mechanical-Electrical Analogies . . . . F. A. Firestone
   Journal of Applied Physics **9**, 373–387 (1938)
6. Studies in Lubrication. I. The Theory of the Thick Film Lubrication
   of a Complete Journal Bearing of Finite Length . . . . . . M. Muskat and F. Morgan
   Journal of Applied Physics **9**, 393–409 (1938)
7. Scientific Training and Its Relation to Industrial Problems . . . . C. F. Kettering
   Journal of Applied Physics **9**, 427–430 (1938)
8. Human Beings and the Motor Car . . . . Carl Breer
   Journal of Applied Physics **9**, 433–437 (1938)
9. Physics of Rubber as Related to the Automobile . . . . W. F. Busse
   Journal of Applied Physics **9**, 438–451 (1938)
10. Some Physical Problems in Noise Measurement . . . . Paul Huber
    Journal of Applied Physics **9**, 452–456 (1938)
11. Photoelastic Analysis Practically Applied to Design Problems . . O. J. Horger
    Journal of Applied Physics **9**, 457–465 (1938)

*The following papers were also presented at the
symposium but were not published in this series.*

12. Some Aspects of the Modern Theory of Solids . . . . Frederick Seitz
13. Some Factors Influencing the Flow of Physics into Industry . . . E. J. Martin
14. The Training of Physicists for Positions in the Automotive Industry J. S. Thomas
15. A Few Instruments Used in Automotive Research . . . . E. J. Martin

Attendance List

Topical Conference on Physics in the Automotive Industry
May 15-16, 1980

Gary P. Agin
Michigan Tech. University

Ralph B. Alexander
Wayne State University

George Arfken
Miami University

Frank J. Arlinghaus
GM Research Laboratories

G. Ascarelli
Purdue University

Robert A. Ayres
GM Research Laboratories

Donovan M. Bakalyar
Dearborn, MI

George A. Ball
Chrysler Corporation

William J. Baxter
GM Research Laboratories

James H. Bechtel
GM Research Laboratories

Charles P. Beetz, Jr.
GM Research Laboratories

John R. Bradley
GM Research Laboratories

George Beard
Wayne State University

Richard J. Blint
GM Research Laboratories

Donald Boys
University of Michigan-Flint

Jeffrey C. Buchholz
GM Research Laboratories

James M. Burkstrand
GM Research Laboratories

Ramon Burriel
University of Michigan

T. Weston Capehart
GM Research Laboratories

Andrew R. Chraplyvy
GM Research Laboratories

W. Dale Compton
Ford Motor Company

Russ Cressman
Bethlehem Steel Corporation

John J. Croat
GM Research Laboratories

M. Czajowski
University of Windsor

Camerson J. Dasch
GM Research Laboratories

Harry Denman
Wayne State University

John Ellis Dickman
Russiaville, IN

Larry Dishman
Wayne State University

Gary L. Eesley
GM Research Laboratories

Robert W. Eshelman
Henry Ford Comm. College

M. Farr
John Deere Prod. Eng. Center

William A. Fate
Ford Motor Company

Frederick R. Faxvog
GM Research Laboratories

Galen B. Fisher
GM Research Laboratories

Sisten John Francis
Madonna College

Mary Fritsch
Madonna College

Martin Gaerttner
Ford Motor Company

John Galli
Weber State College

Aaron D. Gara
GM Research Laboratories

Jack G. Gay
GM Research Laboratories

Edward Gelerinter
Kent State University

Roger George
American Motors Corporation

Walter Gessert
Eastern Michigan University

Donald M. Ginsberg
University of Illinois

Martin Goodson
Delta College

David F. Griffing
Oxford, OH

William L. Grube
GM Research Laboratories

Daniel R. Gustafson
Wayne State University

Joe Ham
Texas A&M University

Keith Hartman
Davison, MI

William W. Havens, Jr.
American Institute of Physics

R. Helbing
University of Windsor

Peter Henriksen
University of Akron

Jan F. Herbst
GM Research Laboratories

Robert Hetrick
Ford Motor Company

John C. Hill
GM Research Laboratories

Robert W. Hoffman
Case Western Reserve Univ.

Dieter Hohnke
Ford Motor Company

S. Huang
Cleveland State University

John R. Hummel
GM Research Laboratories

Robert C. Jaklevic
Ford Motor Company

Frank E. Jamerson
GM Research Laboratories

R. N. Jeffrey
Wayne State University

Wayne Johnson
Ford Motor Company

Patrick Keating
Bendix Advanced Tech. Cntr.

John E. Keem
GM Research Laboratories

Howard H. Kehrl
General Motors Corporation

William H. Kelly
Montana State University

George L. Kelsh, Jr.
Ferris State College

Patrick F. Kenealy
Wayne State University

Iam-Choon Khoo
Wayne State University

David Klick
Ford Motor Company

Ronald A. Kobiske
Waukesh, WI

Donald P. Koistinen
GM Research Laboratories

David K. Lambert
GM Research Laboratories

Lee E. Larson
Denison University

Robert W. Lee
GM Research Laboratories

Abe Liboff
Oakland University

Robert J. Lieb
W. Virginia Instit. of Tech.

Lawrence A. Linden
Office of Science & Tech. Policy

Wayne Lo
GM Research Laboratories

E. M. Logothetis
Ford Motor Company

James Lunan
Chrysler Corporation

Philip A. Macklin
Miami University

Kenneth Marko
Ford Motor Company

Caren Marzhan
Michigan State University

Laurence R. McAneny
Southern Illinois University

S. L. McCarthy
Ford Motor Company

J. A. McClennan
Bethlehem Steel Corporation

J. W. McConkey
University of Windsor

Daniel Mioduszewski
Detroit, MI

G. Paul Montgomery, Jr.
GM Research Laboratories

Richard D. Montgomery
Flint, MI

Fred Morgan
York University

Nils L. Muench
GM Research Laboratories

William Mykolajenko
University of Michigan-Flint

Barbara Niewibecka
University of Windsor

Harmon D. Nine
GM Research Laboratories

Frank V. Nolfi, Jr.
U.S. Department of Energy

Dale L. Partin
GM Research Laboratories

Howard Petterson
Albion College

Harry T. Pinnick
University of Akron

Brian Pohl
Madonna College

S. M. Puri
Northeastern Illinois Univ.

Ruth A. Reck
GM Research Laboratories

John R. Reitz
Ford Motor Company

Lajos Rimai
Ford Motor Company

David M. Roessler
GM Research Laboratories

Donald Roiseland
Waverly, IA

Peter Roll
University of Minnesota

Phillip Roll
Michigan Technological Univ.

Bahman Shalid Saless
Michigan State University

Richard Sands
University of Michigan

Joseph A. Schoefer
Loras College

Peter Schroeder
Michigan State University

Jeffrey A. Sell
GM Research Laboratories

Michael Shulman
Ford Motor Company

Edgar B. Singleton
Bowling Green University

George W. Smith
GM Research Laboratories

John R. Smith
GM Research Laboratories

John W. Snider
Miami University

N. Spielberg
Kent State University

Mary Beth Stearns
Ford Motor Company

Francis C. Stephson
South Euclid, OH

Robin Stevenson
GM Research Laboratories

Mel Stewart
Wayne State University

Richard E. Teets
GM Research Laboratories

M. J. Throop
Ford Motor Company

Gary G. Tibbetts
GM Research Laboratories

W. Toothacker
Wayne Community College

J. Charles Tracy
GM Research Laboratories

Alan E. Van Antwerp
Ferris State College

Ray G. Van Ausdal
University of Pittsburgh

Robert H. Wagoner
GM Research Laboratories

William J. Walsh
Argonne National Laboratory

Dale Winder
Ford Motor Company

Margherita-Zanini
Ford Motor Company

Marguerite R. Zielesch
Harper Woods, MI

AIP Conference Proceedings

		L.C. Number	ISBN
No.1	Feedback and Dynamic Control of Plasmas	70-141596	0-88318-100-2
No.2	Particles and Fields - 1971 (Rochester)	71-184662	0-88318-101-0
No.3	Thermal Expansion - 1971 (Corning)	72-76970	0-88318-102-9
No.4	Superconductivity in d-and f-Band Metals (Rochester, 1971)	74-18879	0-88318-103-7
No.5	Magnetism and Magnetic Materials - 1971 (2 parts) (Chicago)	59-2468	0-88318-104-5
No.6	Particle Physics (Irvine, 1971)	72-81239	0-88318-105-3
No.7	Exploring the History of Nuclear Physics	72-81883	0-88318-106-1
No.8	Experimental Meson Spectroscopy - 1972	72-88226	0-88318-107-X
No.9	Cyclotrons - 1972 (Vancouver)	72-92798	0-88318-108-8
No.10	Magnetism and Magnetic Materials - 1972	72-623469	0-88318-109-6
No.11	Transport Phenomena - 1973 (Brown University Conference)	73-80682	0-88318-110-X
No.12	Experiments on High Energy Particle Collisions - 1973 (Vanderbilt Conference)	73-81705	0-88318-111-8
No.13	$\pi\text{-}\pi$ Scattering - 1973 (Tallahassee Conference)	73-81704	0-88318-112-6
No.14	Particles and Fields - 1973 (APS/DPF Berkeley)	73-91923	0-88318-113-4
No.15	High Energy Collisions - 1973 (Stony Brook)	73-92324	0-88318-114-2
No.16	Causality and Physical Theories (Wayne State University, 1973)	73-93420	0-88318-115-0
No.17	Thermal Expansion - 1973 (lake of the Ozarks)	73-94415	0-88318-116-9
No.18	Magnetism and Magnetic Materials - 1973 (2 parts) (Boston)	59-2468	0-88318-117-7
No.19	Physics and the Energy Problem - 1974 (APS Chicago)	73-94416	0-88318-118-5
No.20	Tetrahedrally Bonded Amorphous Semiconductors (Yorktown Heights, 1974)	74-80145	0-88318-119-3
No.21	Experimental Meson Spectroscopy - 1974 (Boston)	74-82628	0-88318-120-7
No.22	Neutrinos - 1974 (Philadelphia)	74-82413	0-88318-121-5
No.23	Particles and Fields - 1974 (APS/DPF Williamsburg)	74-27575	0-88318-122-3

No. 24	Magnetism and Magnetic Materials - 1974 (20th Annual Conference, San Francisco)	75-2647	0-88318-123-1
No. 25	Efficient Use of Energy (The APS Studies on the Technical Aspects of the More Efficient Use of Energy)	75-18227	0-88318-124-X
No. 26	High-Energy Physics and Nuclear Structure - 1975 (Santa Fe and Los Alamos)	75-26411	0-88318-125-8
No. 27	Topics in Statistical Mechanics and Biophysics: A Memorial to Julius L. Jackson (Wayne State University, 1975)	75-36309	0-88318-126-6
No. 28	Physics and Our World: A Symposium in Honor of Victor F. Weisskopf (M.I.T., 1974)	76-7207	0-88318-127-4
No. 29	Magnetism and Magnetic Materials - 1975 (21st Annual Conference, Philadelphia)	76-10931	0-88318-128-2
No. 30	Particle Searches and Discoveries - 1976 (Vanderbilt Conference)	76-19949	0-88318-129-0
No. 31	Structure and Excitations of Amorphous Solids (Williamsburg, VA., 1976)	76-22279	0-88318-130-4
No. 32	Materials Technology - 1975 (APS New York Meeting)	76-27967	0-88318-131-2
No. 33	Meson-Nuclear Physics - 1976 (Carnegie-Mellon Conference)	76-26811	0-88318-132-0
No. 34	Magnetism and Magnetic Materials - 1976 (Joint MMM-Intermag Conference, Pittsburgh)	76-47106	0-88318-133-9
No. 35	High Energy Physics with Polarized Beams and Targets (Argonne, 1976)	76-50181	0-88318-134-7
No. 36	Momentum Wave Functions - 1976 (Indiana University)	77-82145	0-88318-135-5
No. 37	Weak Interaction Physics - 1977 (Indiana University)	77-83344	0-88318-136-3
No. 38	Workshop on New Directions in Mossbauer Spectroscopy (Argonne, 1977)	77-90635	0-88318-137-1
No. 39	Physics Careers, Employment and Education (Penn State, 1977)	77-94053	0-88318-138-X
No. 40	Electrical Transport and Optical Properties of Inhomogeneous Media (Ohio State University, 1977)	78-54319	0-88318-139-8
No. 41	Nucleon-Nucleon Interactions - 1977 (Vancouver)	78-54249	0-88318-140-1
No. 42	Higher Energy Polarized Proton Beams (Ann Arbor, 1977)	78-55682	0-88318-141-X
No. 43	Particles and Fields - 1977 (APS/DPF, Argonne)	78-55683	0-88318-142-8
No. 44	Future Trends in Superconductive Electronics (Charlottesville, 1978)	77-9240	0-88318-143-6

No.45	New Results in High Energy Physics - 1978 (Vanderbilt Conference)	78-67196	0-88318-144-4
No.46	Topics in Nonlinear Dynamics (La Jolla Institute)	78-057870	0-88318-145-2
No.47	Clustering Aspects of Nuclear Structure and Nuclear Reactions (Winnepeg, 1978)	78-64942	0-88318-146-0
No.48	Current Trends in the Theory of Fields (Tallahassee, 1978)	78-72948	0-88318-147-9
No.49	Cosmic Rays and Particle Physics - 1978 (Bartol Conference)	79-50489	0-88318-148-7
No.50	Laser-Solid Interactions and Laser Processing - 1978 (Boston)	79-51564	0-88318-149-5
No.51	High Energy Physics with Polarized Beams and Polarized Targets (Argonne, 1978)	79-64565	0-88318-150-9
No.52	Long-Distance Neutrino Detection - 1978 (C.L. Cowan Memorial Symposium)	79-52078	0-88318-151-7
No.53	Modulated Structures - 1979 (Kailua Kona, Hawaii)	79-53846	0-88318-152-5
No.54	Meson-Nuclear Physics - 1979 (Houston)	79-53978	0-88318-153-3
No.55	Quantum Chromodynamics (La Jolla, 1978)	79-54969	0-88318-154-1
No.56	Particle Acceleration Mechanisms in Astrophysics (La Jolla, 1979)	79-55844	0-88318-155-X
No. 57	Nonlinear Dynamics and the Beam-Beam Interaction (Brookhaven, 1979)	79-57341	0-88318-156-8
No. 58	Inhomogeneous Superconductors - 1979 (Berkeley Springs, W.V.)	79-57620	0-88318-157-6
No. 59	Particles and Fields - 1979 (APS/DPF Montreal)	80-66631	0-88318-158-4
No. 60	History of the ZGS (Argonne, 1979)	80-67694	0-88318-159-2
No. 61	Aspects of the Kinetics and Dynamics of Surface Reactions (La Jolla Institute, 1979)	80-68004	0-88318-160-6
No. 62	High Energy e^+e^- Interactions (Vanderbilt, 1980)	80-53377	0-88318-161-4
No. 63	Supernovae Spectra (La Jolla, 1980)	80-70019	0-88318-162-2
No. 64	Laboratory EXAFS Facilities - 1980 (Univ. of Washington)	80-70579	0-88318-163-0
No. 65	Optics in Four Dimensions - 1980 (ICO, Ensenada)	80-70771	0-88318-164-9
No. 66	Physics in the Automotive Industry - 1980 (APS/AAPT Topical Conference)	80-70987	0-88318-165-7
No. 67	Experimental Meson Spectroscopy - 1980 (Sixth International Conference, Brookhaven)		0-88318-166-5
No. 68	High Energy Physics - 1980 (XX International Conference, Madison)		0-88318-167-3